This Is a Picture
and Not the World

THE SUNY SERIES IN
POSTMODERN CULTURE
Joseph Natoli, *Editor*

This Is a Picture and Not the World

◆

Movies and a Post-9/11 America

Joseph Natoli

STATE UNIVERSITY OF NEW YORK PRESS

Published by
State University of New York Press, Albany

For information, address State University of New York Press,
194 Washington Avenue, Suite 305, Albany, NY 12210-2384

Production by Marilyn Semerad
Marketing by Fran Keneston

Library of Congress Cataloging-in-Publication Data

Natoli, Joseph P., 1943–
This is a picture and not the world : movies and a post-9/11 America /
   Joseph Natoli.
      p. cm. — (SUNY series in postmodern culture)
   Includes bibliographical references and index.
   ISBN-13: 978-0-7914-7027-5 (hardcover : alk. paper)
   ISBN-13: 978-0-7914-7028-2 (pbk. : alk. paper)
1. Motion pictures—United States. 2. Motion pictures—Social aspects—
United States. 3. Motion pictures—Political aspects—United States. I. Title.
II. Series.

PN1993.5.U6N39 2007
791.430973'09051—dc22
                                                                2006013427

10 9 8 7 6 5 4 3 2 1

It's 1895, everyone's favorite moment in film history—the time of naivete when the cinema was born. The audience that turned up for the Lumiere brothers' pioneering exhibition, in Paris, was not yet comfortable with the idea of illusion. The image on screen was not a picture of something real; it was reality itself. That idea hasn't quite faded: to some degree, many of us still believe that the cinema has a scandalously intimate connection with life.

—David Denby, "The Quick
and the Dead," *The New Yorker*

There is no higher calling than to make pictures that show you the true world.

—E. L. Doctorow, *The March*,
Random House, 2005

Contents

Behind the Scenes

A Preproduction Q & A

Kevin Nicholoff interviews Joseph Natoli, whose new book, *This Is a Picture and Not the World: Movies and a Post-9/11 America,* is currently in press.

———◆———

KEVIN NICHOLOFF: This is a picture and not the world. You have in mind the neoconservative picture of the world?

JOSEPH NATOLI: That's the picture President Bush adopted right after 9/11 as true to the world and the prompt for my title. The screenplay format introduces characters who may not have accepted that picture as true though everyone certainly has to deal with it. I call it the resident reality.

KEVIN NICHOLOFF: And movies somehow reveal this resident reality?

JOSEPH NATOLI: All art is what Wolfgang Iser calls "at play" with the world and we in turn are "at play" with the movies we see. Popular film needs to be where we are in our imaginations, but not just be there to soothe us but to haunt us as well, haunt us with what already haunts us.

KEVIN NICHOLOFF: Such as Al Qaeda?

JOSEPH NATOLI: An inordinate amount of fear after 9/11 when you consider what other countries have faced and continue to face. It's the kind of traumatizing fear that a canny politics would find useful—and did. Potentially crippling for the Dow Jones though. The neocons wanted to leverage the disaster in their direction while the traditional market conservatives wanted everything to return to normal as soon as possible. If you look at the country through one lens, you could say nothing has changed after 9/11. I mean, we were urged to go to the mall to shop and go to Disneyland and we went. That we haven't changed haunts some, mostly the older generations I think. Our own history tells us we have done more than go to the mall and go to Disneyland. Americans live in a story of their exceptionalism, and that's been severely challenged. On the neocon end, fear has to be kept on the boil so that a tongue-tied, born-again president from Texas can appear to be a laconic, heroic westerner like Gary Cooper "come to bring 'em to justice." We're caught between manufactured fear and not supposing to care, and what shows up on the diagnostic screen looks like cultural post-traumatic shock.

KEVIN NICHOLOFF: You think the market boom of the 1990s set us up for this? You remember that PBS special "Affluenza," the virus of the 1990s?

JOSEPH NATOLI: Set us up for a super-sized portion of fear? Sure. The invisible hand of the market doesn't direct us to thoughts of our own mortality. That's counterproductive. Death is the nemesis of shopping. That's glib, but it points the way; it's revealing. Of what? Of thoroughly privatized souls.

KEVIN NICHOLOFF: As opposed to what? Thoroughly socialized souls?

JOSEPH NATOLI: I'm not joking. I'm serious. When you live totally within the cocoon of your own self-creation, which is a product of your own personal choices, which is itself a product of your infinite freedom to choose, which is fed by an economic system that thrives on the maximization of choices . . .

KEVIN NICHOLOFF: X-Box or PlayStation choices. We're not talking about existential choice or moral imperatives or what's the sound of one hand clapping. Ugg boots or flip flops.

JOSEPH NATOLI: You're choosing products from a shelf or from a catalog.

KEVIN NICHOLOFF: Or more likely now from a computer screen.

JOSEPH NATOLI: We've privatized and personalized and uniquely designed our lives to the exclusion of anything outside ourselves. Your cell phone has a personal directory of your world. There's nothing outside you. But bin Laden got their attention.

KEVIN NICHOLOFF: Outside us? You mean like what religion supposedly gives us?

JOSEPH NATOLI: I'm impressed by how little the 700 Club is unimpressed with 45 million people not having health care and a minimum wage below subsistence level and the polluting of the planet and the savagery produced by the market's invisible hand.

KEVIN NICHOLOFF: I thought it was God's hand that upheld the world? What did Dylan say? You gotta serve somebody?

JOSEPH NATOLI: I think you have to attend to more than your own navel. Whether it's poetry or philosophy, nature or socialism, genealogy or science, fate or the stars, the point is that when we think of death within any of those narratives, it is in *medias res*; it's not closure. It has a place within a story outside ourselves. And that story includes not only other people but history. And the future. Not just of ourselves but of others, of the so-called lower orders, of the country, of other countries, of the planet.

KEVIN NICHOLOFF: Yeah, but it is. Death is closure. Regardless of how you spin yourself.

JOSEPH NATOLI: Ah, but the story—call it a spin—of reality is what we live in. No one lives in reality as it is in itself, directly. We humans live in a "world" that is an instantaneous mediation of the stuff of the planet and ourselves. Animals may live directly, which is what we may mean by instinctually. But we will never know. The story that everything now and forever means only what it means to me is just that. A story. It's a piss-poor story, historically speaking, but who's young and paying any attention to history? And I'm saying that kind of story reacts to 9/11 very, very badly.

KEVIN NICHOLOFF: So you're saying the story Americans live in after 9/11 . . .

JOSEPH NATOLI: . . . is a story of fear of a certain kind resulting from an excessively privatized way of being in the world.

KEVIN NICHOLOFF: And it's the vulnerable spot that was targeted by the neocons to lead us to preemptively strike Iraq, and it was Karl Rove's same target in his politics of fear campaign in 2004.

JOSEPH NATOLI: We've not much concern for things outside. You can measure our curiosity by measuring the distance anything is from our own face. Neighbors have become the more nebulous "network." The notion of a society of mutual aid has become something over with, gone with the Socialists and their quaint sense of "solidarity." What's hip is the notion that government has to be drowned in a bathtub otherwise it will interrupt your life of personal choosing. Europe is "old" and doesn't "get it." We keep "reaching out" to the rest of the world and they remain unappreciative. We're all alone in here. But of course we're not. 9/11 was a knock from outside our cultural solipcism.

KEVIN NICHOLOFF: So would you say our lack of curiousity also has made us vulnerable?

JOSEPH NATOLI: Mark Hertsgaard calls us the "oblivious empire." We're sidetracked by a lot of really personal interests, all of course, as I repeat, generated by our free enterprise system. Wasn't it the 9/11 commission that pointed to a failure of imagination? You know today if you took a long walk in the woods like Wordsworth did, you'd be hit with 3,000 commercial messages. No space, man, for the imagination to get exercised.

KEVIN NICHOLOFF: Distraction, seduction, repression, overstimulation. You keep repeating this stuff in everything you write.

JOSEPH NATOLI: Hey, repetition does the trick for the president. Repeat. Repeat. Repeat. Stay on message. Anytime cultural ADD kicks in and out, the message is there. I do think if the most inventive minds in the country and the best in high-tech weren't directed 24/7 at keeping us productively consuming, we just might become something. Fear would diminish. Not just ours but fear *of* us. Given the lesson of our preemptive attack on Iraq, Iran is not foolish for seeking a nuclear "deterrent." Our cultural inability to think and feel beyond the box of our own self-interest doesn't exactly make other countries feel safe.

KEVIN NICHOLOFF: Okay. This is what we're like post-9/11. But what does popular film really have to do with all this?

JOSEPH NATOLI: How do I know what we're like? Right now. At this moment. Should I wait for a definitive sociological or political study? Tune into Fox News owned by Newscorp, a corporate leviathan? Pay attention to PBS's *Newshour* sponsored by venture capitalists, Wall Street brokers, and a global food broker? Pay attention to the polls? Do my own five-point empirical study? Google it? Wait for the mathematics? Apply Rational Choice theory or go cognitive?

KEVIN NICHOLOFF: You go to the movies.

JOSEPH NATOLI: I go to the movies. Why? Because popular culture sets out to connect with the imaginary of the masses, not transcend it or instruct it or critique it. Reality frames change with time and pop culture keeps up. It has to if it wants to sell tickets. If you want to know what the American mass psyche is after 9/11, one of the places you can go to find out is the movies. Sure, it's escapist and it's entertainment, but the real draw is in touching the hot spots in the cultural psyche, and successful pop film often does that.

KEVIN NICHOLOFF: Is it true that your work focuses on audience reception and not on film itself?

JOSEPH NATOLI: I don't go to the movies to look at the audience. I go to look at the movie. However, I'm not a film theorist or critic or historian.

I'm not a formalist. I'm a guy looking to connect what I read in the headlines with imaginary transformations of the same. Why? Because we live in a world we first imagine. Popular films help us see how we've imagined ourselves and are imagining ourselves. I look to film worlds the same way I look to literary worlds (*Mots D'Ordre* 1992): as imaginary "as if"-they-were-taken-to-be-real worlds. Such playful, picturing worlds are not discursively bound, so they disclose not only a conscious order of things but also what we struggle to represent. Popular film shows us our reality-making ways of the moment or, more precisely, puts us at play with those ways.

KEVIN NICHOLOFF: So popular film reacts to us, and we react to it, and then it reacts to our reactions? You know we came before the movies.

JOSEPH NATOLI: None of us came before stories of us. Advertisers, marketers, trial lawyers, political candidates, telemarketers, TV evangelists, football coaches. . . . They want to create a narrative we adopt as our own, totally possess. You buy the story, you buy everything in it. But movies can hit gold by projecting whatever story we're in, including the gaps, the holes, the fissures. No story of reality can be reality so every story is fractal. We all know that. We all don't want to know that. Movies don't want to fabricate us the way the market does; movies can play into the haunting and electrifying spaces of our fabrications.

KEVIN NICHOLOFF: Okay. Or, as your students would say, "Whatever." So if we don't go to the movies, what happens?

JOSEPH NATOLI: You don't go to the movies but you fall in love with someone who went to the movies and you play out *her* script of what love is. My point is that you play out somebody's script. Even Shakespeare had Holinshed. You think you can lock yourself away from Walt Disney, MTV, Rupert Murdoch, Time Warner, Viacom, and all the rest? Look, American culture is four parts Hollywood, five parts Madison Avenue, two parts MTV, one part Disney . . .

KEVIN NICHOLOFF: More Disney, I think. And all *American Idol*. Here's the thing. If we're all living these totally privatized lives as you call them, how come we're scripted? Pre-fab, as you like to say.

JOSEPH NATOLI: Ah, there's the con. To be manufactured as Chomsky says and yet to think you're unique. I said our mantra is "free to choose," but that doesn't mean we are. Our choices are constrained by the cultural surround, which in the United States . . .

KEVIN NICHOLOFF: . . . is five parts Victoria's Secret, three parts *Survivor* . . . I got it. Even if we don't go to the movies, we're in a movie.

But you're in it too. If you aren't, where are you? Our culture's a thing marketers and filmmakers and Jack Abramoff and Karl Rove create. But not for you. We're all in this matrix, but you're like Neo who is outside the matrix.

JOSEPH NATOLI: No, I'm in it. I just keep telling myself when I'm watching a movie that what I don't see outside the movies I can see here. I start looking for disclosures, for an unconcealing. And when I'm outside the movies I keep telling myself that this world we humans create has to be treated like a movie. I start looking for the writer, the producer, and the director. I'm not living in my own private imagining. I'm living in somebody else's. A lot of people. Living and dead. It's not a conspiracy and it's not rational. There's no beginning, middle, or end. We may go from Act One to Act Two, but Act Two may be from another script.

KEVIN NICHOLOFF: Movies reveal something hidden about reality . . .

JOSEPH NATOLI: About the picture of reality we're in at the time.

KEVIN NICHOLOFF: And to understand the reality you're in—or we're in—we have to treat it like a movie. I've got it but I don't have it. Know what I mean? What keeps what you say about a movie or about American culture or their connection from being nothing more than your personal take? And what about things that are not human culture like nature and asteroids and bird viruses and atoms and . . . gravity.

JOSEPH NATOLI: Okay, my personal take. I don't see "personal take" as any more establishing of the personal than "free to choose" is establishing of free choice. Take Huxley's *Brave New World*. How many unique individuals all expressing their own personal take do we have? One guy. Almost. I'm in the box of the moment just like everyone else. But I'm in a story that says it is a box; it's a stage set. So I'm just looking up and around and down and seeing the walls. Which are changing sets. And I'm looking to other people for confirmation on what I see. This isn't a personal screening. We're in a hierarchically narrated world.

KEVIN NICHOLOFF: If we're so *Brave New World*, how come we have so much difference and conflict and . . . red and blue states and we hate Bush and we love Bush and pro-lifers and pro-choicers. Everyone in a war of all against all. If we're in the same box.

JOSEPH NATOLI: All of it, and I mean all of it, arises out of a reaction to—positive or negative—our "show *me* the money!" mantra. Everything is narrated in reference to the master voice of the market, which outshouts and overwhelms every other voice. Because it's so pervasive it's reached an invisible status, like air. In its apparent absence, we seem to be arguing over other, independent matters. But all our conflicts can be traced to what will not enter our discourse because it is beyond the need of discourse. It's gone beyond the need for alibi. Our free-enterprise system, after the collapse of the Soviet Union, is in the nature of things. It is as foolish and useless to critique it as to . . . critique our own mortality, or our need for oxygen, or whether technology isn't necessarily progress, or the motives lying behind 9/11. We're prefabricated not to think that we are mostly prefabricated within a dominating discourse that like the notion of God in the view of the Christian Coalition has disappeared from the scene because it is unarguably self-evident.

KEVIN NICHOLOFF: I'll let you argue that with the Christian Coalition, not to mention the Libertarians. What happens when you go to the movies? Let's get back to that. Oh, first tell me how you get nature into your movie.

JOSEPH NATOLI: You know when Berkeley's idealism that it was only perception that made things real reached Dr. Johnson he kicked a stone and said, "There, I refute Berkeley." A real foot hit a real stone and it moved and Dr. J's foot hurt. Was that a refutation? Not if Dr. J was scripted to see the stone move. You could say that Boswell saw it too but Boswell's verification could have been part of Dr. J's script. What I'm saying is we go into the woods we see a deer, we play out *Bambi* or *The Deer Hunter* or a story of the guy down the road dying of deer TB. Blake put it best when he noted that when some see a tree they see a green thing standing in the way—they're into a land developer story—while others see the handiwork of God—they're in a God story.

KEVIN NICHOLOFF: Okay, you're not in the woods. You're in the movies.

JOSEPH NATOLI: Well, I go to see a picturing of the world I'm in that the movie is at play with but maybe I'm not at play with. Maybe it's because I don't picture the world in that way or maybe it's because I haven't consumed and responded to the world in the way the movie does. Film is an imaginative "as-if-it-were-the-world" creation, and therefore it abides by the laws of the imagination, working into levels of emotions, senses, and imagination that, say, rational choice theory or discourse analysis or whatever can't get to. I'm not looking for an original theme or startling message. I don't care what popular film may have to *say*, plotwise or subjectwise. On this imaginative level, however, popular film can become an analogue to the world we are in, one which by its very picturing of that world has an integrity independent of our own minds. We can be put into play with what may be projections of what is in us but we can't deal with, we can't represent.

KEVIN NICHOLOFF: For a guy who says he doesn't have a film theory it sounds like you do have a kind of film theory and approach. Right down to it, what's invisible here that the film may reveal is this invisible free-market stuff. Or something else?

JOSEPH NATOLI: It could be something else, but right now, both before and after 9/11, certainly since Reagan, the repressed and suppressed cultural dominant is how free-market economics let loose in a global arena totally drives the politics of our democracy. And since the bottom line of one is not the bottom line of the other, you can see the need for a cloaking of this dominant.

KEVIN NICHOLOFF: But popular film isn't all about uncloaking what this democracy fears to recognize. I mean where's the popular in that? We are talking commercial enterprise. Selling tickets. This isn't a PBS enterprise.

JOSEPH NATOLI: Sure. The fact that's it's commercial and therefore striving to be widely accessible makes it effective in shaping the culture. It also needs to do more than stroke that culture. It can't for commercial reasons repeat where we're at, but at the same time it has to reassure us that where we're at is okay. In both cases—if it's redundant or if it unsettles us—we'd walk out.

KEVIN NICHOLOFF: And the way it walks this tight rope?

JOSEPH NATOLI: Popular film has to present itself within a naïve realist mode of presentation; otherwise it would fail to be popular. The need here is to bring the viewer into the picture of reality being presented in such a way that the viewer is reassured that his or her own grasp of things is solid, that he or she knows what's going on and is in control. But the film can't rest there, because such redundancy, such repetition of how the viewer is already in the world, doesn't elicit the kind of box office smash appeal that sells tickets. There has to be an unnerving aspect, there has to be a threat to and unsettling of everything naïve realism has worked to create. I call it a haunting passage or moment, a plugging into what seizes and electrifies the viewer. We are taken beyond our sense of realism, beyond the order of our reality making, set against our own order of things. Then the film draws back and away and works to recover what it has disclosed so in the end we are not left unsettled but with the feeling once again that we are in control of the world around us, that our picture of the world is indeed not a picture but the world itself. Not all popular films do this, of course, but I have found that the more popular a film is the more certainly I will find such haunting passages.

KEVIN NICHOLOFF: Wouldn't you say that art or independent film and not box office would be more likely to reveal something to us about the world we're in?

JOSEPH NATOLI: One of the reasons popular film has something to reveal on these subliminal levels of desire and fear of what we are is because it has a close relationship with the American populace. That necessity is market driven. That populace goes to popular movies and ingests and reacts to those movies. In turn, in order to be popular, popular film has to work itself into this populace, alternatively giving it the escape it seeks and jolting it with what it's escaping from. As none of this is on a rational, conscious level of exposition and critique, there's no unifying second level of grand meaning. It's an endless circle of fabrication, seductions, and consumption. Critically acclaimed films that are rarely seen by anyone but an elite few invariably are critically acclaimed because they attempt to end this round of insensibility. However, they might be able to change it but they can't end it. And popular film by its very nature creates change and also responds to it much more rapidly and reliably than art film can.

KEVIN NICHOLOFF: I'm sure every serious film student will give you an argument on that. And all this is important because . . . we need to be insensible?

JOSEPH NATOLI: The ways we imagine the world lead to the ways we narrate the world, and these are the stories of reality we live within. It's important to know what reality you're in, what the new rules of the game are, what Wittgenstein called the language game being played. Science and its wannabe-science brood want to discover and explain reality, expose falsehood, even if they can't find truth. In the end, they come up with stories of discovery and explanation. The kind of cultural studies I do focus on the stories and story-making process itself and attempts to track them to our imaginations, our cultural imaginaries, because our own individual imaginations are, with rare exceptions, culturally bound. We may stay calmly within certain imaginaries or we may suddenly experience what our imaginations struggle to represent or repress, to defend against by demystifying or deconstructing. We run in all different directions from what haunts us.

KEVIN NICHOLOFF: And after 9/11 we're living in a different picture of the world? How do you prove that?

JOSEPH NATOLI: I can't. I don't. I leave the five-point statistical survey behind. I go to the movies and I am aware of the difference. If a good part of how we imagine ourselves and the world eludes us because it remains inconceivable to our resident conceiving-making ways, we either reconfirm and more deeply impose that resident reality, as do conservatives; protest the unreliability and inadequacy of such a reality, as do liberals; or remain in an undecided posture, as do the so-called swing voters. We haven't come to terms with what we've become for a very long time. "Greed is good," Gordon Gekko says in Oliver Stone's film *Wall Street* in 1985 and that picture of us stunned some and inspired others. Bin Laden also brought us a picture of ourselves, so you can say that 9/11 raised the stakes, raised the intensity levels of both what haunts our cultural imaginary and our defensive responses.

KEVIN NICHOLOFF: I keep choking on this idea that there's only one cultural imaginary.

JOSEPH NATOLI: And that I'm the guy who can reveal it.

KEVIN NICHOLOFF: Hey, you've got a take and maybe we're all more in the same box than in different boxes, but if it's all a matter of story choice, I'd like to be able to know the difference between being in a movie theatre watching a flick and driving my car on the interstate. I'd also like to think Karl Rove isn't renting all my brain space. You know the WMD story was totally bogus and everybody gave a shout-out on that. Well, almost everybody. After awhile. Reality trumped story. Maybe we could do that every time, like we used to, if this postmodern virus hadn't gotten inside our heads. Now, is all that I've just said out of a movie script?

JOSEPH NATOLI: Well, let's say, for the moment, that what I've been saying are just my personal connections with the films and the politics. It's the way a certain kind of leftover Leftist riddled with postmodern ideas would think. Then they won't stick in anyone's mind because they spring from purely personal soil. But if a connection is made not only between film and headlines but also between the reader, that implies a mutual sharing of something. I say we are at this moment sharing a very powerfully constructed cultural imaginary. Maybe it's the virus, as you say, of postmodernity that created this imaginary, or maybe postmodernity is the "cultural logic" of what created this imaginary, or maybe postmodernity is what enables us to recognize what the invisible hand of the global market has made of us. Maybe we'd prefer to be back in a world where realism and rationalism rule, but we're now in a world in which both provide spin and alibi for our cultural dominant—market globalization.

KEVIN NICHOLOFF: Which is shared because it's so powerful?

JOSEPH NATOLI: I'm repeating myself, but transnationalized capitalism has pretty well defined the dimensions of that imaginary. You can be caught black or a woman or poor or illiterate or "downsized" or gay and so on, but it's the dominating values and meanings of globalized capitalism that narrate all that.

KEVIN NICHOLOFF: Let's get to the book. You use characters because?

JOSEPH NATOLI: Using characters is a form of sampling or quoting the population. I sample well-known film characters who bear with them film worlds that picture or are at play with former American realities. I do this in order to create a level of historical contrast. I engage in a sort of dialogic, a sort of endless Q&A that floats more balloons than it brings to ground.

KEVIN NICHOLOFF: And the Blogosphere that ends the book is similarly a sampling?

JOSEPH NATOLI: Let's say you try for a trustworthy picture of the world with a mass of characters in a number of screenplays. After all, why not use imaginative means to track the imagination? Is there some universal law that keeps us divided, reason and imagination, in our writing? So, I write screenplays with characters to reach toward our cultural imaginary after 9/11. What I get are epiphanies, but no unified, clear picture emerges. How do I supplement this? You go to the Internet, the new Google Delphic Oracle, and what do you find? A battle of narratives, each narrative a discursive thrust, say, rant, into the heart of darkness, promising to deliver a true picture but in the end only inciting a counter-picturing. My use here of blogs is a satiric parodying; there is no space within these blogs for a revelation of what haunts the cultural imaginary, but there is such revelation, I think, in a fabricated clash of narratives, of blogs. These are meta- or sur-blogs, not read for the message alone but read with an awareness of construction, intent, and context. That as Duchamps' urinal showed us in another century fires up more than our everyday, conscious awareness. The screenplay format and the blogospheres attempt to picture, not capture or mirror or analyze, a post-9/11 world. And I find the style suitable to the subject: movies and reviews.

KEVIN NICHOLOFF: But how do you get from movies to the Bush administration, which seems to be the main focus of your attack? Clearly regardless of how many character parodies you use and how many pseudo bloggers, there is an underlying unified voice of rage against neocons, the Bush regime, and capitalism itself. Do the movies reveal this, or do the movies give you a chance to do what the bloggers do: rant your case?

JOSEPH NATOLI: The glue connecting the Bush administration—call it neo-cons—and the movies is this equal immersion in an unchecked globalized capitalism. Popular film needs to plug into that connect not because it wants to critique it but because it has potency. It has power over us. Why? Because it's repressed in the cultural imaginary. It's a psychodrama on a cultural scale. How then does an undisclosing of that connection reach us? As a rant. How else would it?

KEVIN NICHOLOFF: Spell out the postmodern in all this for me.

JOSEPH NATOLI: How do you go from art to reality? From picture or word to world? As a postmodernist, I think that we live in a buffer zone of stories about the world. Of course, "hard pragmatists and Scot realists" like to say they live in world not fancy. The more they set about "explaining" that "hard realist" view, the more we see the act of narration. Hayden White pointed all this out in regard to our "objective" accounts of the past. We make a world of reality by the very act of narrating that reality. We are "worlding" in Heidegger's view, that is, we are transposing at the moment of intentional perception something not "out there" but rather something we are "already in" into a human life-world. That's what humans do. The irony is that they want to escape this by narrating stories of escape. Stories of power—of government, politics, corporate lobbying—are part of our narrative frame. Movies concoct stories within the same buffer zone. They intersect and interrelate.

KEVIN NICHOLOFF: So you won't object if those who feel there are disciplinary boundaries and methodologies to be respected can't find your purpose or your contribution here?

JOSEPH NATOLI: I don't have a story of escape. And that, at this moment, is not a very viable position. We act out what we imagine, and movies, the art form of the twentieth century but not the only one, both script that imagining and put us into play with it. But I don't have a methodology. I don't know what discipline can track our imaginations to the world, or what methodology tracks art to emotions, or indeed can tie pictures to world. We live in pictures of the world we—first person plural—ourselves have imagined. We can probe the imagination itself or we can probe the world or both. What I do is probe a product of imagination and world, a picturing of the world movies present. And I don't take up political analysis or discourse analysis or argument analysis to do it. I have no theoretical bottom to do any of that; my theoretical bottom is postmodern, and the subplot of *This Is a Picture* is trying to perform nothing more than an attitude or disposition.

KEVIN NICHOLOFF: I kind of disagree that you don't have any theoretical bottom. It sounds like you've got a lot of. . . . Let me ask you this. At a time when being post-9/11 America also means—to many—that we're post-postmodern, you connect what you see as a movement from modern to postmodern film with our post-9/11 awareness. Why? How so?

JOSEPH NATOLI: There's been great success since 9/11 in knocking off not only postmodern thought but Enlightenment as well. We could have taken the view that bin Laden and al-Qaeda are picturing the world in a way we can't understand, or, we could have declared The Truth that they're evil and we're good. The former is postmodernist, the latter naïve realist. It doesn't follow that in trying to grasp fully the story of reality al-Qaeda is in that we are condoning the actions of 9/11, giving up our moral compass, being liberal-soft on crime, or hoping for a Utopia where we "all get along." But knowing how the world is pictured and knowing how that picture convinces anyone that it is not a picture but indeed the world itself puts us in a far better defensive posture than throwing bin Laden and al-Qaeda in a handy historical bin of "Evil," a signifier absolutely empty of any pertinent conceptual force.

KEVIN NICHOLOFF: Wouldn't just being more scientific about everything been the best defense? Not that I think scientism is the answer for everything, but we did fail to analyze some pretty far-out intelligence, so called.

JOSEPH NATOLI: The Enlightenment had also to be replaced by the reigning naïve realism, a mode dominant in the Middle Ages, so that any application of a Kantian critical reason to reasons as to why we should attack Iraq after 9/11 was considered unnecessary. Why? Reason is unnecessary when faith rules. And we had faith after 9/11 that "evil" covered the crime and nothing more than a Dark Ages approach was needed. Besides, faith—not critical reason—won Bush the White House in 2004. Rove's problem with Bush from the beginning was that he couldn't possibly represent the Enlightenment but as a repentant drunk and born-again Christian he could front faith. I forget what else you asked me.

KEVIN NICHOLOFF: You relate a movement from modern to postmodern film with film before and after 9/11.

JOSEPH NATOLI: We are now aware of how we are aware. What Bush and his neocon mentors made of 9/11 has made us too aware of the power of spins to shape our world. At least for those who weren't made aware already by the film *Wag the Dog*. This sort of hyperconsciousness that we are inevitably living in a hyperreality brought to us by resident power-brokers is what we bring to the screen and what the screen now brings to us. Were we first put into play with this postmodern awareness by the movies? Or did our picturing of the world postmodernize and the movies followed along?

KEVIN NICHOLOFF: Something like every small town becoming a Twin Peaks after Lynch's TV show.

JOSEPH NATOLI: Sure. Theory set me up for it but David Lynch's work in fact put me into play with the far-reaching implications and consequences of our imaginative mediation of reality. Movies shaped themselves within this postmodern attitude and showed us the power of our own fabrications. This too is now what haunts us—we've somehow constructed this dark world we are now in, dark in spite of the daily, bell-ringing buoyancy of Wall Street and perhaps more dark because our globalized, capitalist foundation seems indifferent to war, death, job loss, poverty, natural disaster, torture, inequality, environmental and species degradation, and so on. But at the same time movies launched themselves to a privileged place within the hyperreal.

KEVIN NICHOLOFF: That's reality plus what we've made of it.

JOSEPH NATOLI: To know what reality is for us at this moment we need to see it from within the cultural imaginary of the moment. That awareness too is part of the hyperreal. We see everything as if it were being screened. What is more hyperreal than airplanes flying into the Trade Towers on a brilliantly clear autumn morning in AD 2001, than a preemptive strike against Iraq for fallacious reasons, than a loss within the tenure of one willfully ignorant president of all the international respect we had earned up till that time? Those jets flying into the World Trade Towers, Saddam's stolid statue being toppled, George W. uttering "I know what I believe. I will continue to articulate what I believe and what I believe—I believe what I believe is right"—these are all hyperreal.

KEVIN NICHOLOFF: I see what you're saying about our responses being contrived. But the attack itself—that was real. People died. That was real. Those towers are gone. That's real.

JOSEPH NATOLI: Sure. It's an historical fact. Place, date, and all. Like Pearl Harbor. Vietnam. Wait. Aren't those historical events, like all historical events, now imagined within the dimensions of a present cultural imaginary? Their existence is at once a matter of representation, which is a matter of cultural mediation. The 9/11 attack was unique in that it happened on our TV screens at the same time it happened in the world. From the very first TV images of a plane and a building the event went through the kind of mediating filtering TV gives to reality and we give to TV. At once, what we saw on TV was like a movie and we could digest it in no other way. Bush's responses were also from a movie, the only way to reach a culture already residing in the hyperreal. He became John Wayne. He had a Texas walk, a tobacco-chawing smirk, a twang as needed, and he cut brush a lot "out at the ranch. It was pure PR genius to give Bush a part in that movie, pure genius to see it all so quickly as a movie.

KEVIN NICHOLOFF: This is a special problem for Americans? And, say, before TV and the movies and the computer and any kind of technology?

JOSEPH NATOLI: To answer the first: we are exceptional in the longevity and success of our use of technology to create new products and new needs and increased profits. The past and the hyperreal? A matter of degree. Patrick Henry or Paul Revere or John Paul Jones and so on get into the mix of a Revolutionary war narrative. There's an imagined community back then through which everything is filtered. But the technology to disseminate their representations are nonexistent or primitive. We now live at a time when the image-making powers technology has produced invade every moment and place in our lives. We are reached as no one in the world has ever been reached before. The image-making machines of Hollywood and Madison Avenue are truly awesome. Everything that happens is immediately massaged to suit market needs. It's ironic that a time when market power can be tempered by governmental power, we hold government the villain and look to the market for relief.

KEVIN NICHOLOFF: But don't you rail against the Bush regime?

JOSEPH NATOLI: That's a regime fully responsive to market power. Nader, I think, called Bush's presidency a "corporate presidency." Theoretically, ideally, and constitutionally, the Federal Government can operate independent of the corporate boardroom. It shouldn't operate in opposition to the free market on the grounds of any principle or ideology but certainly on behalf of the democratic and egalitarian ambitions of this society, which, everyone realizes, far exceed a bottom line of profit to shareholders. There was no mention in the Constitution of profit or shareholders.

KEVIN NICHOLOFF: Now doesn't this kind of partisan rage put your whole project here in jeopardy?

JOSEPH NATOLI: I think more rage should have been shown by the press, by the Democratic Party, by university faculty and students, by an American public more concerned with the latest special at Wal-Mart than with where President Bush was taking us. I don't apologize for rage. It's biblical. And whether I've presented just my own rage and rant or have gotten into other lifeworlds, other characters, is up to the reader to decide. I think I put the reader into play with clashing lifeworlds and clashing views and although there is no grand summation or resolution, no original revelation or stunning closure, there are, I hope, some windows to a new awareness, some fresh incitements as to how we imagine ourselves and the world.

KEVIN NICHOLOFF: Do you think Hillary Clinton will get some red state votes if she runs for president?

JOSEPH NATOLI: Not a one.

KEVIN NICHOLOFF: That's what I think about you getting red state readers for this book. Good luck.

JOSEPH NATOLI: I won't need it. This interview is going to draw them in.

KEVIN NICHOLOFF: I see post-traumatic shock hasn't missed you. But maybe you're right. People will read this and go on to read the book: *This Is a Picture, and Not the World: Movies and a Post-9/11 America.* Was that spin as good as Rove after 9/11?

Introduction

September 11, we were told repeatedly, had created a "new normal," an altered condition in which we were supposed to be able to see, as the *Christian Science Monitor* explained a month after the events, "what is—and what is no longer—important."

—Joan Didion, "Politics in the 'New Normal' America,"
The New York Review of Books, October 21, 2004

Even in this post-9/11 period, Senator Kerry doesn't appear to understand how the world has changed.

—Vice President Dick Cheney,
Republican National Convention, 2004

The more that I look into it and study it from the Taliban perspective, they don't see the world the same way we do.

—Rear Admiral Stufflebeem,
Deputy Director for the Joint Chiefs of Staff

WRITER: First of all, this is a story about what used to be called "the pictures," which were never ostensibly taken to be the "world" but hopefully an escape from it. I say "story" about movies because I am not a film historian perpetrating upon an innocent readership a definitive, determinate history of film. This is a story I, an inveterate expounder of postmodernity . . .

PRODUCER: Cut! This is dead. I mean postmodern anything in a post-9/11 climate. We're premodern if anything. Certainly post-history.

WRITER: But I need it to describe how we see the world differently. 9/11 caught us at a postmodern hyperconscious moment. We're aware of spins and spinmeisters but ironically . . .

PRODUCER: Irony is dead also. Roger Rosenblatt said so in *Time* magazine.

WRITER: May I go on? Ironically we're obsessed with "raw reality." We're living in a picture of a post-9/11 America and we know it.

PRODUCER: The blue states know it. Maybe. But the red states don't.

WRITER: Everybody knows it. But at the same time we're going at things as if we were rational and realistic. We're fighting a War on Terror based on very poor picturing of the world. We're being led by a president who we all know has only a paint-by-numbers ability to picture the world. If this isn't an ironic situation, I don't know what is. You know why it all has the feel of a Hollywood movie? Because when we go to a movie we know this is a picture and not the world. When we watch TV, cable smashmouth news or reality TV or listen to squawkbox radio or watch a presidential press conference or a Rumsfeld war briefing we also know this is a scripted picturing and not the world. We're not naïve realists anymore.

PRODUCER: So it's all a movie? Flying planes into the Trade Towers was a movie?

WRITER: No, but we've been picturing it differently since 9/11. Western Europe, Middle East, the United States. And in the United States itself. If you picture things via the scientific method, the reality of 9/11 is open to investigation. The president served it up immediately in an older frame—a moral frame. This was evil and you don't scrutinize evil; you eradicate it. As it turned out, the reality of 9/11 succumbed to neoconservative politics, fitting in nicely with the dreams of the *Project for the New American Century.*

PRODUCER: And the movies reveal all this?

WRITER: No, actually post-9/11 movies, like post-9/11 TV, have adopted the naïve realist stylings of the Bush administration. We're not deconstructing the programming coming out of the White House.

PRODUCER: That's because deconstruction is dead.

WRITER: How often did the Catholic Church say the Enlightenment was dead? Unfortunately for the Church, the Enlightenment mindset was already occupying cultural brainspace. Look, contemporary movies have been picturing a shifting from realistic and modernist mindsets to a postmodern one. The planes that flew into those towers flew into an America that brought the world to meaning in a style learned from Hollywood movies, and those movies have often in the last twenty-five years been reflecting how we picture and narrate the world and then live within those depictions. Some movies were drawing attention to their own constructive ingenuity, to their own reality-making powers. And some movies were all about the Hollywood magic of convincing us this picture we're watching *is* reality. If you investigate that change, you're automatically investigating a changing America. And since 9/11 had been a culturally traumatizing event, we can't picture the world or talk about any past picturing of the world without those 9/11 lenses on. That's postmod too.

PRODUCER: Did we get this on film? Okay, make it part of the intro. Intro. Take 2.

WRITER: This is a story I, an inveterate expounder of postmodernity, tell about the screen without concealing that what I have already seen on the screen adjusts the lens of my seeing and telling. I look at movies within the horizon of all movies I've gone to. My moviegoing, like yours, contributes greatly to what you could call an a priori mindscape. I could claim that I rise above and out of the way I see, the dispositions and predilections, the curvature of my lens, but that's a story I've neither been able to verify in my own life nor in any account of the day's news, including Fox News.

As a postmodernist then I admit that the way I look at the world and think about the world has a lot to do with the big screen. Simply telling myself that this is a picture and not the world doesn't at all prevent me from linking picture and world, from adopting the reality-making ways of movies in my real life, in my life outside the movie theatre. Most of how I hook up with the world has to do with not what I've directly observed in my life outside the movie theatre but what I've gleaned from stories and pictures, words and images, of the world. Perhaps then if I didn't read or go to the movies or watch TV or listen to others, including my parents, I would have a way of looking at the world that was totally shaped by my direct encounters with the world. However, at the getgo, my mother and father started telling me things about the world and about myself so that I have a suspicion that the very first time I ventured out into the world there was already the beginnings of a filtering process, a cultural lens shaping, that has matured into the extreme myopia of my adulthood.

So pictures have done a lot to picture me as I now represent myself. But this book's title is not a lie: As a postmodernist I believe that there may be something as big as the Grand Canyon between how the world is pictured—in film, photograph, painting, book, newspaper, magazine, lecture, sermon, formula, campaign speech, blueprint and so on—and what the world may actually be. Every picture tells a story—and every story has no way of validating its accuracy except by offering yet another story.

This is a picture and not the world, and now I mean my account of how movies reflect and pilot changes in American culture. I tell that story through Hollywood's own formational system: film genres. They were created in response to what kinds of pictures audiences seemed to want, and, in turn, Hollywood mapped out its pictures of the world within this genre grammar. Because it was an audience-response grammar, genres changed, faded away, returned remodeled, or blossomed. There's no such categorization of human life in the world that these modes correspond to or reflect. And they weren't created, as for instance Northrop Frye's anatomy of literary criticism was created, in response to what he thought was an inhering structure in literature. Genre categories responded to a commercial need; they were a marketing device, very convenient hooks to haul in the ticket buyers.

I'm just as pragmatical: I take advantage of these Hollywood categories in order to focus on changes in their presentations, their picturing, of the world. My premise is that you can trace the ways we bring the world to meaning through these genres, and that because we have gradually shifted toward a postmodern way of representing ourselves and the world we are within, we're going to find signs of this shifting in the genres themselves. I am primarily concerned with this paradigm shifting, an ontological as well as epistemological shifting. Both surround and players change over time, and chance, as in 9/11, plays a hand, but none of this necessitates a change in how we perceive and think about these changes. Such a cataclysmic perceptual revolution occurred from medievalism to modernity, but unfortunately we have no movie archive of this. However, the change from modernity to postmodernity has been captured and is being captured on the screen. Indeed these are pictures and not the world, but they are pictures *of* the world. If we look carefully, we can see the postmodernizing of our picturing and our viewing. Because genres were created in the beginning by Hollywood to tap into a world, an audience, outside Hollywood, we can continue to look at the audience—ourselves in the world now—in order to recognize and confirm changes on the screen. This is my license to venture into "off-screen" reality, which is of course no more than venturing into "off-screen" pictures of reality. These are all pictures and not the world, but we and our mediations, our scripts and directing, are what is pictured.

At this point I admit that the pragmatics of my own project here do not entirely correspond with the pragmatics of the old Hollywood studio system. I start with an "outtake" I call postmodern screwball, by which I mean the multiple clashing realities of classic screwball comedy combined with the ludic nature of a postmodern awareness come close, I imagine, to a micro-atomic chaos. It's an "outtake" because it's best in this sort of book to begin with a beginning that removes itself as a beginning. Beginnings often promise to lay a cornerstone that ends with a cap-stone conclusion or experience, and I certainly don't want to promise that. And whether we're now prepared to see it or not, screwball creates at least part of the atmosphere of our post-9/11 world.

The next chapter, entitled "Futurescape," concerns our need to pic-ture and then live in our own cultural paranoia. Like the Krell in *For-bidden Planet*, we have been creating our own monsters. Or have we? "Frontierscape" traces the Western iconography that runs from the Lone Ranger to George W. Bush. "Noirscape" refers to the film noir genre, style, and period. How is classic film noir's dark angst from 1941 to 1955 different from post-9/11 dread? Writing this after the 2004 Christ-mas holiday shopping frenzy that took so many working class Ameri-cans into Wal-Mart, I wonder if the film noir's "sympathetic fugitive," disenfranchised by fate and corporations and hounded by a class-strati-fied "order of things," has any parallel in this post-9/11 world where fear is a political orchestration—that makes a two-term president of George W. Bush—as well as creating a market opportunity to get Amer-icans "shopping for security."

The chapter I call "Magic Town" delves into the "Heartland of Security," a Disneyland/Main Street that is no more illusionary or less real than the paradise of many virgins pictured in the Koran. But this is not a genre any film genre scholar has ever heard of, although in a ter-rified world this idea of a "magic town" where life is not threatened, the atmosphere is not heating up, and one's job and one's future are secure may yet take the twenty-first century American psyche by storm.

The Shortscape chapter on melodrama faces the dilemma of being outrageously "unrealistic" at a moment when "reality TV" assures us that all the flim-flam of fiction and spin have been deleted. Melodrama unapologetically creates, directs, and produces a picture of reality, whereas "reality TV," as we all know, serves up Reality Raw. We Amer-icans were "just for the facts" long before 9/11; to paraphrase a won-derful moment in a wonderful film, *Sideways*, a moment when would-be novelist Paul Giamatti is asked what kind of book he's writing and he replies a novel, an admission that produces frowns. He reassures his friends by saying that a good part of the novel is based on the facts of his own life. *That's fine*, is the reply, *because there are too many serious things going on in the world right now for us to be wasting time with make-believe*. The "Never Far from Melodrama" chapter reviews the United States since 9/11 as mounting one melodrama after another, some over-the-top such as our memories of the 2000 Florida chad count, some so tragic that we would as a nation weep if our much-touted com-passion had not been detoured already by presidential campaign strate-gies and shopping manias.

Following the bombast of melodrama, we run a documentary entitled "The Short-Term Memory Detective," which does a close-up of a post-9/11 American attentiveness, or lack of. This might be called a subgenre of mystery, and it may prove to be a short-lived affliction of our cultural historical memory.

The next chapter, "This Genre Does Not Exist," struggles to picture a film genre that exists perhaps only as a subgenre of the Thriller, namely, the Political Thriller. However, distinguishing such a genre at a moment when "everything is political"—and therefore all movies are—is an impossible task. At the same time, because "everything is political," it would be absurd not to have a chapter on what is so pervasively present, especially at a moment when we are exporting our nation-building politics throughout the world. I would argue that even two 2004 blockbusters—*Shreck 2* and *The Incredibles*—though delightful family animations, suit the regnant political mood of the country.

The chapter "Fearscape/Thrillscape/Nightscape" probes into the heart of our post-9/11 fears, tracing the continuum of fear, both personal and cultural, as revealed on the screen. Even pre-9/11 films awakening pre-9/11 fears are re-seen and infused with new fear. In *The Sixth Sense*, for instance, Bruce Willis tries to help a young boy filled with fear because dead people seek him out. In the end the boy helps Willis realize that he is one of those dead people, that he had not indeed survived being shot by a deranged patient, that there was no post-shooting existence. Post-9/11 we hook up this way: Did we really survive? And where are we now? Is this what survival looks like?

I present another trailer at his point—the first being the trailer midway in the Frontierscape chapter, a trailer called "Dead Man." The trailer here is entitled "The Jesus Genre," the nonexistent genre that may have mobilized the red states in the 2004 presidential election but certainly knitted nicely into President Bush's "faith-based" theme, from "faith-based" prisons and pharmaceuticals to "faith-based" national parks and wilderness areas.

The last chapter, appropriately, brings to our attention another fictitious genre, "American Cool." However, American "cool" is the "soft power" that the United States peddles throughout the world. What is "cool" in a post-9/11 world, and what can Madison Avenue peddle but the escapism of narcissistic self-stylings, from botox and colonic treatments to collagen and silicone supplementations? The bedrock foundation of the "Ownership Society" must be "American Cool."

PRODUCER: Okay, that's a wrap. Let me get this straight. You're writing about post-quantum screwballness, fear and paranoia, short-term memory loss, "coolness" in an age of terror, Jesus power, cartoon politics,

Cowboy George W. Bush, dead as a doornail melodrama, and magic towns, whatever they are. These are cockamamie, no?

WRITER: In screenplay format. I'm writing about them in screenplay format.

PRODUCER: Okay, here's what I'll need. Every script has to be doctored. I want the script doctor rewrites along with your screenplay. Also, you know that you're going to be blogged to death by every crank who ever saw a film. Plus, you diss film genre, so the real and serious film scholars will also jump in with their blogs.

WRITER: You're giving me writer's blog.

PRODUCER: Here's what we'll do. We'll put the bloggers' reviews into the production. Okay, redo the ending.

WRITER: Finally, I tell this story of film genres and bogus film genres by using what I call "filmscapes" (think of the family of scapes: landscape, seascape, cloudscape, dreamscape, timescape, mindscape, filmscape). Each filmscape presents parodies of characters from the films of that genre as well as contributions from the producer, a stable of script doctors, and assorted members of the tech crew. A voice-over sets the scene and establishes the approach, an approach that may at once be challenged by a script doctor. The writer behind the scenes is a postmod cultural commentator who began in *Hauntings* in 1992, a project in which "I crisscross between the lived experiences (I scour the headlines, listen to the talk shows, follow the campaigns) of our present culture and popular film in the hope of bringing to a consumable and respondable level some of what haunts us" (94). The writer continued that project in *Speeding to the Millennium* (1995), *Postmodern Journeys* (1998), and *Memory's Orbit* (2002), intent on finding in popular film of the 1990s the outline of changing American realities, of an American cultural imaginary daily altering its mix of conceivables and inconceivables, of the privileged and the haunting.

PRODUCER: It's a wrap. Run the bloggers before the credits.

THE BLOGOSPHERE

Blog: www.postmodisdead.com

Hello? Irony is dead. Postmod is dead. I quote: "Whatever may be said of the perpetrators of Tuesday's slaughter, they're not cowards." Susan Sontag, *The New Yorker*. So they were brave, heroically brave? It's this sort of offensive interpretation that results from Natoli's postmodern nominalism: It's possible to produce in a post-9/11 America a movie that sees the devils of 9/11 as "not cowards" and to have *that* devilish "picture" of reality trump reality and find a hospitable place within what he calls the American "imaginary." He goes on as if an imaginary filled only with Hollywood B movies swept aside our sense of realism and rationality as well as every bit of our moral sense. Sure, we suspend all that briefly for entertainment's sake, but we don't go back to being a tabula rasa. This is just another Baudrillard spin: The hyperreal has replaced the real world. Here's news: Critical realism has replaced the hyperreal with the real; critical realism has deconstructed deconstruction. President George W. Bush's second term isn't proof that a spin reality can replace reality. It's yet another indication that we're going to elect a man who doesn't confuse being in a movie theatre with being in a real post-9/11 world.

Blog: www.antirelativism.com

Thoughts on Natoli's project:
    "Academia . . . is a hotbed of fancy foreign notions, a den of dangerous relativists who can't talk straight, can't think straight— and don't even want to try. . . . Very little harm would be done if literary critics and postmodernist anthropologists, lawyers and the like were told to go and get real jobs" (A. C. Grayling, "Relative Thinking," *The Guardian*, November 18, 2004).

Blog: www.ironyisneeded.com

Irony can't be dead just at the very moment we need it the most, Joan Didion mused in her piece for *The New York Review of Books*: "Fixed Ideas: America Since 9.11" (January 16, 2003). It would indeed be ironic if it was.
    Whoever named Bush's still murky plans of retaliation "Infinite Justice" was dangerously devoid of irony, not to mention a sense of Islamic theology. Here is one definition of irony: "Incongruity between actual result of a sequence of events and the normal or expected result." That kind of irony might note that America, for all its efforts to shine a beacon of freedom throughout the world, is seen as an empirical oppressor by large swaths of the Islamic world. That kind of irony would wonder if, in this new battle on behalf of freedom, we may rush to strip away civil liberties. That kind of irony would wonder whether this new kind of war, waged to make us safe from terrorist attacks, might plunge the world into a far more dangerous conflagration.

Blog: www.postmodtracker.com

The latest jihad against the signifier "postmodern" is our post-9/11 jihad as the conservative right invokes the September attacks in an effort to score a decisive victory in the culture wars. The postmodernists would be unable to condemn the attacks in any unqualified way, since they reject universal values and ideals. "There Are No Postmodernists in a Foxhole" was the title of a *Fresh Air* commentary on August 20, 2002. *U.S. News & World Report* announces that colleges are preaching "the postmodern conviction that there are no truths or moral norms worth defending." It's a slippery slope after this. *National Review Online* publishes pieces titled "Postmodernism Kills" and "Dangerous Ideas." Stanley fish comes to the rescue in the *New York Times* and then in an article in *Harper's*: Everybody has postmod wrong. Sure it holds for universal values and ideals, but the problem is we can't justify "our response to the attacks in universal terms that would be persuasive to everyone, including our enemies" ("Condemnation Without Absolutes," *New York Times*, October 15, 2001).

Bog: www.showmetheresearch.com

Here's what I get out of the intro to *This Is a Picture*:

1. Postmodernists say we live in pictures of the world we ourselves create;
2. We go to the movies to find out what reality is, and in turn we make movies to show us that reality;
3. If you want to find out what post-9/11 America is like, go to the movies;
4. If you look at film "genres"—mostly not real film genres but ones made up by script doctors—you'll see not only how we've become hyperconscious and deconstructive (that is, postmod)—but also how we've changed as a country.

I totally disagree. First, sane, rational people live in reality first and then picture it; second, we go to the movies not to find reality but to escape it; third, if you want to find out what post-9/11 America is like, don't go to a place that's trying to get as far from that as possible, namely, the movie theater; fourth, if you want to know what finally killed off postmodernism, check out 9/11. And if you want to study the difference between pre-9/11 America and post-9/11 America, wait for the real research to be done.

THE BLOGOSPHERE

Blog: www.moralclarity.com

If irony hadn't been declared dead by Roger Rosenblatt, I would dare to say that it's ironic that Hollywood and its moral decadence—which the red states triumphantly turned away from in this election—is what the writer here advises us to look to in order to see what we've become as a country after 9/11. My response: We've become a moral country that doesn't need to go to the movies to find our moral compass. No moral clarity can emerge from this book, or screenplay, or whatever it is.

Blog: www.blowingsmoke.com

Joan Didion found some smoke!
    "Postmodernism was henceforth to be replaced by 'moral clarity' and those who persisted in the decadent insistence that the one did not necessarily cancel out the other would be subjected to what William J. Bennett would call—in *Why We Fight: Moral Clarity and the War on Terrorism*—'a vast relearning' . . . the reinstatement of a thorough and honest study of our history, undistorted by the lens of political correctness and pseudo sophisticated relativism" (Joan Didion, *The New York Review of Books*, January 16, 2003).

Blog: www.realityisreal.com

The writer should preface his screenplay with this from Aldous Huxley, but of course he won't:
    "If films were really true to life, the whole of Europe and America would deserve to be handed over as mandated territories to the Basutos, the Papuans, and the Andaman pygmies. Fortunately, they are not true. We who were born in the West and live there, know it. But the untutored mind of the poor Indian does not know it. He sees the films, he thinks they represent Western reality . . ." (*Jesting Pilate*, 1926).

Blog: www.cheapcommercialism.com

I thought Leftists were dead way before irony and postmodernism were dead. Both the Old Left and the New Left were buried with the Soviet Union. Now here's a Leftist who factors economics out of the equation. I mean, is Hollywood all about profit to shareholders? How come we're looking to movies—which will "picture" anything as long as it goes over on a mass-market crowd—to see how America has changed since 9/11? If you want to look at aesthetic changes, or computer-generated changes, or distribution changes and all that, okay. But you can't stretch movies into the real world, especially not into post-9/11 America. Anyway, here's what Nick Clooney says in a book worth reading about how movies changed us:

"[S]o many of us actually saw on our television screens the second sleek jet liner slice cleanly through the splendid geometry of the remaining World Trade Center Tower. . . . For many, that chilling, indelible picture made cheap and vulgar the guilty pleasure we had derived from watching dozens of similar pictures created by Hollywood in an increasingly frantic effort to shock us into buying tickets" (Nick Clooney, *The Movies That Changed Us*, 2002).

Hollywood films cheapen reality; they don't reflect it. And if they try to change us, it's something our real values and moral sense will resist.

Blog: www.everythingispost.com

In writing about horror film as "postmodern" Andrew Tudor points to three levels of analysis, the third being what I think the writer is up to:

"At the third level, the argument is as much about postmodernity as postmodernism. Yes, it claims, there are aesthetic attributes properly to be considered as postmodern [in recent horror film]; yes, there is an emergent pattern of postmodern cultural and moral change; however, all this must be seen as part of the historical social transition from modernity to postmodernity. To this extent, postmodernity is indeed 'post,' markedly different to what has gone before'" ("From Paraonia to Postmodernism? The Horror Movie in Late Modern Society," in *Genre and Contemporary Hollywood*, ed. Steve Neale, BFI, 2002).

Blog: www.thisisapremodernworld.com

I ask my reader: what's easier to parody than film genres? They're recognizable. This from *www.filmsite.org/genres.html* (a real Web site unlike most in *This Is a Picture*):

"[Film genres] are various forms or identifiable types, categories, classifications or groups or films that are recurring and have similar, familiar or instantly recognizable patterns, syntax, filmic techniques or conventions—that include one or more of the following: settings (and props), content and subject matter, themes, period, plot, central narrative events, motifs, styles, structures, situations, recurring icons (for example, six-guns and ten-gallon hats in Westerns) stock characters (or characterizations), and stars. Many films straddle several film genres."

THE BLOGOSPHERE

THE BLOGOSPHERE

But the writer is not parodying film genres as a way of carrying through in a postmodern form with his view that film has been mirroring a shifting from a modern to a postmodern America. I mean, until 9/11, a moment when we reverted back to whatever the world was before it was modern. But he uses pastiche characters; they're not parodies of well-known film characters because they don't really undermine those characters, or expose their constructed nature, their fabricated "reality." Maybe they are parodic on some really stretched-out connection, but I don't see it. What I see is that using send-ups of recognizable characters to talk about the genres they're connected with confuses film and reality, film research, commentary, criticism, and films themselves. It's like the writer is saying "If you want to talk about film you need characters to do it. You can't have a monologue. You have to produce, direct, script, and shoot your 'account.'"

None of this will work at a premodern moment. Consider this: In presenting his argument to President Bush that the United States should not pre-emptively attack Iraq, Secretary of State Colin Powell was advised to reduce his position to one page and then be prepared to further condense that one page into a five-minute oral presentation. Message? This is not a moment when reading and criticism are in flower. We, in fact, went to war in spite of what knowledge was readily available. No, this is not a time to experiment with boundaries between the discursive and the nondiscursive, between reason and imagination, between fact and fiction, between creativity and criticism.

Hollywood can take over the presidency with a Reagan and probably a Schwarzenegger, and George W. Bush can turn the United States into the world's "nightmare on Elm Street," but if some crazed writer tries to show that we're script-doctoring reality all the time, that there's no place in this red and blue America that's not a Hollywood set, that we're all characters in a Madison Avenue production, that 9/11 was a horror that script doctors were hired to turn into the America in which we're now living—why that writer will wind up on the "No Fly" list, one of those "postmodern intellectuals [who] have weakened the country's resolve." I'm quoting Stanley Fish.

Blog: *www.classificationisall.com*

Westerns, comedies, and sci-fi are real genres.
   Documentary is a nongenre.
   Trailers are not genres.

The detective film is a subgenre, as are film noir, melodramas, and political thrillers.

Magical towns do not a film genre make, nor does American Coolness or Jesus.

Pace Borges, but rational, well-defined classification is not only possible but necessary at this time in our post-9/11 existence.

THE BLOGOSPHERE

Outtake

Postmod Screwball

> . . . and God help you if you use voice-over in your work, my
> friends. God help you. That's flaccid, sloppy writing. Any
> idiot can write with a voice-over narration to explain the
> thoughts of a character.
>
> —Robert McKee, Adaptation,
screenplay Charlie Kaufman

Voice-over: A blog on TV shock humor asserts that reality is the
new king of comedy. "Audiences are getting increasingly jaded, so
that a scripted scene of a man getting hit in the groin with a golf
club isn't enough; they want the real thing." What else could explain
the huge popularity of "reality TV" except this hunger for reality,
for "the real thing" in an age where we are, to paraphrase Baudrillard, offered more and more information and less and less meaning, in an age, to paraphrase Debord, of spectacle and not reality.
After the Enlightenment the picture of the world changed from
medieval to modern but the essence of that change lay in the realization that we do indeed picture the world. We, in short, don't live
in it as God made it but rather as we picture it. For modernity, however, we could accurately picture the world through right reason so
none of the alarms were set off. Modernity could empirically and
rationally generate an accurate picture of the world. However, the
postmodern awareness that the way we reason went on within the
picture frame and not outside it—a Nietzsche observation—did set
off the alarms. We indeed were picture makers but also those
already pictured: We were not the distanced, objective observers of
the scene but rather adopting roles already scripted. We, and our

reasoning, were in already existing pictures of the world. We could picture reality wrongly at any time and place and not see our error; we could be the blind man holding the tail of the elephant and testifying to the snakelike shape of the elephant. Shock humor is a defiant naysaying to this postmodern awareness. Things can be done without intervention, either of thought or feeling, so that in total crudeness unfiltered reality can undeniably be on display. The goal is laughs, because this is a revolutionary gesture and, as George Orwell suggested, "every joke is a tiny revolution." But the question remains: Is there a postmodern comedy? A comedy wrought not in defiance of the postmodern awareness but deriving from it? And because postmodernity, according to its critics, leads to chaos and anarchy and an "anything goes" climate, one thinks of all that brought to the screen in classic screwball comedy which flourished roughly from the mid-1930s to the mid-1940s. One thinks: Ah! there's a beginning . . .

———◆———

Characters: *Parodies of the twin brothers in the movie Adaptation—Lee and Chaz.*

———◆———

LEE: You go inside Malkovich's head in the movie *Being John Malkovich* (1999) and what do you find? A midget with an oversized Malkovich's head. The first part is not funny. The midget is funny.

CHAZ: But look, brother, you can't just have the midget with Malkovich's head. You need context. You need to put the head in the same surround a twenty-first century audience is in. And they're in a postmodern world. The comedy comes out of that: sharing the surround, the zeitgeist. You put both of us in a medieval world, brother, and we might be laughing when everybody else is crying and vice versa. A Martian can't tell a joke on Earth, brother, and we can't tell one on Mars.

LEE: So our surround is postmodern? I don't know what that means, bro'. Besides confusion. Confusion is not comedy.

CHAZ: We live in stories deep inside our heads. We project those onto the world. Two stories here in this movie: One, Americans want to jump inside the skins of celebrities. Two, Americans are not self-reflective but instead project a mirror reflection of themselves and their egos and desires upon the world. Malkovich is funny because he's a parody of all that. The movie is funny beyond the farce of seeing the midget with Malkovich's head because the movie observes in a witty and clever way what we recognize is true, that is, our own egomania.

LEE: That's confusion, bro'. Nobody's laughing because of all that. If that's the context you say funny needs, then we're not talking about normal funny. Nobody's anyplace in their head they don't understand. They're in a normal world. You do something to the normal and you got funny. Like Charlie Chaplin did.

CHAZ: The Little Tramp is not in a Depression-era world, brother?

LEE: He's funny because he takes us out of it. Otherwise, he wouldn't be funny. There's nothing funny, bro', on the breadline.

CHAZ: But that's just it, brother. The bedrock of Chaplin's comedy is the Depression surround. Without it, Chaplin's not Chaplin. Keaton's iron face wouldn't register. They'd be guys we just couldn't place.

LEE: I say Chaplin is still funny now because his comedy wasn't dependent on the surround. He's a classic, bro', cause his humor is timeless and placeless. He's probing the human heart, bro', and that doesn't change. It's all about human nature and the foibles therein. Unchanging at what you call bedrock level, bro'.

CHAZ: I don't think you'd recognize what was called "the human heart" in earlier centuries, brother. Or human nature. They change, but who's there to recognize the change? Let's say the next generation could never find butter or eggs or milk in the stores but only some chemical substitutes. But they still called those substitutes "butter" and "eggs" and "milk." Did anything change and who's to point out that change?

LEE: Let me get this straight, bro'. You're saying if somebody laughs at Chaplin now they're not laughing at what they laughed at back then?

CHAZ: We've got a couple of generations out there already, brother, who have to overcome what they see as obstacles to silent comedies: No one talks and there's no color up there on the screen. They have to be motivated to jump those before they ever get to anticipating being amused. Plus the fractured nature of digitalized timescapes that are computer- and TV-generated puts the contemporary young audience at odds with the analogue, linear, causal-sequential timescape of the silents. You've got the same problem with film comedies after the talkies came in, right up to, oh, I'd say, right up to Woody Allen, Monty Python, and the old *Laugh-In* TV show. You get a radical ontological break that has a lot to do with creation of cyberspace and virtual realities. I mean the brainpan is flooded with marketing messages that at the same time suppress older modes of world interaction. You might say that in order for the pace of both transmission and reception to be speeded up older neural networks have to become extinct, go out of business. The way we laugh is a cultural creation, because it's a part of the way we perceive, or preliminary to the way we perceive. And that, brother, has gone through a digital/global market revolution.

——◆——

Off Camera:

DOLLY GRIP: I thought this was going to be a big production? A lot of set changes and equipment assemblage? What we got here is one set and just two guys talking.

KEY GRIP: We're here, we get paid. Want to keep it interesting? Name your favorite comedy and why.

WRANGLER: Easy. *Ed Wood* (1994). Tim Burton's movie about the worst film director ever, Ed Wood. He's the guy who made *Plan 9 from Outer Space* (1959).

GREENSMAN: That's funny? That was the worst movie ever made.

WRANGLER: Get this. Ed Wood is doing a film backed by these Baptists who want him to make the film he's doing more Christian, so Ed Wood yells out: "These goddamn Baptists are killing me!" and then he rushes into a closet—he's being played by Johnny Depp—and comes out dressed like a woman. He slides into a pink Angora sweater and he says it makes him feel better. The guy's totally whacko; his films are whacko; all his friends are whacko. They don't have a clue. It's hilarious.

DOLLY GRIP: I worked that job. I liked when one of Ed Wood's friends, this guy Criswell the Great, Seer Extraordinaire, who floats future realities like so many balloons, tells Wood "If you predict something with absolute confidence, people believe you. I make it all up." That's what Karl Rove's been telling Dubya.

WRANGLER: Okay, a guy who makes movies about people on the edge of the mainstream—Tim Burton—makes a movie about a guy, Ed Wood, who's out there who made out-there movies that were so bad. And who could put a spot on that whole world better than Burton?

DOLLY GRIP: Yeah, well I was going out with the dialogue editor of *Ed Wood* and she said the whole film was revealed in one line. It's when Bill Murray who plays Bunny Breckenridge, a tranny, who's playing the role of the alien brain behind a plot to resurrect the Earth's dead and turn them against the world, is so perfect in the part that Johnny Depp/Ed Wood yells out, "Now, that's an alien!" She said Tim Burton was like Ed Wood in that both of them were all about expanding what she called our repertoire of alternative realities. Ed Wood's head was multiplex and Burton was trying to show that now we weren't in the split-level ranch of the 1950s that Wood was caught in but in a postmodern multireality world.

WRANGLER: There's a whole lot of cultural conservatives and born agains out there who aren't in that world and want to shut it down.

KEY GRIP: Obviously, the movie wasn't funny to them. They liked *Elf* (2003). A cute freak. Let's get back to work. One of those guys is talking again.

———◆———

LEE: Wow! I'm thinking you don't find any of the contemporary movies funny, bro', cause you're not, like you say, digitalized. I mean you didn't think *Elf* was a riot?

CHAZ: No, brother, I didn't.

LEE: Okay, bro', now we're down to it. It's all a matter of taste. What you think is funny. Totally subjective.

CHAZ: What about the classic comedies you were talking about? The funny that transcends time and place?

LEE: That's just what the film critics say are classics. You know what a great painting is, bro'? It's a painting that they hang on a museum wall and everybody looks at because it's what you do when you go to a museum. Some fancypants critic tells you your opinion is stupid and you better start learning about what his opinion is. But, you know, with movies people still have the freedom to their own subjective opinion. Especially with comedy, bro'. If it don't strike me funny, I ain't laughing.

CHAZ: Subjectivity is subject to time and place, brother. You like to think you're your own man, brother, but unless you've got the sense of humor of a psychopath like Hannibal Lecter, your funny bone is part of the cultural body, which has various appendages. But you can trace all of them to the trunk of what's playing in American culture right now. And right now you've got a cultural split between the cyberspace generations and the baby boomer/analogue generation. And that doesn't have to do with just how we attend to something, our attention span, our sense of boredom, our necessary rate of stimulation, our need to make accompanying sense of something. It has to do with our tolerance for what was constructed from within a timescape different than our own. Now that tolerance is part of the analog timescape. Why? Because the present doesn't trump the past. The past is prologue to our understanding of the present. There's connectedness, sequence, causality, precedent, linkage. In the analog timescape you look for continuity. Fragments have to be sewn together. Meaning derives from making the right connection amid fragmentation. In the digital timescape, fragmentation fuels an attentiveness that is already over-stimulated, which means that attentiveness fails quickly and boredom follows.

LEE: You know, bro', they say the Prez has to have everything reduced to a one-pager for him and then he doesn't read it. Somebody has to summarize it. And they've got about two minutes to hold his attention.

CHAZ: The past is itself an unneeded fragment because sense-making has itself become fragmentary. Things don't make sense because they add up. Sense-making is dropped in favor of consumption. You keep consuming a new stimulation. In sense-making you're trying to respond to things; you're trying to real-ize things. You're trying to conceptualize, interpret, understand, and then respond based on all that. But in the digitalized timescape, there's no time to real-ize things. And there's no inclination. That's over with. That's old, over, and adios. Consuming a fragmented reality that's packaged to stimulate incites you to act, not to think. You consume the advertising, the images, and the spectacle, and then you go out and consume the things they represent. This is the ultimate capitalist encounter with the world, bro'. Your way of seeing is consumed, your sense-making is consumed, the world is reduced to hyperkinetic Web pages.

LEE: That's heavy, bro'. And not at all funny. So why do I like *Elf* and you don't?

CHAZ: Have you ever seen *Being There* with Peter Sellers?

LEE: No. When did that come out, bro'?

CHAZ: 1979. Peter Sellers plays the part of a naïf. As does Will Ferrell in *Elf*. Sellers plays Chance, whose only contact with the world has been through watching TV and gardening. Then he's suddenly turned out into the world, and everything, for him, is as if it were a TV show or a garden. The confrontation between Chance's picture of the world and what the world is is hilarious. Will Ferrell's Elf is equally worldless, except he's from Elfland, which is meaningless in terms of giving viewers a recognizable frame of reference. Therefore, there is no hilarious contrast with the world beyond the laughs some viewers get from seeing a big guy like Ferrell dressed as an elf. That had very limited funny in it for me, brother. I only smiled, once and after that I was depressed, and you know why?

LEE: I'm really afraid to ask, brother.

CHAZ: Because everybody around me was laughing because what they're seeing Ferrell do is as if it were a *Saturday Night Live* sketch. In other words, brother, the whole audience has become TV products, just as Chance was in *Being There*. There's no surround in *Elf*, neither on the screen nor in the audience. It's all simulacra, brother. Film and audience.

———◆———

Off Camera:

KEY GRIP: Okay, Take Five. What's your favorite comedy, Best Boy?

BEST BOY: *Fargo* (1996). You've got two sets of absolutely nutso characters. You've got Marge and Norm Gunderson. She's a sheriff, and he's a bird painter hoping to get a bird on a stamp. Their town is Brainerd, which is Mayberry all over again except it's white with snow and ice. Then you've got Karl and Gar. Steve Buscemi is Karl, and Karl is a total sociopath. He hates any sign of authority, even a guy in a toll booth wearing a uniform. He's teamed up with a silent psychopath named Gar. And who and what brings these two worlds together is Jerry Lundegaard, played by William H. Macy, who wants Karl and Gar to kidnap his wife so he can get the ransom money from his wealthy father-in-law. Why? Jerry says he's in a bit of trouble, but it's personal so he doesn't tell Karl and Gar. We don't know what drives him, but he may be the craziest guy in the movie. And Sheriff Marge from Brainerd is on the case and she's going to solve the whole thing.

KEY GRIP: You know what I'm thinking, and mind you, I've been listening to these brothers rap about film comedies and I've been behind the scenes. . . . I worked as Best Boy on *This is Spinal Tap* (1984) . . . and a lot of comedies. You throw people from different walks of life together and you get laughs. You get a little jarring too if you come from Brainerd. Remember what Sheriff Marge says to Gar when she's caught him stuffing Karl into a wood chipper. "There's more to life than a little bit of money, don't you know that?"

BEST BOY: And here you are and it's a beautiful day. I just don't understand it.

KEY GRIP: Wherever the guy is, it's incomprehensible to her. I mean she comes from a Brainerd way of understanding.

BEST BOY: What about when she runs into her old schoolmate, Mike Nagageeta, and he lays down this whole story that Sheriff Marge later finds out is totally bogus. Here's her reaction: "Jeez, that's a surprise."

KEY GRIP: Every time that lady takes a step out of Brainerd she's in for a surprise because guess what? The U.S. of A. has popped its Brainerd fences and has grown outside the gates of what they understand. It's like they're frozen in a whole mindset, caught in an iceage.

BEST BOY: Man, I was surprised too when Mike turned out bogus but seeing that dopey look on Sheriff Marge's face and hear her say she was surprised made me not want to get caught anywhere in her naïve world.

KEY GRIP: Yeah, you laugh but then you get nervous. I got nervous like that with *Being John Malkovich* when Malkovich goes into his own head and sees everybody around him with his face.

BEST BOY: Is there a funnier scene, dude? Why'd you get nervous?

KEY GRIP: Why'd you step back from wondering what was going on with Mike Nagageeta when you saw that Marge had the same reaction? They put a finger on where we're at in our heads and they showed us where we needed work. You didn't want to be caught in Brainerd and I didn't want to be caught in Malkovich's head. Brainerd, I mean, being a picture perfect town but not the world and being in Malkovich's head too much a reminder that we're all egoists picturing the whole world with our face on it. Hey, they're starting up again.

——◆——

LEE: I hate to tell you this, bro'. But you're an egoist. You only hear your own voice and you only see your own face on everything. And an elitist. For all your B.S., what it comes down to is when you laugh at a movie it's a funny movie. If I laugh, I'm shallow and thin.

CHAZ: Brother, don't get angry. But the market has created a mook mind out there. Unreflective, uncritical, uninterested in what dead people might have written or filmed, and needing constant stimulation. Have you seen *Road Trip* (2000) with Tom Green, brother? Or, *Jackass, The Movie* (2003)? What I'm saying would be clear if we had a list of the top one-hundred comedies compiled by people under thirty.

LEE: What would we see, bro'?

CHAZ: More what you wouldn't see. *Some Like It Hot* (1959) is number one on the AFI list. But it's black-and-white and no one under thirty would recognize any of the actors. *Dr. Strangelove* (1964), also black-and-white. Doomed. But doubly doomed because it's a satire, which means you have to float two balloons to appreciate it, and a parody, which means you'd have to be aware of what was being parodied.

LEE: Something like someone writing about film comedies through character parodies from Charles Kauffman's film *Adaptation* (2003)? You know the twin brothers. Charles and the other one.

CHAZ: Look, brother, Chaplin's films are already becoming culturally extinct. The *Gold Rush* (1925) is number twenty-five on the list, *Modern Times* (1936) is number thirty-three, *The Great Dictator* (1940) is number thirty-seven, and *City Lights* (1931) number thirty-eight. *When Harry Met Sally* (1989) is rated higher than all the Chaplin movies. Is it funnier than Chaplin ever was? No. It's more culturally amenable, more culturally accessible and assimilable. Meg Ryan's face is a face that countless women in the audience want to have. They share the same reality frame and timescape as her. She's a cultural icon of the present. But, you know, brother, seventy-five years from now that face and that comedy will have been already culturally extinct for sixty years. And *Airplane!* (1980) as number ten on the list will itself make people laugh.

LEE: I don't know, bro'. Then why are any of those old movies on the list at all? I mean, if no one can hook up with them like you say?

CHAZ: My prediction brother is that when the baby-boomer generation is gone from the scene all those old movies will disappear too. They'll take analog perception, linear, causal thinking, and patience with the past along with them. There will be nobody left to hook up with old movies as funny.

LEE: What about that postmodern screwball comedy you're always talking about? That's just coming on the scene. That's not leaving.

CHAZ: You know *Bringing Up Baby* (1938) and *The Philadelphia Story* (1940) are fourteen and fifteen. The Marx Brothers' *Duck Soup* (1933) is behind *Tootsie* (1982).

LEE: I told you funny was totally subjective, bro'. There's your proof. You won't find two people who agree with that list. So what about the postmod screwball? Is that analog or digital?

CHAZ: Both, brother. It's an awareness of how we filter the world. Where does that awareness come from? I'd say it's a response to the timescape switch, what the philosopher of science, Thomas Kuhn, called paradigm revolution and Michel Foucault called episteme. Let's call this stuff the hardware, brother. The software is all the cultural stories we are born into. But it's the hardware that brings them to us, manipulates and mediates the software. Postmod isn't partisan to IBM instead of McIntosh or vice versa. It doesn't believe or advocate either one. It's just a notation that hardware is involved in the way we perceive, realize, feel, imagine, think, dream.

LEE: And that makes a difference between, like, the golden age of the screwball comedy from mid-1930s to the early 1940s, and postmodern screwball comedies, which are, like what comedies, bro'?

CHAZ: Brother, as soon as you mix an analog timescape with a digital one, you get an upset, you get disruption, you get disjointure, you get a messing around with our sense of realism. And comedy is closely allied with all that. Wit is the sudden joining of what's normally disassociated. It crashes into anticipated causality and makes a striking detour. Funny is seeing the world—as it's imagined at that time—turned upside down; maybe it's Chaplin spinning on a banana peel or maybe it's John Malkovich being flung out of his own head onto the Jersey freeway.

LEE: And traditional screwball, bro'?

CHAZ: In my opinion the manic vibe of screwball comedy is a kind of post-Depression visitation of chaos and madness. It's revolutionary, like Dada and surrealism were. It's countercultural in terms of conventional middle-class values.

LEE: Maybe it's a hangover from the Roaring Twenties, bro'. You know all that roar got shut down in 1929. Something went wrong. The world went screwy. The winners were throwing themselves out windows. Screwball is like a dip into what-does-it-matter-anyway-so-let's-rearrange-the-living-room attitude.

CHAZ: It's an odd mixture, brother. You take three tablespoons of the Dadaism of a Marx Brothers' movie like *Duck Soup* (1933), two tablespoons of a Depression-generated class warfare, one tablespoon of Mae West mouth like in *I'm No Angel* (1933), a tablespoon of streetwise fast-mouth from films like *Angels With Dirty Faces* (1938), a teaspoon and a half of a Busby Berkeley extravanganza, and a pinch of the New Deal and you get screwball. Take one of my favorites, brother. *Bringing Up Baby* (1938). Katherine Hepburn's performance as the rich, spoiled, disorganized, daffy Susan is a riff on Carole Lombard's performance in *My Man Godfrey* (1936). Cary Grant, though, creates the part of a mild-mannered but rational man trying to pursue his work who suddenly gets swept into the vortex of Susan's whirlwind. He spends the whole movie trying to counter her screwball with real sense until she finally blows him off course, and he gives up and accepts their romance. In *Arsenic and Old Lace* (1944), he's similarly trying to batten down the hatches of reason and sanity, but his whole family is straight out of the booby hatch, and he's frantic the whole movie trying to do what can't be done. In *His Girl Friday* (1940), Grant assumes the role of the screwball himself, as if he had given up trying to be a light in the storm, and jumped overboard himself. In *The Awful Truth* (1937) and *My Favorite Wife* (1940), Grant and Irene Dunne take the vicissitudes of marriage for a zany ride.

LEE: They say George Clooney in *Intolerable Cruelty* (2003) reminded everybody of Cary Grant. He was, you know, screwball like Grant in those earlier films. So, bro', if the surround changes comedy like you say, how come it doesn't?

CHAZ: It does, brother, and you just proved it. You're watching Clooney's performance as double coded. You're bringing Grant and his screwball movies right up there on the screen with Clooney in this movie. What do you get? Brother, you get a sure realization that 2003 isn't the 1930s. Clooney is sampling Grant, and it adds another dimension to the part, but it also reminds us that Grant isn't up there. He's absent. And there's a lot of what naturally made people laugh in the early screwball comedies that's also absent now. We're being wagged and we're aware of it. We're canny about how we're being moved toward laughter. Our laughter is an echo of a real laughter now out of our reach.

LEE: That's true of all postmodern screwball?

CHAZ: Look, brother, classic screwball is screwball because it monkeys around with the everyday order of things at the time, conventions of behavior and speech, the protocols of sanity, the proper development of relationships, orderly expectations, personal comportment and public restraint, the hierarchies of class and gender, tacit social understandings and unquestioned assumptions regarding respect, values, desires, and ambitions. In other words, it jostles the order of things, kicks up the mania level, confounds reality. But it doesn't multiplex reality. The whole world has gone screwball in these comedies, and everybody in the audience is trying to put it back together and having no chance of doing that. But in the postmodern world, the whole world doesn't stay whole.

—— ◆ ——

Off Camera:

KEY GRIP: Break. Hey guys, meet our film editor. Favorite comedy of all time?

FILM EDITOR: Naturally it's a film I edited. The Coen brothers' *The Big Lebowski* (1998), which these two characters should talk about as an example of a postmodern comedy, but they won't get around to it until I edit all their chat down.

KEY GRIP: *The Big Lebowski* is multiplex realities like this Chaz brother is saying?

FILM EDITOR: Think of the Dude as the dude not from another planet but from another time period.

BEST BOY: The 1960s.

KEY GRIP: Seattle Seven. The Dude plus six other guys. A little sampling of the Chicago Seven. What does the Dude do? Soaking, toking herb, the occasional acid flashback, listening to CCR, a penchant for White Russians, and bowling. He's a flashback dripped like acid over the entrepreneurial American 1990s. He's what's now called a Loser, and the Coen brothers fascination with him proves they're not in grown-up reality. That comment was made by a film reviewer in the *New Yorker* (March 1998). Everyone is now bowling alone in our fiercely all-against-all society, except the Dude. He has buddies. The spirit of egalitarianism abides in the Dude.

BEST BOY: So when you throw the Dude into a world whose hero is not the Dude but, say, Gordon Gecko from *Wall Street* and the real-life Donald Trump, then you get a clash that produces sparks. Look at the way the Dude goes up against the big fraud, the Big Lebowski. "Your side has lost, Mr. Lebowski. Get yourself a job."

FILM EDITOR: What's that but the voice of Newt Gingrich from back in the *Contract With America* days telling us that the whole countercultural revolution was a wrong turn in American history and we're now on the winning road?

KEY GRIP: Okay, if I'm getting this right, it comes down to this: we're in a culture war . . .

FILM EDITOR: Which plays out in our red vs. blue states in politics.

KEY GRIP: And postmodern comedy comes out of pitting different realities . . .

FILM EDITOR: Sampling or quoting different realities.

KEY GRIP: Which can get very funny if you're not already sidled up with what you picture as reality.

FILM EDITOR: But you don't picture. You already know what reality is. Yours isn't a picture; it really is the world.

KEY GRIP: Then all these other realities being sampled are not only wrong but a lot of them, say, like in *Ed Wood* or in *Boogie Nights* (1997) or in *The Big Lebowski*, are downright degenerate and immoral.

FILM EDITOR: And clearly, therefore, not funny.

KEY GRIP: Yeah, so do you have to be a postmodernist to laugh at postmodern comedies?

FILM EDITOR: I went to see *Ed Wood* with some friends who have the kind of jobs where they problem-solve and spreadsheet all day long. For the first half hour they sat there wondering what I was laughing at. My laughter got them to re-invest in what was going on on the screen. Maybe I opened up a doorway into the movie and out of their normal way of hooking up. It was keying them to what was there and transmitting, but they weren't on the channel to receive. They started to laugh along with me. Comedy and laughter are infectious like that, like they bypassed your filtering lens. But you have to experience it to become infected. There's a reason why most people who attack movies have never seen them. I'm thinking of recent attacks on Michael Moore's *Fahrenheit 9/11* (2004). *Fight Club* (1999) was dismissed as a star vehicle macho movie, *The Big Lebowski* as an "empty frame." *Pulp Fiction* was pop-culture chaos. Laughter is revolutionary; postmodern parody takes us out of one narrative frame and into others. And that has political consequences.

KEY GRIP: So Hollywood was too liberal, too leftist, and now it's what? Too postmodern? Cameras are rolling.

———◆———

LEE: I know you think you're saying something, bro', like the whole world isn't whole, or, reality is a duplex on Mulberrry, or, Cary Grant isn't up there. Maybe he's down there. Or, screwball is a tablespoon of Mae West. That's all screwball, bro', if you know what I'm saying. You're bowling an empty frame with me, bro'. It's too postmodern.

CHAZ: It's simple, brother. In postmod the whole world breaks up into a lot of worlds, each with their own sense of realism. You know what's screwball to one world? Another world they can't understand. And your comic sense comes out of the reality you're in. The awareness of all this is what I call the postmodern awareness. And all these worlds are in motion, some just emerging, some fading, some clashing, some so privileged we assume they represent the whole world. It's like saying screwball comedy captures reality as it is. Not melodrama, or tales of the wild West, or sci-fi, or mystery, or romance. But screwball. In the postmod view, all of a sudden at a certain time Hollywood put on a screwball lens and began to filter the world in that way. It was a lens that was forged by the culture at that time and, therefore, it found a response in that culture.

LEE: So will there be a time when the postmod lens will wear out and get replaced?

CHAZ: Well, this is a lens that reminds us we are always using one lens or another. So when you say replacing the postmodern lens I don't think we can replace that awareness with unawareness. But you can put on a lens that relegates a postmodern awareness to a "so what?" level. If you find yourself asking the question "how can I maximize profits with this postmodern awareness?" or, "how can I increase profit to shareholders with this postmodern awareness?" then you've put that awareness in the service of a more dominating story. You're looking at postmod through the lens of market value.

LEE: But we've got some comedies made with the postmodern lens? And George Clooney isn't in one?

CHAZ: The Coen Brothers are sampling romantic screwball comedy in *Intolerable Cruelty* where George Clooney samples Cary Grant. In *O Brother, Where Art Thou?* (2000) the Coen Brothers are not only sampling Preston Sturges's great comedy *Sullivan's Travels* (1941) but Homer's *Odyssey* too. Clooney himself samples not only the golden-tongued Odysseus but every golden-tongued, thin-mustached, fast-talking, narcissistic leading man of Hollywood's golden era, from John Barrymore and William Powell to Clark Gable. The chain gang is out of *I Am A Fugitive From a Chain Gang* (1932) with Paul Muni; the legends of Baby Face Nelson, the notorious bank robber, and Robert Johnson at the crossroads selling his soul to the devil are sampled; shades of Elvis shadows the scene when they walk into a small southern studio and record a song that becomes an overnight sensation; the coffin that saves the three at the end bobs up out of the water—a flood right out of the Bible—like Ishmael's coffin in *Moby Dick*. The movie is filled with the stories of our culture. But it's not simple pastiche, brother. Sullivan went in search of the poor in America, hoping to make a movie he called *O Brother Where Art Thou?* The United States is on an Odyssey today, a journey to find its soul, to find its lost brothers, both at home and elsewhere. Everything sampled serves as a measuring device for where we are now.

LEE: It doesn't sound screwball, bro', the way you put it. But it was screwball.

CHAZ: *Dr. Strangelove* (1964), *Magnolia* (1999), *Fargo* (1996), *Being John Malkovich, Pulp Fiction* (1994), *Boogie Nights* (1997), *Ed Wood* (1994), *Edward Scissorhands* (1990), *Adaptation, Pleasantville* (1998), *Mars Attacks!* (1996), *Zelig* (1983), *Purple Rose of Cairo* (1985), *The Player* (1992), *Bob Roberts* (1992), *Sleeper* (1973), *Annie Hall* (1977),

Manhattan (1979), *Broadway Danny Rose* (1984), *Deconstructing Harry* (1997), *Stardust Memories* (1980), *Love and Death* (1975), *A Midsummer's Night Sex Comedy* (1982), *Do the Right Thing* (1989), *The Big Lebowski*, *Clerks* (1994), *Jay and Silent Bob Strike Back* (2001), *Dogma* (1999), *Rushmore* (1998), *Ed TV* (1999), *The Cable Guy* (1996), *The Truman Show* (1998), *Wag the Dog* (1997), *Don Juan de Marco* (1995), *Mystery Science Theatre 3000* (1996) . . .

LEE: Whoa, bro'! So what makes these postmod screwball?

CHAZ: Each of these films displays a degree of postmodern awareness, some more than others. All of them quote what I call a classic realist and/or modernist frame. But *quote* is the operative word here. They don't rest unreflexively on either classic realist or modernist underpinnings. Comedy is traditionally a variation on a reality that is itself unquestioned. Chaplin and Fields and Keaton are at play within an uninvestigated reality; they have fun within that shared reality. Screwball comedy is that same thing but not shared; screwball comedy people are frenzied up there on screen being watched by people who haven't caught that fever. And the audience's reality and sense of realism are pushed to the limit. Postmod screwball isn't at play *within* a shared reality; it's at play *with* reality and the assumption that it's shared. What's projected are various representations of reality that implicitly show us that reality is many pictures running in many different theatres.

LEE: Cineplex. Multiplex. I get it, bro'.

CHAZ: Take films like *Zelig, Purple Rose of Cairo, Pleasantville, Ed TV, The Truman Show.* The postmodern vibe to these comedies is all about representation and reality. In the postmod view, reality is there, but when we come to represent what's there, all we've got is . . . well, a movie of it. Film dialogue. Images on the screen. So when characters on the screen literally interact with people in the audience, as in *Purple Rose of Cairo* . . .

LEE: Or Steve Martin in *Dead Men Don't Wear Plaid* (1982). I love that movie.

CHAZ: . . . and the question of who's more real than who, who's a character and who's a person, comes up, we walk into a postmodernizing of the world.

LEE: In *Wag the Dog* there's no real war, but Dustin Hoffman, a Hollywood director, stages one and that becomes the real war.

CHAZ: Remember, brother, in *Citizen Kane* (1941) when the young Kane fires off a telegram to a reporter who said there was no war? "You supply the photos, we'll supply the war." Kane's philosophy is if the news isn't big they can make it big by putting it into the headlines. And that's a philosophy Orson Welles followed also. Remember, brother, when Kane was shown on a balcony with Hitler? And then standing next to Teddy Roosevelt? Woody Allen will use that same kind of historical revision in *Zelig* when Zelig appears with real life historical figures. But they both have to thank Buster Keaton for being the first to step across the threshold from reality to representation. In *Sherlock, Jr.* (1924), Keaton is a movie projectionist who falls asleep but a wraith of himself walks into the movie theatre and then jumps into the screen where he becomes a character in the movie.

LEE: Reminds me of *Pleasantville*. And *The Truman Show*. I mean, Jim Carrey doesn't know that he's in a TV show. Twenty-four hours. He thinks he's in reality.

CHAZ: The situation we're all in, in the postmod view. If you take a whole world of people living in different TV shows, let's say, then what you're doing is always running into people who are interacting with you but from within different TV shows. I know that sounds crazy . . .

LEE: And that makes postmod screwball.

CHAZ: I think so, brother. If a movie represents even a fraction of that kind of interaction, there's no way it can't be screwball. And if the film parodies a reality frame because it reveals its source in simulation . . .

LEE: The TV show it comes from.

CHAZ: Madonna singing Happy Birthday in Marilyn Monroe style. Self-parodying because Madonna has indeed sampled Monroe in order to launch her own career. Or Tab Hunter parodying Tab Hunter in *Lust in the Dust* (1985). Tim Robbins parodying Hollywood producer with power in *The Player* and conservative hypocrite in *Bob Roberts*. Brando parodying himself as the Godfather in *The Freshman* (1990). Paul Thomas Anderson parodying the Bible in *Magnolia* . . .

LEE: I'm thinking of *Galaxy Quest* (1999), bro'. Total parody of *Star Trek* flicks. Mass confusion when these actors wind up in real space dealing with aliens who believe they're real because their culture was totally brought up on the *Galaxy Quest* TV show.

CHAZ: You know what makes the comedy *Dick* (1999) funny, brother? A Dick Nixon seen through the eyes of a couple of daffy teenagers. All the darkness surrounding Nixon—Watergate, impeachment, Cambodia—hovers around the whole movie, which is screwy at the center.

LEE: Yeah, Nixon. But you know who totally takes apart the Indiana Jones dude hero?

CHAZ: Michael Douglas in *Romancing the Stone* (1984)?

LEE: No.

CHAZ: Kurt Russell in *Big Trouble in Little China* (1986)?

LEE: He's good, bro' but I'm talking totally.

CHAZ: Arnold Schwarzenegger in *Last Action Hero* (1993)?

LEE: I'm talking about Bruce Campbell in *Army of Darkness* (1993). Last film in the *Evil Dead* trilogy.

CHAZ: The greatest send-up of the rational detective who arrives on the scene and solves the mystery is Johnny Depp in *Sleepy Hollow* (1999). He's the screwball Doctor Von Helsing from the Dracula flicks; he's the screwball Sherlock Holmes; he's the screwball Dr. Frankenstein.

LEE: None better than Mel Brooks's *Young Frankenstein* (1974) with Gene Wilder.

CHAZ: Mel Brooks pulls you into a topsy-turvy world, but he doesn't set up clashing realities. He'll parody the Western, the historical saga, the monster flick, the sci-fli flick, but the parody is at the service of farce. In Brooks's world, farce is everywhere; at the center of things, there's farce. But in postmodern screwball, parody serves to call up and re-see what is being parodied, put it in a contrastive relationship with other reality frames. Tom Cruise as the sex guru in *Magnolia* is a parody of every media prophet from the Reverent Ike to Dr. Phil. If Brooks were to film that world he'd bring out the implicit farce in this character and his world, but there would be no escape to other worlds. What Paul Thomas Anderson does in *Magnolia* is float the Cruise character's world alongside a number of others.

LEE: You thought *Magnolia* was funny, bro'? I'm also thinking *Pulp Fiction* wasn't funny. Or *Boogie Nights*. Or *Ed Wood*. But you said they were postmod screwball.

CHAZ: I think we're back to my original point, brother. Funny comes out of the surround; change the surround, you change funny. When the world was modern—by which I mean it was the dominant lens of viewing—what was funny and what wasn't funny obliged the specifications of the lens. If comedy is no more than a certain artful rearrangement of our sense of realism, and our sense of realism comes out of way of realizing, or deeming things real or not real, rational or irrational, normal or absurd, anticipated or not, then any change at this foundational level changes everything.

LEE: So the surround has changed to postmodern . . . for some people and they'd see those films as funny. But for me . . .

CHAZ: The thing to keep in mind about the postmod lens, brother, is this: It's a multifaceted lens. A realist way of seeing is part of that lens. So is what I call an Enlightenment way of seeing. So is a twentieth-century modernist way of seeing. You have to adjust the lens to the movie. And you have to be willing to do that. And to be willing to do that, you first have to be aware that this is the way we inevitably see the world—through a lens, through a lens shaped by the culture, the society, and ourselves, to varying degrees. You have to keep telling yourself this is a picture and not the world.

LEE: And then there's no way of saying something is funny for everyone.

CHAZ: Yes, brother, but that's not because everyone has a unique funny bone. It's because from where they are, where they are positioned, nothing funny can be seen, although someone else, positioned at a different time and place, would see what was funny. Once you have that postmodern awareness, that humor is not part of your unique individuality and that what you see is never seen in a neutral way, then you can tinker with the lens. I mean you can step back and try to see where and how you're positioned and what's there to be seen that you're positioned not to see, not to respond to.

LEE: You know, bro, I think we're all post-9/11 in the same place—a place of fear. Classic screwball comedy is over because we're not living in the 1930s anymore. And I know you're not going to like this, bro, but just like screwball had its brief moment, postmod and all your duplexing and multiplexing of reality has already had its short run. We're in a dark, subterranean basement now waiting for a dirty bomb to go off. Reality set in, an awful reality, and we're all nailed to the same spot.

CHAZ: Not all of us, brother. You forget the people doing the nailing and I'm not talking about al-Qaeda. Mass paranoia works politically, like pulling Willie Horton out of the bag at election time, or raving about feminazis to working-class stiffs listening to Rush Limbaugh, or doing the old bait and switch in the 2004 election with gay marriage wiping Iraq from people's minds . . .

LEE: You think somebody is laughing at us watching *Survivor* shows when the real survivor show is in Iraq?

CHAZ: If we can't imagine any other reality but a reality of fear and escape, then maybe you're right, brother. We're in a place where funny is just another victim of our collapsing attention span, and that's collapsing because we can't look too long at anything without the screen growing dark.

LEE: I think you're forgetting that laughter is spontaneous, bro'.

CHAZ: It doesn't detour the brainpan, brother.

LEE: Unless somebody is tickling you.

CHAZ: Now don't, brother . . . I'm ticklish . . . Stay away . . .

———◆———

THE BLOGOSPHERE

Blog: www.tarantinoisempty.com

Postmodernism empties comedy of a very necessary ingredient: a grounding psychological, emotional, or social presence shared by creator, characters, and audience. There are plenty of laughs in Tarantino's *Pulp Fiction*, but the laughter is a quick high, like Vincent, played by John Travolta, seeks in the film, a high disconnected from anything real in your life. Here's Gary Groth in *The Baffler* quoting James Wood:

"Literary critic James Wood writes that 'Tarantino represents the final triumph of postmodernism, which is to empty the artwork of all content, thus voiding its capacity to do anything except helplessly represent our agonies (rather than contain or comprehend). Only in this age could a writer as talented as Tarantino produce artworks so vacuous, so entirely stripped of any politics, metaphysics, or moral interest.'"

You take a screwball comedy like *My Man Godfrey* (1936) or *His Girl Friday* (1940): As far from reality as you think you get in these films and as screwball as it gets, you still need the real world to get your bearings and it's there in those films. You might say that the genius of screwball is keeping sight of land no matter how far out you go. And, I'll add, fully appreciating the difference that differing points of view can make. You're not where you were, but you don't lose sight of where you were. In Tarantino's *Pulp Fiction*, you're offshore but you don't know what a shore is. Let's say it's a picture of a shore, a picture Tarantino is sampling. We're detached from the sense of realism that was in that sampled picture, a world in an endless number of multiple worlds or realities. But, meanwhile, an audience is within a real surround, a real context, and if there's no respect for that, then all we've got is an evanescent screwball, something like a hiccup and then it's gone. Screwball isn't now playing in the hyperreal; it's playing within a surround that's trying to empty itself. The laughs won't last.

Why would I expect to see the end of this kind of comedy? Because being in a post-9/11 world matters; it's a surround we can't empty. There are really no multiple, clashing realities in this terrorized America: The blues and the reds are equally terrorized. We can't empty our surround and render it inconsequential by filling it with clever sampling of pop culture. But we can escape our terror for the duration of a movie. And *Elf* is funny in this clime because it escapes it; it doesn't seek to turn reality into papier-mâché or into a Chinese box of pictures within pictures. And I would say that because this nonpostmodern comedy doesn't try to confound our basic ontological notion of who we are and what it's like to be in the world, there's a certain foundational persistence and continuance that will make this sort of comedy funny in the future. Context, or surround, then, have enduring aspects, because we as humans have enduring aspects. A postmodern comedy that the writer tries to describe here empties the surround of not only the realities of the moment—post-9/11 at this moment—but also of the realities of self and world.

Blog www.parodyhasheft.com

I disagree with the Tarantino-is-empty blogger. I'm not prepared to say that Tarantino's sampling clashes rise to the level of a critically edged parody, but you certainly can have a postmodern screwball that doesn't fly off into endless pastiche. The writer mentions *Being John Malkovich* and *Adaptation*. You can add Kaufman's latest, *Eternal Sunshine of the Spotless Mind* (2004). *Malkovich* is a hyperconscious film about hyperconsciousness and, therefore, quintessentially postmod. But at the heart of the comedy is a critique of "the cold wintry economic climate" and the people in it; *Adaptation*'s theme is how representation—the picturing of the world—has to adapt to an existing formula for realism. *Eternal Sunshine* is about de-programming or de-narrating or de-picturing our minds and trying to start again but winding up inevitably filling our minds with yet another portfolio of pictures.

Blog: www.bananapeel.com

Screwball comedy was running from the Depression just like comedy now is running from 9/11. Now our comedies are computer-generated animation films, because Hollywood needs to animate faster to keep our digitalized attention span, and classic screwball, as fast with the dialogue as it was, couldn't kick up the visuals. Computer animation can. You get a double escape with these also:

First, they're funny; second, you don't have to worry about seeing something that reminds you of a plane flying into a Trade Tower. And, sure, comedy doesn't need context, at least not the kind that shows up in the headlines. That's always a downer. What gets somebody in post-9/11 U.S.A. laughing at a W. C. Fields movie, for instance? Fields takes a fall in the 1930s and seventy-five years later Will Ferrell takes a fall. Laughs both times. That's the eternal in comedy.

Blog: www.bodylaughs.com

Banana peel comedy detours the brainpan; it's laughter that comes out of the body, not the brain. That's why Woody Allen's comedies are—to put them in present U.S. demographic context—blue state comedies while a comedy like *Elf* is solidly red state. Allen's a quipster, a wit, a satiricist, a guy who loads a scene with all kinds of ironies. What do you need to respond? You need the cultural mêmes. In Woody Allen's case, they're urban, allusive, frenetic, idiosyncratic, irreverent, argumentative, artsy, and dismissive. None of that is particularly keyed to, say, the Heartland where the cultural mêmes might run something like this: woodsy, laconic, leatherneck, middling, respectful, conciliatory, utilitarian, and familial.

The comedy that unites us, that you could say is universal, is comedy targeting the body and not the head; we "belly laugh," "chuckle," "snort," "rip," "roll over," "cry," "shake," "fall down," "slap," "jump," and so on. What's universal here? We all have brains and we all have bodies. But bodies do something that has absolutely nothing to do with cultural mêmes and socioeconomic demographics. Bodies die. The ritual and grieving and so on may be culturally different, but the event transcends the cultural. Death doesn't wait for a narrative of death. Death rolls over time and place and is relative to no society or culture. We all face it and everybody that's died has done it. It doesn't matter how much time you spend in cyberspace or in the hyperreal, death calls you back. It doesn't matter how hard shopping malls work to keep time and death out of sight, we bring its shadow in with us. Death is not like anything else; it escapes our knowing, our recognition. It never becomes familiar. The wisdom of a three-day wake with an open coffin with a body for all to see is this: When death visits the body, the body too becomes unfamiliar to us and we see all the time this person was alive the body was something other, not a husk or a shell, but something other, something persistently real and other in spite of our ideas, beliefs, feelings, dreams. Something is always

THE BLOGOSPHERE

there in this body that is not his or her personality, not his or her difference; we are all bodies and join in this sameness.

How can comedy emerge from the body and death? You're asking your mind for an answer, and the only answer is that it does and it does so universally, persistently. And sometimes we see it on the screen; you only have to watch Chaplin and you'll see all the connections.

People laugh more at funerals, in the smoking rooms, outside in the parking lot; people have been laughing more at the movies since 9/11. There have been more comedies—the body's response to 9/11.

THE BLOGOSPHERE

Futurescape

He who fights with monsters might take care lest he thereby become a monster. And if you gaze for long into an abyss, the abyss gazes also into you.
> —Nietzsche, *Beyond Good and Evil*, Aphorism 146

The future would simply be the present infinitely repeated— or, as the postmodernist remarked, "the present plus more options."
> —Terry Eagleton, *After Theory*, 2003

I know combating terrorism may require extreme measures, but if you have no control over such . . . once you turn loose those dogs, they can easily turn on you. Society then becomes the victim of its protector.
> —PRWeb Press Release Newswire

At some point, we may be the only ones left. That's OK with me. We are America.
> —President George W. Bush,
> reported by Bob Woodward

Voice-over, in the stentorian tones of James Earl Jones: When *Star Trek* first aired on TV in September of 1966 its first plot episode struck the same thematic note as the 1955 sci-fi classic movie *Forbidden Planet* (1956): out of the depths of the unconscious we can call up the monsters, the alien forces, that will bring us to destruction. The cause of our paranoia is rooted in a heavily repressed death wish that we externalize, give a form and face to. In the 1950s we are in a cold war against Communism, and that paranoia took us to the jungles of Vietnam till the mid-1970s. In the 1980s, Ronald Reagan brought our Frankenstein back to life, a clever political as well as psychological solution to Jimmy Carter's probing into our own American cultural imaginary as our problem: There was an underlying malaise within that imaginary Carter hypothesized. With the fall of the Soviet monster in 1989, America bemused itself with a globalized digitalized superhighway to prosperity, a high-tech revolution that would lay the old economy's cycle of growth, inflation, recession to rest and rock the Dow Jones to 40,000. A whole generation was built on an optimism that would find any darkness at the heart of the American cultural imaginary as inconceivable. But that bubble burst and with it evaporated a bullish exuberance that had done nothing more during its brief tenure than exacerbate the divide between Haves, Have Mores, Have Increasingly Less (the old middle-class) and Have Nots and left Americans wondering if all they stood for was encompassed in the "Show *Me* the Money!" mantra of the 1996 film *Jerry Maguire*. Behind the curtain of high-tech optimism and a globalized capitalism outdistancing workers' rights, consumer and environmental protections there stood once again a dark wizard: our awareness of our own destructive powers and an attending awareness that we were attached to systems out of control, beyond our control. The need to once again project this haunting awareness outside ourselves and into the world was ultimately satisfied on September 11. Terrorists were now the alien force seeking the end of our civilization, and these antagonists, unlike the Soviets who unexpectedly vaporized, would and could never disappear. We would have to learn how to live in a perpetual state of alertness: yellow to red. We would have to learn to deal with a constant threat outside ourselves that had nothing to do with ourselves except in this one thing: "They hate us because we love freedom." After 9/11 it seemed to be once again crystal clear that Americans were not paranoic: The enemy was real and it wasn't us, nothing threatening us could be connected to what we ourselves were and had become. We weren't picturing the world after 9/11 as paranoics; 9/11 was real. We had an enemy and it wasn't us. All those American critics of America "on the left" could shut up and go home.

In his "malaise speech" in 1980, President Carter had gone where no man had dared go before—looking for an alien within—and had lost to Reagan; but sci-fi film also dared . . .

——◆——

Characters: *Captain Becark, of the Farship Enterpride; Commander Deja; Lt. Warp; Chief Engineer Gordie LaGorge; Counsellor Joy; Dr. Crush*

———— ♦ ————

CAPTAIN BECARK: I don't know if everything we humans have become was prefigured in those sci-fi films of the twentieth century, Mr. Warp.

LT. WARP: A barbaric period, sir, in Earth's history. A Clingon was a kind of plastic wrap, I believe.

COUNSELLOR JOY: I think I look something like Ursula Andress did in the movie *The Tenth Victim* (1965).

LT. WARP: I saw that movie. You do not.

GORDIE LAGORGE: I don't think what they called hyperdrive in the movie *Forbidden Planet* is anything like our warp drive, Captain.

COMMANDER DEJA: And might I remind you, Captain, that Robbie the Robot in *Forbidden Planet* can in no way be connected to my own positronic brain?

CAPTAIN BECARK: Yes, but Deja, the very idea of a man-machine can be traced to the 1926 film *Metropolis*. The mechanical creature that is given a human face is your ancestor, Deja, whether you like it or not.

COMMANDER DEJA: According to Arnold Scharzenegger the machine didn't reach consciousness until 11:15 A.M. in the year 2001. I'm quoting the movie *The Terminator* (1984).

DR. CRUSH: Wasn't he the president of the United States?

COMMANDER DEJA: Hardly, Doctor. He was defeated by a liquid metal cyborg in *Terminator 2—Judgment Day* (1991).

COUNSELLOR JOY: Aren't you confusing movies with reality, Deja? Aren't we all doing that by having this discussion? What movies show us are fantasies. We've become what we've become through science. Reason not imagination.

———— ♦ ————

Script Doctor: I think we should add some discussion of the 9/11 Commission Report in July 2004 in which they concluded that our lack of preparedness on September 11 had more to do with a failure of imagination than a failure in intelligence reports. You want early on, here, to indicate a radical rescripting of the American psyche from a sense that communities are rationally engineered, constructed, and protected, or arise most successfully out of the free play of market values, to a sense that we live in imagined communities, in line with what Benedick Anderson reveals in *Imagined Communities*. The systems analysts and the intel gleaners only pave the road that imagination blueprints. Why did the whole CIA's close scrutiny of the USSR fail to see it was ready to fall? Because they were seeing within an imaginative scenario, within a script, written in the cold war: Namely, the USSR was the major threat to American security. Recall this amazing admission of imaginative failure by Admiral Stufflebeem: "The more that I look into it and study it from the Taliban perspective, they don't see the world the same way we do."

— ◆ —

CAPTAIN BECARK: Reason and imagination. Are they so distinct, Counsellor? Or is it more true to say that one is affected by the other?

COUNSELLOR JOY: I don't understand, Captain.

CAPTAIN BECARK: We reason within the country of the imagination. Our science pursues what the imagination has already mapped out.

LT. WARP: I, for one, am very clear where I am if I am watching a stupid movie such as the ones watched on *Mystery Science Theatre 3000* or if I am watching my control panel to see if the ship is on course. There is reality, Captain, and an escape from reality.

COUNSELLOR JOY: The imagination takes from the real world, Captain, and it does fanciful things with it. But they are separate domains and we know when we have to leave fancy and get back to reality.

CAPTAIN BECARK: Do we, Counsellor? Or are the products of our imagination already in the world around us? We see the world through them. And we may deceive ourselves into thinking that at certain moments at will we leave our fancy, as you call it, behind and can get back to reality, but do we? Can we?

DR. CRUSH: If I'm following you, Captain, you believe that old movies have done more to shape our encounter with space than science has?

CAPTAIN BECARK: I wouldn't even accept that divide, Doctor. We already do science within the boundaries of our imaginations. It isn't as if we could break free of the hold movies have on us and get back to science. Science is the fulfillment of our imagination. It goes where we have dreamed of going.

LT. WARP: An astounding statement, Captain.

COMMANDER DEJA: I think I have an example, Captain. One of my favorite sci-fi movies is called *Galaxy Quest* (1999). This movie is about actors who have been on a very successful but now defunct TV sci-fi show. All the fans of the show confuse the actors with the characters on the show and they gather in huge numbers to see and hear these actors at show reunions. Meanwhile, these actors are unemployed or now doing very humble work. They have personal problems and their lives are not going well.

COUNSELLOR JOY: There you have it, Captain. There is a definite difference between the parts they play and their real lives.

CAPTAIN BECARK: Go on, Mr. Deja.

COMMANDER DEJA: These TV shows have been watched by a humanoid species from an Omega galaxy who arrive on Earth to seek the help of these TV actors. They are being threatened by a Klingon-like species.

LT. WARP: I will not listen to this.

CAPTAIN BECARK: And what occurs, Mr. Deja?

COMMANDER DEJA: The actors discover that everything they fictionalized on their TV show is really occurring in space. They also discover that they are as heroic as they pretended to be on the TV show.

LT. WARP: I don't understand the point of this story.

COMMANDER DEJA: I will point out that the humanoids seeking the help of the TV actors were already totally immersed in the plots of all these TV shows. Therefore, they responded to their plight by accessing those TV-show memory banks. They were imaginatively scripted to respond.

CAPTAIN BECARK: And the TV actors, Mr. Deja?

COMMANDER DEJA: They slipped across the divide between performance and reality, Captain, and discovered what they had pretended to be for many years had become what they were. There was no separate self-image grounded in a reality untouched by images.

CAPTAIN BECARK: And movies, my friends, are the premiere transmitters of images.

COMMANDER DEJA: I would also like to point out, Captain, that this movie did refer to a very popular TV series of the late twentieth and early twenty-first century called *Star Trek*. There were several generations of actors on this show who went around the country appearing at what were called Trekkie conventions. There was also Web sites for Trekkie fans who wished to communicate with each other regarding picayune details of every episode of the show.

CAPTAIN BECARK: So if one were watching the film *Galactic Jest* . . .

COMMANDER DEJA: *Galaxy Quest*, Captain.

CAPTAIN BECARK: Yes, of course, one would be aware of the reference to that TV show and to the characters on that show. One's experience of that movie would have a certain depth of field, wouldn't you say so, Mr. Deja? The impact might be particularly telling if one were oneself a Treppie.

COMMANDER DEJA: A Trekkie, Captain. Yes, and that depth of that field would be increased if, for instance, we were ourselves characters in a sci-fi TV show who had gone on to make sci-fi movies and who also attended fan conventions.

CAPTAIN BECARK: If that were the case, Mr. Deja, our discussion of what affect sci-fi movies had on our own present circumstances would be deeply biased since we ourselves would already be products of those movies.

COMMANDER DEJA: We wouldn't be real, Captain. It would be necessary to find someone to write uncorrupted by sci-fi movies who had never seen sci-fi movies. I think then we could get the most objective, realistic account of those movies.

CAPTAIN BECARK: I especially would avoid finding someone who employed sci-fi movie characters to carry on the discussion.

———◆———

> **Outtake:** Note the multiplexing here: The writer takes up a discussion of sci-fi movies through sci-fi characters who take up a discussion of whether or not a discussion of sci-fi movies can be objective and whether or not such premised objectivity leads to realism, and the nonhuman—the android who is programmed without subjectivity—concludes logically that only a human who had never seen a sci-fi movie could render an objective account of sci-fi movies, to which another character facetiously remarks that at the very least someone should be chosen to write about sci-fi who doesn't use characters to carry on the discussion. Every voice echoes other voices putting the reader on the trail of the origin or grounding voice, the "Natoli-author" signifier, which links to us through characters considering the complexities of communicating outside the frame of one's own observations, one's own always-already-present cultural scripting.

———◆———

COMMANDER DEJA: I merely point out the paradox here, Captain. If it is true that we can only be real in the way we imagine ourselves to be real, and reality for humans is always mediated through what they imagine, then what we mean by *reality* and *real* is not an ummediated reality but always a mediated one. The human who is already a product of an ever-present cultural mediation of reality cannot tell us about an unmediated reality just as the human who has never seen a sci-fi film can never tell us about the reality of sci-fi films. Paradoxically, humans abide by definitions of reality and real that demand the extraction of subjective and cultural mediation of reality. This is not a paradox faced by an android with a positronic brain such as myself. I am incapable of watching the world within the surround of old movies; I am equally incapable of watching old movies within the surround of the world. I do not in point of fact watch anything. I receive transmissions. The selectivity of my scanning gaze is modulated by . . .

CAPTAIN BECARK: Yes, yes, Mr. Deja. That's quite enough. You're a marvel, but, truth be told, I would not give up one second of sitting in a movie theatre waiting for those words "Klaatu, barada, nikto" in *The Day The Earth Stood Still* (1951) to . . . scan the gaze, or whatever it is you do.

LT. WARP: So you are proud to say, Captain, that you are not real?

CAPTAIN BECARK: What I am to you, Mr. Warp, is what you imagine me to be. What I am to myself is also what I imagine myself to be. Inevitable. And thus real.

LT. WARP: You are a very tricky conversationalist, Captain, but a Klingon laughs at what is unrealistic. I laugh at all those old sci-fi movies. Humans may see something real there, but that is a seduction a warrior does not fall into.

CAPTAIN BECARK: Come now, Mr. Warp, surely there must be one sci-fi movie that you find compelling?

COUNSELLOR JOY: What was that you said before, Warp, about those *Mystery Science Theatre 3000* TV shows?

LT. WARP: I enjoy that show, because I too sit in the movie theatre, as do Tom Servo, Crow, Gypsy, and Joel, to mock the movie being shown, to show how ridiculous and unreal these sci-fi movies were.

COMMANDER DEJA: This was a very popular American TV show in the last decade of the twentieth century, Captain. It is a good example of multiple fields of reality being screened. We are the furthest screen out, if you will, Captain. We are watching a TV show whose premise is that a janitor at the Gizmonic Institute is now in space watching cheesy movies, most of which are sci-fi, as part of a secret experiment. The janitor and the 'bots he creates to keep him company are being watched by the experimenters as they watch the cheesy movies. As they watch these movies, they make comments that break the spell of the movie and cause viewers to re-evaluate the connections they have been making with the movie and to add another level of commentary on the running commentary of the janitor and the 'bots.

CAPTAIN BECARK: A kind of multilevel continuous commentary on the movie's conventions of realism.

COMMANDER DEJA: Precisely, Captain. Since most of the movies were done in the 1950s and the three characters in the audience, whose heads appear in dark shadow just below screen line, are in the late 1990s, there is a constant clash of timescapes. Love and sex evoke the most hilarious commentary.

CAPTAIN BECARK: Yes, but I would expect that sword of satire to be double-edged, Mr. Deja. For instance, what might appear in one of those earlier movies might be something that in the later period had become extinct—such as an egalitarian spirit—or degraded—such as worker and environmental protection.

COMMANDER DEJA: I believe, from what Lt. Warp has said, he finds nothing to cry over in those movies.

CAPTAIN BECARK: And yet you watch that old TV show, Mr. Warp? For what reason?

LT. WARP: The 'bots amuse me. They disdain the falseness of unreal and hokey representations of reality as I do.

CAPTAIN BECARK: And yet they're fictive characters. What did you call them, Mr. Deja?

COMMANDER DEJA: 'bots, Captain. Robots. Made of junk parts the janitor finds about the space station. Tom Servo has a glass bowl head like a candy machine. Crow has a pie-plate body, and Gypsy has a vacuum-cleaner head. Very unrealistic, Captain. We are a very long way from a positronic . . .

LT. WARP: I do not believe they are real or realistic, Captain.

CAPTAIN BECARK: And yet you say you share the same view of reality as they do. They have your critical eye. Could it be that something of how your critical eye is formed is formed by these unreal 'bots, Mr. Warp?

COUNSELLOR JOY: Captain, you would agree there's a difference between our experiences in and out of the holodeck?

CAPTAIN BECARK: We change timescapes and play parts in our virtual programs in the holodeck, Counsellor—in other words the setting of our experiences—but the way we experience in the holodeck is not fundamentally different than the way we experience outside the holodeck. In fact, we don't just employ the holodeck for recreational purposes. We use it to learn by experiencing beyond the circumstances of what our life aboard this starship allows.

GORDY: I wonder if I could go back to your original question, Captain. I've been thinking of a way we could find out just what we owe these old sci-fi movies—I mean, what we may have inherited from them. We could program the holodeck to run a sample of films . . .

DR. CRUSH: And use parodies of the janitor and the 'bots to comment as we would comment.

CAPTAIN BECARK: Make it so, Mr. Deja. Let's enter Holodeck 3 and join our 'bot buddies.

— ◆ —

In Holodeck 3: Becark, Deja, Warp, Joy, Crush, Gordy are joined by 'bots Tom Servile, Gypsum, Krowe, and janitor Joe L.

CAPTAIN BECARK: We've been watching *Starman* (1984) for at least a half hour, Mr. Deja, and the 'bots haven't made a comment.

COMMANDER DEJA: That's because I've programmed them to respond to our comments, Captain.

GORDY: You could have told us that, Deja.

LT. WARP: The Starman is clearly technologically superior to these humans. He should not have to run from them. This is clearly a movie made by humans.

COUNSELLOR JOY: I think you're forgetting, Warp, the terrible reception aliens received in all the sci-fi movies. Poor Michael Rennie was shot upon arrival in *The Day the Earth Stood Still*. And his gift to us was broken. A cure for all known diseases. Or something like that. And it's absolutely unforgiveable the reception given *E.T. the Extra-Terrestrial* (1982). And all he wanted to do was phone home.

TOM SERVILE: Reagan wasn't going to pick up the tab for that long distance call.

KROWE: Speaking of *Star Wars* (1977–1983) . . .

JOE L.: Okay, who got a better reception? The thing with the big fishbowl eye and the snakes coming out of its head in *It Came from Outer Space* (1955) or the aliens in *Close Encounters of the Third Kind* (1977)?

GYPSUM: They treated The Thing like he was a head of cabbage in *The Thing from Another World* (1951).

TOM SERVILE: Richard Dreyfuss reprised his roll from *Jaws* (1975). When he played Richard Dreyfuss for the first time.

JOE L.: So you want to talk about creature features, eh? Who was more scary? *Them!* (1954), *The Thing from Another World*, *Alien* (1979), *Predator* (1987), *Godzilla* (1954), *King Kong* (1933), *The Fly* (1958, 1986), *Eraserhead* (1977), or Keanu Reeves?

TOM SERVILE: Der Ahnald Schwarzenegger as governor of California, by a mile.

JOE L.: I think you have to remember that George W. Bush achieved consciousness at the Harvard Business School.

CAPTAIN BECARK: Computer, freeze program. Mr. Deja, we seem to be in some sort of mindless spin here. Can you get us back on track?

COMMANDER DEJA: I've switched to *Terminator 2: Judgment Day* Captain. I am fascinated by the way humans want to be cyborgs. Frankly, Captain, I cannot understand the desire.

CAPTAIN BECARK: You know, Deja, humans are propelled by their imaginations, but their imaginations are filled with instinctual desires and fears. It's these that we wish to escape. And perhaps rightly so.

KROWE: Tim Burton's *Mars Attacks!* (1996) does it right. The Martians start kicking butt as soon as they land. Shades of George Pal's *War of the Worlds* (1953). Squash 'em like ants.

——— ◆ ———

Voice-over: It's impossible to ignore the connection these two last-mentioned films have with 9/11: precipitous, unexpected attack that causes catastrophic mayhem and fear. Even though both films show us a war between Earth and aliens from another planet, the sudden attack is on the United States, battleground Midwest in the 1953 George Pal movie, and Washington, D.C., in the 1996 Tim Burton movie. There's an attempt in both movies to talk to the invaders, to assume, in liberal, politically correct fashion, that at heart all beings, regardless of what 'hood they were raised in, are good. Those peaceful overtures and idealistic assumptions are zapped into extinction by the aliens. Two years before Pal's film, when a flying saucer lands in Washington, D.C., the alien who emerges is greeted with a bullet. The film is *The Day the Earth Stood Still* and it's a pacifist's paen. In terms of 1951 American politics it's a vote on the side of the United States standing with the UN in opposition to Gen. Douglas MacArthur's advocacy of strategic attacks against the Chinese, who had joined with the North Koreans against the United States. Two years later, in 1953, Republican Sen. Joseph McCarthy's communist witchhunt was in full swing, Julius and Ethel Rosenberg were executed for selling atomic secrets to the USSR, and cold war fear of the Soviets, of a sudden nuclear strike, generated post-9/11-type fears. *War of the Worlds* plays into a cold war paranoia whose panic attack can be cathartically relieved by bringing haunting fears to life—I mean to the big screen—bringing Americans into the heart of their own contrived darkness and then dissolving it. It's a masterful cultural catharsis. Burton's *Mars Attacks!* (1996) is a more difficult film to see in relation to its mid-1990s surround: The Soviet Union has collapsed, the cold war is over, al-Qaeda is unimagined, the Dow Jones is kicking, Bill Clinton is leading winning preemptive strikes against every Republican position by co-option, and the whole country seems gradually to be moving toward difference, of every kind. Yet the Martians who attack are a devilish breed of alien. No chance to move toward their difference. Only the plaintiff sounds of country music destroy these aliens and save the planet. The film ends with Tom Jones high in the mountains singing "It's not unusual to be loved by anyone." The film is like a bad dream, filled with a surrealistic instability, a hopped-up wasteland where the country is saved by an addled old lady, a redneck kid in a pickup truck, and a former football player dressed like a gladiator in Vegas. The president is a *Mad Magazine* creation, a man at a feast of the rich. This is a cartoonish attack on American soil, not a cathartic expulsion of fear by the whole country, not an expulsion of lunacy but a full immersion in it. Our cultural fears of extermination, perhaps once again put into gear by the approaching millennium, are as laughable here as we are. Burton mocks the millennial fears of a society whose defense weapon is plucked from the heart of its own cultural banality. This is a culture that had earned its enemies, its attack, its fears; this is a trash or be trashed culture, a culture dreaming of salvation through trash. By September 11, others besides Burton have adopted this view. *Mars Attacks!* is *War of the Worlds* done again, but this time with the 1950s screen vision of the American Heartland turned into the *fin de siecle* glitz of Las Vegas, the White House turned into a Mad Hatter's tea party, and the movie's lovers subjected to an alien science that severs their heads and reattaches them to the bodies of animals, where indeed their love persists. And is quite unusual.

———◆———

JOE L.: I thought I heard a voice. An overvoice. Did you hear a voice? Do you think the Borg queen in *Star Trek: First Contact* (1996) owes her role to the ant queen in *Them!* (1954). The exterminator was the hero in both movies. I'm talking about the liquid-metal Exterminator.

TOM SERVILE: Shock and awe! Get them before they get us. Think: All aliens are terrorists. All terrorists are aliens.

JOE L.: I think John Ashcroft should decide who's an alien.

KROWE: Absolutely William Kristol. He's the Chair on the Project to Build the American Empire.

JOE L.: I thought Paul Wolfowitz was.

TOM SERVILE: He's the man behind the man who was liberated from the welfare roles to join the Army.

KROWE: I thought Donald Rumsfeld was the man behind the man who was behind the man who actually went to Iraq.

JOE L.: No, that's Karl Rove.

GYPSUM: Anyway, the war in Iraq is a neocon rendition of *Star Wars: The Empire Strikes Back* (1980).

———◆———

Script Doctor: Okay, at this point you desperately need a voice-over to cover the Reagan vs. the Evil Soviet Empire connection with the Jedi and the Force vs. Darth Vader and the Dark Side of the Force. Nothing was to be gained if one assumed that darkness of evil, either Vader or the Soviet Union, didn't exist. Had we made more of the Soviet threat during all those cold war years than we should have? Or, had we acted in a bold confrontational way sooner, in a Return-of-the-Jedi fashion, would we have pre-empted those cold war fears? The lesson George W. Bush and associates learned from Reagan—and Star Wars—was that you can't coddle evil. And the worst thing you can do is blame yourself for its existence, or, still worse, assume that its origins are in your head, that you somehow brought this evil into being because your civilization is not civilization but some dark force threatening the existence of the entire planet. Maybe Dubya and associates didn't want to take time out to investigate what we might have done to trigger 9/11 because he knew we weren't totally innocent in our long history of dealing with the Middle East but the game on the table wasn't search-your-conscience but survival. Maybe Dubya and associates didn't want to take time out because he was facing a post-Vietnam generation of baby boomers who would link Iraq with Vietnam and go into all that soul searching, never finalized, which would eventually lead to a discovery of guilt lying at the heart of the American cultural imaginary and a death wish lying right beside it. As far as sci-fi unrelentingly pointing to such a death wish, you only have to cite films like *Starship Troopers* (1997) and *Independence Day* (1996), films of the 1990s, to see that sci-fi films back survival at any price in the face of real enemies. And a classic film like *Invasion of the Body Snatchers* (1956) may reflect our paranoia about becoming brainwashed by communism, but as the film shows, there is an enemy, and unless that enemy is stopped, our identities, our independence and freedom, our democracy will be taken from us.

———◆———

JOE L.: Do you realize that the man behind that empire was James Earl Jones? *Brother from Another Planet* (1984).

———◆———

Script Doctor: Two films released at the end of Reagan's first term: *Starman* and *Brother from Another Planet* present a kind of compassion, a brotherly love and concern, that were missing in Reagan's America. There were twice as many people in prison in 1984 as there had been in 1974; a woman was executed for the first time in twenty-two years; Reagan signed a bill permitting detention without bail during peacetime, and so on. No compassion, is what I'm saying. By 2000 the Republicans have learned the power Bill Clinton's teary-eyed "I feel your pain" approach has, and they borrow a trick from Clinton's bag: They launch a "compassionate conservative" presidential candidate: George W. Bush. What you want to write toward here is this American mass psyche dilemma. On one side: We're only four percent of the world's popular and yet we consume 40 percent of its goods; somebody is going to stop us. On the other side: We believe we're the good guys, that we give more foreign aid than anyone, that we're loaded with compassion; that we bleed for the downtrodden. Is that represented in the results of the 2000 and 2004 presidential elections? Can the Republicans pull off compassion at the same time they are attacking liberals for their "bleeding hearts," their lust to tax and spend on behalf of the losers? In short, can we make George W. Starman?

——— ◆ ———

TOM SERVILE: That was Joe Morton not James Earl Jones. My point being that Joe Morton was also the scientist in *Terminator 2* who did the science that brought the machine to consciousness. Now, in *Brother from Another Planet* you ask the question whether he was alienated because he was black, or alienated because he was an alien? In *Terminator 2* you ask: Did he bring the machine to consciousness to wipe out white people, or was he just doing the science?

CAPTAIN BECARK: If I might get a word in, gentlemen.

KROWE: Oh, pardon us, your Baldness.

CAPTAIN BECARK: I think you gentlemen overlook the fact that sci-fi gives us ample justification for our defensive ways. Aliens surreptitiously came to Earth and deposited pods that literally snatched our bodies away in *Invasion of the Body Snatchers* (1956, 1978). And need I remind you that the alien hunter in *The Predator* (1992) is preying on humans as if we were trophies. How soon we forget the alien spitting in the face of the President of the United States in *Independence Day* (1996)! And if it weren't for the common cold germ, the aliens in *War of the Worlds* would have destroyed our planet. No, gentlemen, we do not, unfortunately, live in the peacenik universe that Mr. Spielberg fantasizes in *E.T.* and in *Close Encounters of the Third Kind* (1977). The world is more like the nightmare world of the sci-fi film he made many years later, *Artificial Intelligence: AI* (2001).

——— ◆ ———

Voice-over: The point I want to make is that we have in sci-fi films a division between good aliens treated badly and bad aliens we crush. At bottom, it's the war between human nature as essentially good and powerfully affected by notions of social justice and egalitarianism and human nature as essentially corrupt and powerfully affected by self-interest alone. A postmodern take that hears only stories of what's essential would model human nature as a story itself that becomes attached to various stories, or to the relative power of various screenings of what that nature is. *AI* displays a confusion of stories, namely Stanley Kubrick's, who commissioned the first adaptation of Brian Aldiss's short story, and Stephen Spielberg's, who rewrote that adaptation. The sensibility that created the dark comedies of *A Clockwork Orange* (1971) and *Dr. Strangelove* (1964) are clearly in *AI*. In Kubrick's world, we are not so much essentially flawed or noble but caught at various levels in the tragic as well as happy results of human ambition, desire, and power. The cultural surround threatens us and also harbors us, but only in accord with where chance and power have placed us. If you look at Spielberg's sci-fi films *Close Encounters* and *E.T.*, you find an entirely less complex and sophisticated view of human nature, power, the cultural surround, chance, and free will. While Kubrick's dark revelations undermine the seductive cocoon that seems to be what we ask of Hollywood—and too often have received from Frank Capra to Walt Disney—Spielberg's technical facility operates to reduce haunting complexities and dilemmas, as if all filmmakers took an oath to be uplifting. There is enough in *AI* to make us all fear and tremble for the future; we are on a course in regard to artificial intelligence in which our robotical creations will pile up in discarded parts in the dark woods of our own conscience. The fact that we will not be deterred from this future—that it is inevitable—is precisely what brings our lurking cultural death-wish into being.

———◆———

Tom Servile: I'm hearing that voice again. Did anyone hear it? I think you gentlemen overlook the fact that the message is clear. Our visions are inspired by strange love, weird science, and, of course, *The Matrix* (1999). The world is more like the world we see in *The Matrix* films where our nightmare is that Keanu Reeves is The One who will save us.

Captain Becark: I appreciate your facetiousness, Mr. Servile, but I don't think it's our sexual appetites that are skyrocketing us to a disastrous end.

———◆———

Script Doctor: Before going on with Becark's speech here I would interject a word or two about *The Matrix* films because here we have a perfect screening of the new digitalized timescape. Neo, the savior-hero played by Keanu Reeves, heeds the advice: "You're faster than you think you are." What does that mean? It means he's been programmed to move in analogue time but he's actually a free agent who can break the constraints of that program and reprogram himself. He's an autonomous free agent. What's more new millennial American than that? The Neo stands for Neoconservative. We're all free to choose, including being free to choose to be free to choose. Meanwhile, back at the Ranch of Reality, we're submerged in a preservative solution with tubes sucking out our élan vital, our *chi*, at regular intervals and feeding the Matrix, which is that same consciousness-achieving computer network that led to Armageddon in *The Terminator* films. So what's being celebrated here and what's being repressed? Number one: You're digitally fast in the Matrix program; everything can move at the click of a mouse, including you. That's cool to a generation who MTV-fracture and re-angle reality twice a second; analogue time is pre-Internet, premultitasking, pre-cell phone, pre-Palm Pilot, predawn of the New Millennium. What's cool too is your autonomy, your potential to challenge your surround—even if it's the Matrix you're trapped within—and choose your own destiny. You can choose to be rich, just like the poor, obviously, have chosen to be poor. Why can't they just assume personal responsibility and their unconstrained freedom to choose and make something of themselves? Okay, so there's your celebration of the neoCon in Neo. But then the film haunts you with the idea that maybe right now you're actually in that teacup having your chai sucked out of you, maybe what you think you are is what you've been programmed to think you are. You're not in reality but in somebody's virtual program of reality. Who could that be? What kind of power is out there programming you to want to announce your freedom through choosing products from a shelf as well as through filling your Internet shopping cart with all the necessities of life? Could it be that your faith in your autonomy, your absolute free agency, is programmed?! Could it be that believing your mind now works in a digitalized multitasking mode prevents you from a continuous critical focus on the complexities of the now globalized cultural web you are entangled within? Here is a film that envisions us strangled in a technological future we are now heading toward, but also a film which envisions us as somehow remaining capable through choice of self-resurrection. Is that sense of personal freedom, of the individual unconstrained by cultural screening, already part of the programming—a very necessary part—or, is it an unprogramable reality? Are we already in the Matrix in post-millennium America, in red and blue America, and is the neo we are waiting for red or blue or neither? There's no coolness in this dystopic vision.

————◆————

CAPTAIN BECARK: I appreciate your facetiousness, Mr. Servile, but I do not think it is our sexual appetites that are skyrocketing us toward a disastrous end. Nor do I think it is our own distaste for the vagaries and aberrations of our own human nature urging us to replace ourselves with machines. I can think of only one movie where the robots are finer than their creators. I refer to *Blade Runner* (1982). Each of these wonderful creations are rebelling against an arbitrary creation, one in which the lifetime they are granted runs out at the very moment they have achieved an awareness of the wonders and beauties of mere existence that humans cannot appreciate. The machines are the victims of capricious whim attached to a science that hides behind its supposed neutrality. Theirs would have been a world superior to our own, but we do not allow them the opportunity to create such a world. I fear that we are the monstrous gods of not only the lower orders of our planet Earth but of the machines we make. Is there any mention in *The Terminator* movies why the machines rose up against humans? Is it simply faulty wiring in *Westworld* (1973) that sets the robots against humans? Or is it finally an opportunity to rebel against the oppressor? Gentlemen, what sci-fi movies has taught me is that we are aware of our own monstrosity, our own alien status on Earth, and that awareness drives us in two opposing directions.

Tom Servile: We can either shrink to the level of *The Incredible Shrinking Man* (1957) . . .

Krowe: Which is a good thing from a holistic, gestaltist, New Age ecological point of view.

Lt. Warp: I am not happy with what has been said about *The Matrix* films, Captain. The impression is being given that the web of the Matrix is a transnational corporate web. I disagree, Captain. It is clear to me that Neo is caught in the web of federal government bureaucracy. The Matrix, Captain, is the tax code. It is all the liberal legislating into our private lives. We can be free of that; we can be free of such control. The Matrix is the iron cage of bureaucracy, not product choice. I have been restraining myself, but I can no longer. Al-Qaeda is a real enemy. Maybe liberals want to assume guilt or even believe that we must commit cultural hari kari for the good of the planet. You can define anyone on the other side of that belief as a Conservative. Evil men exist and must be destroyed. You cannot stop evil by swaddling it in endless chatter resulting in endless legislation. Neo took action, as did President George W. Bush. I am sorry, Captain, but I cannot allow such a transparent anti-Big Government movie such as *The Matrix* to be swallowed up in your reflections.

Tom Servile: I'm looking at my reflection in this mirror. I drop the mirror. My reflection shatters into hundreds of pieces, and each piece is a tiny me.

Krowe: *Evil Dead II* (1987). Bruce Campbell is attacked by a gang of Lilliputian-size replicas of himself.

TOM SERVILE: The smaller we get, the nastier we get. Except for the dwarves in *Ice Pirates* (1984).

KROWE: We can become *Dr. Cyclops* (1940) and engage in a campaign of global shock and awe against the little people, wiping them out before they get warp drive.

TOM SERVILE: It's why they remade the *Island of Dr. Moreau* (1996) with Marlon Brando as the island. More rear drive knock-out capability.

CAPTAIN BECARK: I don't think we can step aside and mind meld with the Borg. Hive mentality. Or wish Earth was another *Planet of the Apes* (1968). No, gentlemen, the course to be set is toward change not dissolution. Not self-destruction or empire building.

KROWE: Open the port hatch, Hal.

GYPSUM: I can't do that, Dave. And you know why. I read your lips. You want to disconnect me. I can't allow that, Dave.

KROWE: We were just playing with you, Hal. Come on. Open the port hatch.

TOM SERVILE: Yeah, we were just messing with you, Hal. Yanking your chain. Raggin' on ya. Some jiving, man. Open the port hatch.

CAPTAIN BECARK: I hope you don't take what the 'bots are saying personally, Deja.

COMMANDER DEJA: That would be hard to do, Captain, as I have not been programmed to be a person. Although I would like to be. I believe that was Hal 9000's difficulty. He computed disconnection as murder and therefore defended himself against that occurring.

COUNSELLOR JOY: Do your really think, Captain, that the persistent subtextual message of all the Earth's sci-fi movies is that machines will rise up to destroy the human race?

CAPTAIN BECARK: Quite clearly in Kubrick's *2001: A Space Odyssey* the replication and magnification of human intelligence in a computer would indeed inevitably lead to a use of that intelligence for self-preservation.

DR. CRUSH: If there was self-awareness, Captain.

CAPTAIN BECARK: Quite right, Doctor. When we speak of an intelligence that rivals or exceeds the human brain, we assume consciousness attends that intelligence. Consciousness of the world and consciousness of self. It seems to go without saying that great intelligence implies great awareness. Mr. Deja is a sentient entity.

COMMANDER DEJA: My positronic net allows me to respond to new stimuli and reorganize the positronic net to re-align itself.

CAPTAIN BECARK: The very definition of learning, Mr. Deja.

COMMANDER DEJA: I am open-minded, Captain.

KROWE: Quiet. I'm on a *Fantastic Voyage* (1966) inside Karl Rove's brain.

TOM SERVILE: It's existential the way *The Invisible Man* (1933) became the *Hollow Man* (2000).

KROWE: Millennial farce. I mean *Hollow Man*.

———— ◆ ————

Voice-over: The average Joe in the United States in 1933 might have wished he were invisible just to avoid the economic hardships of one of the worst years in the Depression. H. G. Wells's invisible man, Griffin, is an English scientist in the same mad-scientist tradition as Dr. Frankenstein in *Frankenstein*; what he becomes in the 1933 film is an avenging spirit, truly an invisible one, an invisible equalizing avenger: "We'll start with a few murders. Big men, little men—just to show we make no distinction." Imagine how powerfully the subtext of Griffin's mad spree against any and all played in the imaginations of those whose very presence in the world meant misery. Absence, escape, freedom: Invisibility meant power to not only escape hardship but wreak havoc on a world that had brought them to ruin. But madness attends the invisibility formula; the scientist explores what is best left alone and pays the price. It is not science, however, that has center stage in the cultural imaginary of 1933; the Depression does. Griffin is a fantasy fulfillment of Every Poor Man who wants to strike back at forces outside himself that have brought him to ruin. The invisible man is a megalomaniac, but in the war he conducts against all those around him he is a radical terrorist, a man filled with anger and revenge. How else can a rebel force who finds the means to strike back resonate with a 1933 audience except as a man who in the American 1930s will be championed by the politics of the Left, the social and economic programs of FDR, and eulogized brilliantly in the 1940 move, *The Grapes of Wrath*? If you find the means to slip by the watchdogs of any social order, you must pay the price. If you stand up and announce that you are at war with the placements of power, you must be a megalomaniac. The film comes out of the cultural surround; the film in turn offers a fantasy escape from that surround. Find the surround of 2000 in Paul Verhoeven's

Hollow Man. It doesn't exist. What is invisible in this film is the divided American cultural imaginary. What this film escapes is any connection with an America that produced, for instance, the haunting election of 2000. Instead, the film relies on computer wizardry to mesmerize the viewer; digitalized spectacle bears its own reason to be and puts the mind into a worldless place, an X-Box, body- and soul-jacked into the greatest escape humans have yet engineered. In revealing this seduction by high-tech the film is itself a bubble within a dot.com bubble that will soon burst.

——◆——

CAPTAIN BECARK: Suffice it to say that we do not clearly know what we mean when we say consciousness. Are emotions and empathy necessarily involved? Hal 9000 felt pride. The interviewer detected that at the movie's very beginning. And if there was pride, would there be a fall? Fascinating, Mr. Deja.

KROWE: Bring me the fly with the white head. That will be your dad.

TOM SERVILE: I've spent my whole life studying Pi.

KROWE: And neglecting the girl next door.

CAPTAIN BECARK: Mr. Deja, let's conclude with a showing of *Forbidden Planet*. It's my belief that man's greatest fear lurks in that movie.

TOM SERVILE: David Bowie fell to Earth looking for water for his planet in *The Man Who Fell to Earth* (1976).

KROWE: Open the port hatch, Hal.

LT. WARP: Do these 'bots not annoy you, Captain?

CAPTAIN BECARK: Mr. Warp. You haven't told us your favorite sci-fi movie.

LT. WARP: *Mad Max* (1979). I also identified with the predator in *The Predator*. He was a skillful and courageous warrior. He reminded me of my ancestors.

CAPTAIN BECARK: Do you think, Mr. Warp, that the violence displayed in sci-fi against those not like ourselves incited continued violence on Earth?

LT. WARP: If I see someone with a big ugly head, Captain, and a menacing look, I will attack him.

COMMANDER DEJA: I believe I know why you are attracted to this film, Captain. Dr. Morbius utilizes the Krell power base to physicalize his unconscious desires.

JOE L.: What's the id, Doctor?

TOM SERVILE: It's in the top drawer of your dresser, alongside *Donovan's Brain* (1953).

CAPTAIN BECARK: In the last part of the twentieth century, Deja, expanding computer technologies promised to physicalize, as you put it, all of humankind's desires. But if those desires were not only out of conscious reach but also dark and terrible . . .

JOE L.: Then the polar ice caps might melt after the United States failed to sign the Kyoto treaty and the whole planet would be covered with water.

TOM SERVILE: Wait. I think I see Kevin Costner in a catamaran on those waters in a multi-billion-dollar sci-fi flick called *Waterworld* (1995).

KROWE: Is it an unconscious desire physicalized?

JOE L.: He's eating through twenty-nine inches of Krell metal!

TOM SERVILE: That's because he has gills.

CAPTAIN BECARK: End program, Mr. Deja. I think we've had enough of the future.

COMMANDER DEJA: The port hatch to the Holodeck seems to be malfunctioning, Captain. . . .

JOE L.: Alright, Hal. I'll go in through the emergency airlock.

TOM SERVILE: Without your space helmet, Dave, you're going to find that rather difficult.

JOE L.: Open the port hatch, Hal.

TOM SERVILE: Dave, this conversation can serve no purpose anymore. Goodbye.

——◆——

Outtake: Captain Becark's fascination with the 1956 movie *Forbidden Planet* captures, I think, an encompassing fascination sci-fi movies have had for catastrophic annihilation threatening us from without as well as within. *Forbidden Planet* displays a mass paranoia that was at the heart of the cold war; it's a film exploring through an extinct race of beings, the Krell, our own fear of attack from a monolithic force—communism—which seemed as real to us as did the monsters threatening the Krell. But the Krell turn out to have been creating their own monsters via a technology that could actualize their desires, including unconscious desires, the desires of the Freudian id. Through technology they had unleashed the dark forces within them, Thanatos as well as Eros, the desire for their own destruction, a death-wish desire.

That fear of not only desiring our own end but being able to accomplish this through the very technology that gives us our economic strength persists in sci-fi movies. In *I, Robot* (2004), a new generation of all-purpose service robots is being introduced, rather like a new and better version of Windows. But a female version of *2001*'s HAL 9000 has taken control of the robots and is now conducting an all-out war against humans. Why will this robot break her programmed robotic laws, the three laws of robotics? The answer lies in the first law: A robot cannot allow a human being to come to harm. What robot intelligence has done is calculate in its own Boolean way that if humans are not stopped they will destroy themselves. Robot intelligence has concluded that humans are on a path to destruction. Robots cannot allow that to happen. Will Smith, the hero, is partially robotic himself; the Terminator arm under lock and key in *Terminator II* is now, so to speak, our hero's arm. We have already incorporated our cyborg desire, our quest to evolve out of our humanity into robotic reality. This desire and this quest we now imagine as ending badly, a destruction produced by our own imaginations propelled by our own cyborg dream.

Why would paranoia increase in a postmodern age? Consider our growing awareness that we are mediating our world through pictures of the world and that we ourselves are producing those pictures. In our globalized economy, made possible by an increasingly sophisticated computer interconnectedness, we facilitate both desires and production. And we do both unconstrained and unchallenged, certainly not by rival economic systems. Our own liberal democracy plays second fiddle to our globalized capitalism. Here then is an entire society locked irretrievably into this kind of scenario: Corporate-sponsored science generates new technology, which produces new patents and products, which produce new sales, which produce profits to shareholders. Desires are stoked, like coals in a hearth, at both ends: Individuals have the same unquenchable thirst for new products as do corporations. The mantras of consumption—"bigger and better," "cheaper and faster," "more and easier"—create and nurture new desires each and every day. We are growing both the economy and ourselves within and through an endless proliferation of desires. We are in the business of human-desire generation, and we have the productive capacity, like the Krell, to fulfill our desires. We are totally invested in an economic system that is proven the most successful in encouraging incentive, in inspiring and fulfilling human desire.

Paradoxically, we are increasingly aware of the consequences in every sphere of this full-hearted adoption of this picture of the world and ourselves. We fear it's a China Syndrome, a chain reaction now unleashed, that will have a catastrophic end. And since we can trace its very beginning to our own imaginations, our own desires, and to a world we have ourselves imagined into being, a world that desires its own end, we are aware that there is no cold war enemy out there, there are no invading Martians, and, most spectacularly, we suspect at heart that bin Laden and al-Qaeda are our own creations, that we have brought them into existence.

In the case of paranoia, a psychiatrist would try to dissolve the inner dream by referring to a real world outside the mind. When, in a postmodern mindscape, that real world is always a filtered world, a world perceived inevitably through a picturing frame, and that real world is already powerfully pictured within a mass psyche paranoia, there is no solution or resolution offered by pointing to an undisputed, unmediated, external point of reference. They simply do not exist for humans, and, in our postmodern age, we are well aware of this. 9/11 stands within the American cultural imaginary as both indisputable proof of an enemy outside ourselves and at the same time as yet another indication that we are unconsciously engineering our own destruction.

From the very beginning sci-fi movies attached themselves to fear; simultaneously, through the use of the computer, they have magnified the screening of our high-tech, our cyborg dreams and desires. Kicking capitalism up a notch, growing it each and every business quarter, can only be done by kicking up a notch our personal and cultural desires—and these now include a desire for our own end. Whether it is a foundational desire lurking in our unconscious, personal as well as collective, a Thanatos force that is locked in a battle with Eros, as Norman O. Brown traced so long ago in *Life Against Death* (1963), or, whether it's the answer we would get if we fed a computer all the details of our "progress" and asked the question: "How can we put an end to an economy of desire that benefits few, impoverishes many, and threatens the biological integrity of the planet and, instead, adopt an economy that fulfills the needs of the many and enhances the ecological diversity of the planet?" our American culture bears a cultural death wish desire.

The real fear and trembling caused by 9/11 has as a surround this fear that we are dooming ourselves, something in the way we can, we are told, generate in our minds, in our depression, cancer.

9/11 is, on one hand, a consequence of the chain reaction we ourselves have initiated. But, once again, it also allows us to project an enemy outside ourselves, unconnected with the scenario of desire I have conjectured. The enemy is not us but really outside us. That's the position the Krell took before it became clear that the enemy was a by-product of their own desires and their ability to actualize those desires.

This is a picture, and not the world. In the world we are in there is now al-Qaeda; there are no twin World Trade Towers. There are no longer the thousands who died on September 11. Our enemy is really outside us and at the same time our creation, the inevitable result of a politics serving without hesitation our economy of desire in a world of need. Our hyperconsciousness of all this is what we picture over and over again in our sci-fi movies. But now, in our postmodern age, we pay more attention to the power of our picturing ways, as well, perhaps, of the possibilities of picturing and therefore creating the world differently. This is the grounding optimism, the driving utopianism, of all sci fi.

———◆———

THE BLOGOSPHERE

Blog: www.brainsnatchers.com

The thesis poking through the blather is that Americans have a "death wish." Why do empires dissolve? Even sci-fi film empires like the Krell in *Forbidden Planet*? Because eventually they have the technical capacity to bring their fears to life. Where does our deep-structure death wish come from? We're "haunted," the writer says, by all our sins. So the United States is like a patient on the couch, but no amount of therapy can detour us from this path of destruction. Let's not bother to face why we've become "a problem from Hell" (title of Samantha Powers's 2002 book probing some of the reasons why we're "haunted") for the rest of the world. We're just destined by a deeply repressed desire to kill ourselves.

I find this sort of diagnosis/prognosis a "couch trip" that runs us past any need to become informed regarding the actions of our government, of our Fortune 500 corporations, of our "military/industrial complex," as well as our Hollywood and Madison Avenue image-making machines. The writer's "Krell" view is just the polar opposite of the "American exceptionalism" view. Dinesh D'Souza in his essay "America the Beautiful: What We're Fighting For" doesn't see us haunted by our own evil past but sees us as a fundamentally good nation. "The millions of Americans who live decent, praiseworthy lives deserve our highest admiration because they've opted for the good when the good is not the only available option." Our destiny here is to transform the baseness of much of the world into our "goodness." And you know what the writer's take on our destiny is.

I don't believe we're so "exceptionally good" that we should remake the world in our image. Nor do I believe that we are so "exceptionally bad" and so haunted by that badness that we're out to destroy ourselves. We're not good and we're not evil: We're oblivious. Let me quote Gerald Celente, who was quoted in *Financial Times*, September 29–30, 2001: "You are dealing with people [Americans] almost childlike in their understanding of what is going on in the world. We never did anything to anybody, so why are they doing this to us?"

Americans aren't living in paranoid fear after 9/11 because of a "heavily repressed death wish" they're driven to externalize. Karl Rove and Company's success with their political campaign strategies of fear didn't occur because Americans are foundationally haunted by fear. Those fear tactics work because Americans are so uninformed regarding political realities. "The embarrassing truth is that most of us know little about the outside world, and we are particularly ill-informed about what our government is doing in our name overseas" (Mark Hertsgaard, *The Eagle's Shadow*). "Although most Americans may be largely ignorant of what was, and still is, being done in their names, all are likely to pay a steep price . . . for their nation's continued efforts to dominate the global scene" (Chalmers Johnson, *Blowback*).

In my view, it's not *Forbidden Planet* that bears a lesson but *Invasion of the Body Snatchers*. Our "brainspace" is a marketing territory that's been targeted and is taking ongoing surgical strikes. Madison Avenue soap advertisers taught MTV how to target the twentysomethings, and then MTV taught Fox News, and then Fox News taught the White House spinmeisters. Our brains have been "colonized." How? We've been witnessing it since Reagan. One quarter of a century. How do you get into a "colonized" brain? Here's where I agree with the writer: You let characters talk and you punch holes in that talk with skeptics, dadaists, pranksters, deconstructors, punsters, fools like Tom Servo, Crow, Gypsy and Joel from *Mystery Science Theatre 3000*.

Blog: www.thefutureisreal.com

You've got a very eccentric use of "paranoia" presented in "Futurescape." The clinical view describes the paranoic as experiencing continual mistrust in what appears to be the case, which is

THE BLOGOSPHERE

somehow threatening to the paranoic and therefore he or she must be ever vigilant and hyper-alert. The "conspiracy theory" kicks in here when the paranoic begins to trace a pattern, what Thomas Pynchon shows so well in *The Crying of Lot 49* for instance. "Visionary paranoia" involves a kind of postmodern hyperconsciousness; you're aware that you're responding to things like a paranoic would, but you're also aware that the things you mistrust are shielded from disclosure by any investigator's fear of losing himself or herself in the delusions of a clinical paranoia. So the visionary paranoic seeks yet another level of awareness: What elicits their mistrust is conspiratorially and purposefully designed to elicit their awareness of self-delusion precisely in those instances where mistrust is aroused. What is "really true" is there to be found and yet any search may dig oneself further into a pit of delusion. This quandary, this dilemma, may itself be the most cleverly laid entrapment of those you mistrust . . . if they indeed exist outside your own mind. The visionary paranoic is like the cabalist seeker who delves beyond the pictured veneer of truth and reality to find hidden truth and reality.

A postmodern age breeds paranoia because it has put everything from "truth" and "reality" to "self," "knowing," "memory," "words," and "pictures" under interrogation. We're swimming in spins. Which ones are reliable? All this, however, does not breed fear and trembling in the postmodernist, because he or she is not driven like Ahab to stab into the heart of the white whale to find the hidden truth. Every picture has its painter, every painter has his or her time and place, every time and place has its deceits and conundrums, its blindnesses and its insights. It takes a clinical visionary paranoic to set off on a path to finally and totally find out. And of course they never do, programmed as they are to eternally deconstruct their own determinations. Ray Pratt in his *Projecting Paranoia: Conspiratorial Visions in American Film* (2001), views "visionary 'cultural paranoia'—widespread in American films, television, and popular novels . . . as a subjective reflection of the perceived powerlessness of the American public." The writer's paranoic isn't looking for hidden clues in the world outside himself; what he suspicions is that on an unconscious level there's a "death wish" desire culturally implanted. Call it the Armageddon wish and George W. Bush and cohorts are marching us there. Why do Americans have it? Why are we on this ruinous road of empire-building that historically always leads to disaster? Because, in the writer's view, in creating the death machinery to defend ourselves we've created what we cannot control, what will eventually bring the whole world to destruction. If we can only build the Death Star we will have eternal security . . . a thought already enacted in the *Star Wars* movie trilogy. But the "collateral damage," the countless innocent dead have worn through our McNamara/Rumsfeld psychic defenses and forged a psychic "death wish." We can't be fooled in our souls. The only way in which we can avoid planetary destruction is by destroying ourselves. Call it a "planetary survival" imperative that trumps the "national survival" imperative. Whatever it is, we are obeying it on an inaccessible level. Therefore, we suspect that this death wish is behind our preemptive attack on Iraq and our reelection of our "Cowboy imperialist" because such actions are clearly "counterproductive" in the battle we are waging with al-Qaeda for the hearts and minds of the Arab world.

We act in support of our death wish; we act in ways that validate its existence. However, we make a self-defensive attempt to project this threat to "villains/evil" outside ourselves. Now the paranoic's nightmare scenario comes into play: We suspect we're walking around with a death wish buried deep and so we run from that by finding real death dealers "out there," but then we deal with them in ways that fill the wellsprings of our death wish. In engaging our future, sci-fi film ranges imaginatively, as does literature, and naturally runs into the repressed desires of the unconscious. For the writer then, sci-fi film reveals, as in a dream, our motivating fears. We are the Krell who went so far as to create machines linked by intent to their own conscious desires but unexpectedly and disastrously also linked to their unconscious desires. And there lurked the death wish, the unstoppable monster fed by the collective death desires of the entire race of the Krell.

This is, as I say, an eccentric presentation of paranoia and one somewhat surprising for a postmodernist since it rests its case on a foundational "desire" or narrative of universal presence, a narrative that is uncontestable. A postmodern paranoic is redundant, because postmodernists hold that whatever is represented as real and true is always something represented as real and true by someone who is always some place, at some time. Every postmodernist is always looking for the clues that unravel this or that construction of the "real" and "true." But the writer of "Futurescape" doesn't treat his subliminal "death wish" as a contestable fabrication; he universalizes it for political purposes.

Americans didn't fly the planes into the World Trade Towers; those weren't deaths we wished on ourselves. Those were deaths laid at bin Laden's doorstep. So when does the cultural paranoic death wish kick in? If it only kicks in at the response level, as I've

THE BLOGOSPHERE

already described, then there are real people out there wishing us dead. We may have an internalized death wish, but we also have real enemies out there. So even if we were to succeed in destroying ourselves—for the good of the planet, of course—we'd be leaving behind our enemies, who would I suppose eventually go through a collective *crise de conscience* and do the right thing—internalize a death wish, purely for the good of the planet.

The postmodern path here, rather than the politically partisan, would have been to set out this counter to the *grand recit* of a death wish.

Even a blog would do the trick.

Blog: www.conspiratoriallycrazed.com

One more turn toward paranoia:

Does America have real enemies? Sure. That doesn't mean we didn't manufacture them, slowly, painstakingly, say, from the implantation of Israel in Palestine, to stationing U.S. troops in Saudi Arabia. A paranoic would say that it's this hidden death wish that engineered it all, from doing nothing after Jeb Bush arranged a victory for his bro' in the 2000 election to reelecting the most dangerous man to the White House in 2004. If we're not setting ourselves up for a fall of the Corporate States of America then I'm a conspiratorially crazed paranoic.

THE BLOGOSPHERE

Frontierscape

In Western iconography, the lineage runs from Hawkeye to Buffalo Bill, from the Lone Ranger to George W. Bush.
—Sidney Blunmenthal, *Guardian Newspapers*,
September 3, 2004

I recall, shortly after September 11, at a time when the President was talking about "those folks," "smoking them out," "getting them running," "dead or alive," reading one morning in both the *Washington Post* and the *New York Times* about how his words were his own, the product of what the Post called his "unvarnished instinct."
—Joan Didion, "Politics in the 'New Normal' America,"
The New York Review of Books, October 21, 2004

Like it or not, America's contribution to mythology is the story of the lone cowboy in the Old West, who brings about justice his own way, with guns a-blazing.
—David Denby, "The Quick and the Dead,"
New Yorker, January 16, 2005

"[E]ither you are with us, or you are with the terrorists." Like Bush's declaration that he wanted bin Laden "dead or alive," this was more cowboy talk, the Wild West sheriff warning "Do as I say or get out of town"—the very attitude that had irritated America's friends and enemies alike for decades. Never mind that many nations already had their own painful experiences with terrorism; they would follow Washington's orders or else.
—Mark Hertsgaard, "The Oblivious Empire,"
in *The Eagle's Shadow: Why American
Fascinates and Infuriates the World*, 2002

Voice-over: Return with us now to those glorious days of yesteryear . . . which is what Clint Eastwood does in his Western *The Unforgiven* (1992), a Western with a legendary gunfighter called out of retirement to champion the cause of a whore who's had her face slashed by a cowboy. Together with his sidekick from the bad old days and a young wannabe gunfighter, William Munny, the gunfighter, sets out on a knightly mission. Their mission is mythic: Don Quixote with his faithful Sancho Panza, the Lone Ranger with Tonto, the Cisco Kid with Pancho, Lash LaRue with Fuzzy Jones, Red Ryder and Little Beaver, Gene Autry with Frog Millhouse, George W. Bush with Karl Rove . . . an endless list of hero and sidekick. Classic too is a really mean sheriff, Little Bill; an elegant English gunfighter, English Bob; and a whore with a heart of gold. This is the picture of the Old West that Hollywood has imprinted in our genes, but it's a picture that Eastwood steps away from and begins to show us the picture-framing, begins to interrogate the slippage between picture and world. Frontierscape filmscape parodies a scene in the movie when English Bob is behind bars after having been beaten to a pulp by Sheriff Little Bill, and the Sheriff is here interrogating Bob's own personal chronicler, the pulp fiction writer Mr. Beauchamp. For our purposes, Little Phil is interrogating Mr. Bullcrank on the Western movie genre itself. Hollywood Bob adds a croak now and then from his cell.

—◆—

Characters: Mr. Bullcrank, a chronicler of the West, author of ecstatic Western pulp fiction; Sheriff Little Phil, a hard-bitten realist and sheriff to boot; Hollywood Bob, a frontier badman who owes his legenday reputation to the writings of Mr. Bullcrank.

—◆—

The Setting: *Similar to the jail scene in Clint Eastwood's* The Unforgiven *when English Bob, beaten and abused by Sheriff Little Bill, lies bleeding in a cell and Little Bill is proceeding to set Mr. Beauchamp, the Western historian, straight on what the West and its heroes were really like.*

—◆—

SHERIFF LITTLE PHIL: This here is purty interesting reading, Mr. Bullcrank. How the Western movie ran out of steam when the U.S. of A. lost its heroes.

MR. BULLCRANK: Yes, but I'm saying the Western movie colluded with the disastrous turn from real heroes with real courage to . . .

SHERIFF LITTLE PHIL: It says here when John Ford's camera focused on a blurred Duke Wayne as the Ringo Kid in *Stagecoach* (1939) and then jumped into a close and tight shot of the Duke standing by the side of the road, saddle at his feet, Winchester in hand, gazing at the approaching stagecoach, the U. S. of A. had a sharp clear view of what being a real man of the West was all about. Well, ain't that something, Mr. Bullcrank.

MR. BULLCRANK: Whether you like it or not, Sheriff, we live through our movie heroes.

SHERIFF LITTLE PHIL: But you say here we can no longer. Let's see (reading). "We can no longer appreciate the moral courage and steadfast sense of duty of Sheriff Will Kane in *High Noon* (1952)." Now ain't that the president's favorite movie?

MR. BULLCRANK: A man of true courage can't rely on his neighbors is, I think, the message. In Mr. George W. Bush's case, he won't spend as much time as Sheriff Will Kane did in *High Noon* trying to get the support of the United Nations. It was a waste of time for a heroic man like Will Kane to opportune the support of cowards, liars, and the gutless. Bush Sr. confused the networking that enables powerful venture capitalists to join together for mutual profit with the useless kind of political networking the U.N. represents. Bush Jr., under the tutelage of his neo-con advisors, corrected that mistake.

SHERIFF LITTLE PHIL: Well, maybe Bush Jr. and his advisors like Gary Cooper in that movie, but you say right here, the twentysomethings think the whole movie is kind of like a CEO who can't cut the mustard. I'm reading your words here: "Youngsters of today think he is a loser who has failed to optimize and maximize and supersize the potential of the network of resources available to him." Why, Mr. B.S., that's a mouth full of words. And confusion sets in, I can tell you. Because here you say you got a whole audience hostile to old-time Western heroes, and over here you say it's the movies' fault for not giving us any more of those old-time Western heroes.

MR. BULLCRANK: Look, Sheriff, if I can just run through a little bit of history for you. Everyone born around Ronnie Reagan's time . . .

SHERIFF LITTLE PHIL: You're not gonna sit there, Mr. Bullcrank, and tell me folks didn't appreciate the stellar heroic qualities of Mr. Reagan in all them B-Westerns he made? Why, he was elected Prez right off the set of *Law and Order* (1953). Recollect that shoot 'em up, B.S.? Reagan cleaned up not only one town of lawlessness and debauchery but two. Two towns. Rode right into the White House after that there accomplishment.

MR. BULLCRANK: My point, Sheriff, is that you can draw a time line between those who understood what the frontier represented . . .

SHERIFF LITTLE PHIL: Which was? Shortlist.

———◆———

Outtake: They loved freedom; they were independent and spent a lot of time out at the ranch, kept off the Washington beltway. That's why George W. spends so much time on his "ranch" in Crawford, Texas. They didn't look to the federal government or their corporate employers to coddle them from cradle to grave. That's why George W. is set on getting the Feds out of the secured retirement business and welfare to dependent children. They were free to choose, which is why those soldiers who died in Iraq on a mission to prevent Saddam from launching those WMDs at us should assume personal responsibility for their choice to join the military. Frontiersmen shopped when and where they wanted to, and that's why George W. told Americans after 9/11 to rush out to their malls and show al-Qaeda that buildings could drop but shopping wouldn't stop. Out in the Old West, fellows competed 24/7 for the ho's and the gold, brought losers to swift justice and swift justice to Geronimo and every last terrorist Indian in the West, right up to Saddam Hussein. Cowboys weren't up to a whole lot of reading outside of the Good Book, and that's why George W. relies on word of mouth to get his info. Our Western forebears were plain-speaking folks who naturally knew what had to be done because God spoke directly to them, like George W., who talks real plain and listens to God. Bottom line: Frontier folk weren't no bleeding-heart liberals from the East with mouths full of empty words that flopped this way and then that way.

———◆———

MR. BULLCRANK: If you put the cyberspace generation in front of a screen where Alan Ladd's Shane or Burt Lancaster's Wyatt Earp or Randolph Scott's Buchanan is riding again—any of the great Western movie heroes—all the cyberspace generation sees is something old, over and adios, something that doesn't compute in their world.

SHERIFF LITTLE PHIL: If we got this here cyberspace generation who are deaf and dumb to the Old West then how come you can't understand Prez W. and everything he's done since 9/11 unless you know what he's seen in them Hollywood Westerns? Iraq's the Hole in the Wall where the al-Qaeda gang is hiding out and we're in there to get them. Bring 'em back dead or alive. Hang 'em high. Bring 'em to justice. I mean, if the frontier spirit doesn't compute with this digital generation, how does the Prez reach them with it?

MR. BULLCRANK: First of all, if we are exceptional as a country, Sheriff, it's because of our frontier past, and though Mr. Bush quotes that past, he's a mockery of it. And those who respond to such hype do so not in a true heroic, frontier tradition but out of the far less heroic incentives of pure greed, hate and vengeance. The true West, I assure you, is forgotten, Sheriff.

SHERIFF LITTLE PHIL: Mr. Bullcrank, you're just a feller that's set on mourning the loss of something that never was. We're talking pictures, and not the West. We only ever got ourselves a picture of that Western world. What the world really was would be hard to say, but Hollywood ain't close, I'm thinking. Hollywood made all them heroes. Pulled them out of the air. Made men bigger than they ever were or ever could be. Just like Karl Rove made Dubya bigger then he is. Just like you made old Hollywood Bob over there . . .

MR. BULLCRANK: Scottish Bob.

SHERIFF LITTLE PHIL: Hollywood Bob is what I call him. In all that dime novel writing of yours you made old Bob into some kind of tough Hondo when all he is a sorry son of a bitch. Ain't that right, Bob?

HOLLYWOOD BOB (from his cell): You object to seeing the nobler side of humanity on the big screen, Little Phil.

SHERIFF LITTLE PHIL: I ain't objecting to seeing that side, Bob. But I'll be damned if I'm gonna sit there and see a sorry side of beef like you being all gussied up as a real hero of the Old West.

HOLLYWOOD BOB: I don't think art should stoop to the muddy mundane where you seem to thrive, Little Phil. Along with the cockroaches and coyotes.

SHERIFF LITTLE PHIL: Well, Bob, I didn't personally expose the legends of the West. Hollywood did that their own selves.

HOLLYWOOD BOB: I'm sure such a learned man as you, Sheriff, can tell us how.

SHERIFF LITTLE PHIL: No, I can't, Bob. But Mr. Bullcrank here can. He's got it all writ down here. Give Bob a read here, Mr. B.S.

Bullcrank puts on his reading glasses and begins reading.

———— ◆ ————

"On the Trail of the Western Movie"

What we call the classic Western demonstrates a classic or naïve realist style of telling a story. That style suited the times and it suited the people of the times. Americans came out of World War II with a new pride in themselves. They had heroically answered the call of a Europe in distress. They had, if you will, walked boldly into a showdown and gunned down the bad guys and rescued the foreign maiden in the bargain. In 1939, when all eyes scanned the horizon for a hero, John "Duke" Wayne, as the Ringo Kid, stood there steely-eyed, gun-ready, looking every inch the rugged Westerner willing and able to step up and do what was called for. Countless B-Westerns with countless laconic, fast-shooting, shy with the ladies and pals to their horses—from Buck Jones and Lightening Tim Mc Coy to Randolph Scott and Audie Murphy (the most decorated United States soldier of World War II)—fill the classic realist Western screen.

And what was the classic realist formula by which a story on a screen became real to its audience? The formula had these ingredients: audience identification with a heroic figure, clear divide between good and evil, cliff-hanging tension wherein the hero and the good seem doomed, final high noon shootout/chase scene leaving the bad guys dead or handcuffed, and the hero riding off into the sunset, alone, or with a loyal sidekick. What the Western adds to a naïve realist formula that worked through other genres was the isolation of the hero in a vast untamed country. This hero was uniquely connected with the American landscape, uniquely American. The formula could be used in a French romance or a British whodunit, but the American Western brought the formula to another level. Here the Western found its representational form and here the form of representation found its screenplay.

— ◆ —

SHERIFF LITTLE PHIL: So what you're saying here, Bullcrank, makes it clear to me why young folks who have no interest in the Old West because they didn't have cell phones or computers back then get corralled by Bush's tough, old cowboy routine. They're just responding to this here naïve, realist way of reducing complex situations to good guys and bad guys and an X-Box or Play Station shootout.

MR. BULLCRANK (sighs): Yes, Sheriff. It's an effective political strategy, although it probably got its start on Madison Avenue with some sharp scholiast who observed the psychology of seduction at work in Hollywood Westerns. May I go on?" (continues reading)

— ◆ —

Frontier life created a self-reliance, an independent, freedom of the spirit that appealed almost on an ontological level to Americans.

The homesteaders in Shane *(1953) band together against their enemy, the cattle baron who doesn't want squatters on the open range. Solidarity will level the playing field. Shane is on the outside looking in. He attends a meeting of the homesteaders but leaves because the group questions his courage. But it's Shane in the end who faces the sadistic hired killer and guns down him and the other bad guys. It's not the community or the commune, the solidarity of a band of "one among equals" that is respected here. What's implied is that going it alone, relying on one's own initiative and courage is preferable to relying on others, including the law.*

It's a 1953 attitude that sweeps a country now imagining itself in a "cold war," a war between the tyranny of communism and the freedom of democracy. Soviet communism means the end of private property; everything will be held in common without private ownership. What is hypothesized here is mutual alliance and reliance, interdependence and cooperation in a spirit of "one for all and all for one." The bedrock freedom American democracy represents is pursuit of private property, of private concern and self-interest promoting a competitive combativeness that leaves some winners and some losers. Individual ownership and control corresponds to the much admired qualities of self-reliance and determination, with all the mystique surrounding "rugged individualism." To be heroic is to stand alone in a war of all against all. To walk along down the main street at high noon ready to face down your adversary . . .

———◆———

SHERIFF LITTLE PHIL: Point of interruption here, Your Historyness, but every damn homesteader is fencing in his own private patch of ground so the whole open range is barbed wired to hell. You're more than likely to ride into a string of barb wire than into one of them fine Western sunsets. Freedom's in the open range, partner, not in barbed wire.

MR. BULLCRANK: Admittedly a contradiction, Sheriff but the fact remains Americans associate private property with individual freedom.

SHERIFF LITTLE PHIL: Even if that individual can't ride a mile without coming to a gate that says "Members or owners only"?

MR. BULLCRANK: (starts to read again)

———◆———

It's not surprising that a president from Texas who emulates Gary Cooper when he talks to the press and retreats to his ranch to get away from the Beltway will take on the bad guy—Osama bin Laden—in typical Western-movie style. Looking to the United Nations for help is like Shane looking to the homesteader bund for help. Recall how impatient John Wayne's Ethan Edwards in The Searchers *(1956) is with the band of farmers he's riding with. Going it alone and not leaning or relying on the group is what the classic realist Western presents as heroic.*

In the same year that Shane *came out, 1953, another president, Ronald Reagan, at that time a B-movie star, made a Western called* Law and Order. *He turned the script of that film into a political platform in 1980 and won the presidency. He, too, retreated to "the ranch" where he would put on the Hollywood cowboy costume once again and treat the media to some "tall in the saddle" photo ops, thus reminding Americans of the connect between the rugged Western hero and his own presidency. It wasn't surprising that he took that classic realist formula into his strategic plan for dealing with the Soviets. He basically gave them until noon to get out of Dodge or he'd be waiting in front of the Longbranch Saloon, guns ready. Luckily the Soviets deconstructed themselves before noon.*

—◆—

SHERIFF LITTLE PHIL: That man finally went it alone, leaving the U.S. Constitution behind when he engaged in real nefarious dealings that came to be known and just as quickly forgotten by the U.S. of A. citizenry as Irangate. Sorry, for the interrupt, Doctor. Head 'em out. I'm listening.

MR. BULLCRANK: (resumes reading)

—◆—

So Reagan's film cuts itself off from the moral messiness of the Earp-Holiday legend and substitutes a blank cinematic righteous horse opera. Reagan contributes a distracted, acting-by-the-numbers performance suited to a film sucked till it's empty of any worldly connect.

—◆—

Script Doctor: Let's have a sneak preview of Jim Jarmusch's *Dead Man* (1996), another deconstructive journey into the heart of the Western mythos.

—◆—

Trailer: Dead Man

Never before has the American West been so exposed!!

Jim Jarmusch's *Dead Man* turns comedy and farce into parody and exposes through that parody the fictions of our naïve realist view of the frontier, a frontier consistently presented in ways that have present-day impact. Here in *Dead Man* the past isn't simply a fabrication of the present, a story told by the present moment to suit itself and its preoccupations, a total rewriting of the past to fit the present's cultural agenda.

Take this wild ride at your own risk!

What we have here is a deconstructive journey into the heart of the Western mythos, a mocking of the ritualistic "go West young man" scenario that spares neither the West then nor the United States now. This is a devastating send-up that provides its audience with no catbird seat from which to enjoy the distance between itself and the object of ridicule, no Archimedian point outside the cross-parrying of postmodern parody.

Dances with Wolves (1990), with its 1990s politics of identity agenda, is programmatic and tendentious and falls into a naïve realist formula that simply reverses good guys and bad guys. *Dead Man* makes no use of naïve realist formula and therefore doesn't meet the expectations of an audience shaped to discard films they "can't relate to." Translate this expression to a transgression of the first point of connection with a movie: someone heroic to identify with or someone clearly identified as comical, tragic, villainous, ingenuous, or hard-boiled.

See Johnny Depp as you've never seen him before!

Johnny Depp is the star of the movie and he has a built-in star attraction. But when he appears in the very first scene in a checked suit, bow tie and porkpie hat à la Buster Keaton and he's therefore immediately exposed as a naïf from the East, he provides the audience with only a laughable image. But the film is clearly not a comedy. This is a puzzler. When Depp then takes a first walk down the main street of a frontier town called Machine, heading for a smoke-spewing metalwork factory that stands at the end of the street like the castle in *Edward Scissorhands* (1990) and the camera focuses on animal skulls adorning every wall in sight, animal pelts piled high in wagons, huge pigs who get Depp running, a man getting a blow job in an alley who pulls a gun on the gazing Depp, a horse sending a steady stream of piss into the street mud, the maddening scream of machinery in the metal works—all captured in a disheartening black and gray—the audience is meant to be repelled. A walk down any street in the old West most likely would have repelled today's mall shopper.

Some are born to sweet delight, some are born to endless night!

When we meet an Indian who wants to be called Nobody and who connects Depp's name—William Blake—to the eighteenth-century visionary poet and painter and who immediately calls Depp "a stupid, fucking white man" and who quotes Blake's visionary poetry throughout the film, we are into territory far more complex that the multicultural agenda of *Dances with Wolves*. Depp Blake arrives in the West looking for a job as an accountant in Machine, home of Dickinson Metal Works, and he winds up William Blake, poet and visionary—and gunslinger.

He #!@#!! his parents, cooked them up, and ate 'em!

He's pursued by Dickinson, an ogre of a nineteenth-century CEO, and three hired killers who do the corporate bidding. Depp Blake also runs into three psychopaths: a religious, murderous racist, and a couple of dimwitted lawmen. But he is victorious over all of them and floats out to sea in a canoe prepared for his voyage into another and better world. It's not just a long train ride from Cleveland to California but a journey across both nineteenth- and twentieth-century American cultural landscapes. Only a vision other than that of the town of Machine and the Dickinson Metal Works can redeem us. And, Jarmusch shows us that vision is not in the Bible quoting of the three psychos Blake runs into or the Bible quoting of the French trader.

See what lay hidden in the forbidden past of the Old West!

The path of the Sacred was forbidden to the Indians of the Southwest by the Spanish explorers. The French quoted the Bible and passed out disease-laden blankets to the Indians. The excesses of the present are there to be found on this frontier, in our past. "The vision of Christ thou dost see is my greatest enemy," Nobody tells the French trader, quoting William Blake.

See how Western legendary heroes are made!

And Jarmusch's double-edged parodying doesn't end here. He shows us how Western legendary heroes are created. The Depp Blake "in the goddamned clown suit" becomes a "legend of the West." "So you're William Blake," someone says at the end of the movie. The impossible has happened. A stupid, fucking white man has become a legend.

Endless night theatens us at every turn!

"I'm William Blake," Depp Blake tells Nobody at the beginning of the movie. "Then you're a dead man," Nobody replies. The visionary

Blake is indeed dead to that Machine world and, unfortunately, dead in our own world. But he walks and rides in this movie, although he has a bullet close to his heart and he repeatedly loses consciousness. It's as if poetry and vision and sweet delight have no life either back then or now. Endless night threatens to take over both our dreams and our waking life, both what was, what is, and what will be. And yet the movie ends with Depp Blake floating (falling asleep? dying? dead?) floating in his burial canoe toward a sun going down on the horizon.

———◆———

Outtake: The sun is going down on the American vision, which was already moribund in our glorious West, and without vision we face the endless night of a new machine age. We are aware of this, too, in our postmodern age, an awareness darkening the landscape of our cultural imaginary.

———◆———

MR. BULLCRANK: (resumes "On the Trail of the Western Movie")

A playful irony extends to Clint Eastwood's own mythic status as unnamed drifter in Leone's spaghetti Westerns. It's Eastwood, however, who resolves the dilemma of wanting to portray the West but at the same time wanting to escape the stigma of a Hollywood portrayal by bringing the matter into the Western itself. The 1992 film The Unforgiven *takes as its themes a desire to question, parody, and undermine the Hollywood Western mythos-making machine, and a challenging desire to reach the foundational reality of the West "as it truly was." The movie succeeds in both desires. Sheriff Little Bill brilliantly deconstructs the fabled legend of English Bob, the Duke of Death, as narrated by English Bob's personal historian . . .*

SHERIFF LITTLE PHIL: And sidekick.

Bullcrank looks up, frowns, and then continues reading "On the Trail of the Western Movie."

———◆———

. . . as narrated by English Bob's personal historian, Mr. Beauchamp. That same deconstructing is also done by Clint Eastwood's character, the legendary gunman, William Munny, who has long since given up drinking and killing when the movie opens. In response to the continued pestering of a young wannabe gunman, the self-styled Kid, Eastwood confesses that it was drink that led him to murderous doings. He has no

recollection of acting bravely or honorably, just drunkenly. "I was mostly drunk in them days, Kid." This is a direct and open confrontation with the issues worrying the Western, namely, we've always heard stories of the West told by unreliable narrators, and we've erected a frontier hero who stands taller in the saddle than anyone else but indeed may have been no different than anyone else except in ways we'd never deem heroic. Billy the Kid shot his victims in the back; the Earps may have been bigger scoundrels than the Clantons; Jesse James was really just robbing trains not championing the victims of the robbery conducted by the railroad magnates.

The result of Eastwood's airing of our suspicions is a greater sense of authenticity in the characters of both Little Bill and William Munny. And the film itself recaptures the "true grit" of the West and its heroes that John Ford had brought to the screen. What we also see is a reinvesting of Ford's Westerns with the genuineness that had been taken from them by revisionist, lampooning, mythologizing, and "great fun" Westerns. The Unforgiven does this because there is a story and there are characters that survive the self-deconstructing of the movie. It's as if the Western had gone through self-purifying fires, an antivirus program that cleansed it of its untruths. And the whole genre benefits from this purgation. It's not that Ford's Westerns, for instance, were no longer classic realist but that there was something true to nature beneath and beyond the spin of that classic realist formula. You could expose it and remove it, as The Unforgiven seemed to do, and discover something unspurious, unfictitious, something sincere and honest, something un-Hollywood.

Ironically then in this "high noon" encounter with the debunking virus that had bedeviled the Western genre for decades, Eastwood succeeds in doing what films like Hang'em High, Joe Kidd, and The Outlaw Josey Wales had failed to do—give a feeling of naturalism, of absolute realism, back to the Western, giving the audience a sense of a new (rather than redundant) experience. They were still in control of what they saw, because now they were the revealers of how they had been deceived in the past. It was a cultural hyperconsciousness that responded to the hyperconsciousness of The Unforgiven. This was a picture that pictured itself as a picture, that questioned all previous pictures of the West that had attempted to show the West as it really was. The Unforgiven was a picture, and not the world, and this self-awareness, in a postmodern age, ironically made the picture more real than its naïve realist predecessors.

———◆———

Script Doctor: More real to whom? The Western is a dead genre for anyone born from Reagan's first term onward. Why? What happened in the American cultural imaginary that its most favored foundation—the frontier—no longer had an impact on the new generation? Drop the history lesson here and do a voice-over about the movie that faces up to this loss of appeal—Kevin Costner's *The Open Range*.

—— ♦ ——

Voice-over: Kevin Costner's 2003 Western, *The Open Range*, makes no apologies for the genre or for releasing an unrepentant Western at a time when two rising generations of Americans are deep into very un-Western genre mindsets. The first is what a *Frontline* special entitled "The Merchants of Cool" called the "Mook and Midriff Generation," the twentysomethings soaked in reality TV, MTV Spring Break romps, Girls Gone Wild contests, tropical island survivor dreams, "going to the bah," "clubbing," "celling" in their SUVs, and lying in tattoo parlors. Just ahead of them are the former overnight dot.com millionaires, raised on Bill Gates, Ronald Reagan, and the Dow Jones soon to be at 40,000. Entrepreneurial to the bone and anxious to privatize everything in sight, from Social Security to Yosemite, this generation "chooses to be rich" and wonders how people in the Old West survived without shopping or surfing the Web. The Old West has as much hold on the attention of both these generations as a position paper on Iraq written by Colin Powell has on George W.

Costner's film directly confronts this younger audience for whom the West is as dead and without significance as last year's fad in unsandblasted jeans. The first point of confrontation is over what we'll call the timescape: slow or analogue time vs. digital time. And here Costner deliberately pitches a pre-remote, pre-mouse narrative pacing. And then he focuses on the generation living at *Matrix* speed. The twentysomething who is bent out of natural shape and the natural flow of time in this movie is Button, the young wrangler who has much to learn. He cheats at cards; he doesn't know the code of riding with such men as Boss and Charlie. He has to learn but he needs to be cleansed of his bad habits.

—— ♦ ——

Outtake: Spell out what Button has to learn; it's in the dialogue: "A man's trust is a valuable thing, Button," Boss says. "You don't want to lose it over a handful of cards." "Every man has to pull his weight," Mose tells Button, to which Button points out that Mose is twice his weight. "I ain't one to take a man's confidence lightly," Mose tells Button and urges Button to remember that when he's riding with men like Charlies and Boss. What does it all mean? In a word, interdependence: Button has to be a person another person can put his confidence in, can trust, and that person in turn will be someone Button can trust. Mutual respect emerges from fulfilling these obligations. Each person trusts that the next person will do his share, will pull his weight, and in this way all burdens are distributed equally, all burdens are shared. Trust, confidence, respect, and mutual sharing are the virtues instilled and required on the open range.

(Bullcrank resumes reading)

———— ♦ ————

So Button becomes that part of American pop that Costner knows won't take to his Western, and he targets them through Button. He slows them down. He gives them an eye for the open range not the computer monitor, the screening of simulation, of pixels and Boolean logic renderings. He gives them a face-to-face encounter with the world out there and an understanding that growth comes from face-to-face dealings with other people. The old, like Boss, who "sure can cowboy," have a purpose. The open range pictured by Costner is not a youth culture world. The twentysomethings don't own it. What Costner's picture of the "real world" contends with is a picture of a bunch of airhead twentysomethings sitting around analyzing their own know nothingness on or off a reality TV show. The real world pictured in The Open Range *is the open range, not reality TV, or cyperspace, or shopping in upscale "neighborhood malls," or spending a weekend at Vegas's faux Venice, or clubbing till dawn, or day trading, driving down an Interstate in an SUV doing 90 mph, or wondering what history, old people, poor people, public transportation, reading and writing, the federal government, red lights, pedestrians, politics, daily family dinners, real bread, lives without computers, Social Security, and lives before plastic could possibly signify.*

This is a world where Costner's own character, Charlie, respects the older Boss, Robert Duvall, because he knows the open range in a deeper and more profound way than Charlie does. Button knows little, but there's a cockiness to him nonetheless. This is a ride back to an open-range picture of America after a quarter of a century of simulacra, of adulation of youth for commercial reasons and a discarding of the old. To be middle-aged is just something to be hidden and you hide it by buying products. Annette Bening shows the wear and tear of her age, but like the free and open range that hasn't been mowed, trimmed, landscaped, and chemically treated, she's a natural beauty and Costner brings that out, just as he brings out the superiority of the natural unvarnished open range as opposed to the city where they found Button.

The film also adopts redundancy—going back and forth to the doc's for instance—and scorns the need for constant new and more startling and more stimulating computer gambits. This is not the Matrix reloaded; this is the natural world brought to your attention. Overstimulation and the overstimulated are slowed down. Life doesn't move at digital speed, at the quick flick of a mouse or remote. What's needed is for you to pan the scene before you with a slow steady gaze. The overstimulated mentality requires constant feeding with no repeats and no redundancy. The rule is to make it new: new products, new looks, new fads and fancies. To go back again and again into the open range is to be able to enjoy a world that is free and not bought at the mall. On the open range, you don't shop; you feast on the natural beauty of the world, as does Costner's camera.

SHERIFF LITTLE PHIL: I'm thinking there's still a lot of open range in Alaska those market boys want to tear up looking for oil. Open range for a guy like Dubya ain't anything more than a field of venture capital opportunity. Bet this ain't a Western movie Dubya's liked.

HOLLYWOOD BOB: On the contrary, Little Phil, I think President George W. Bush found his own brand of Western justice. You recall that Costner plays the part of a gunman who's tried to leave that life behind but it's his prowess with pistols that saves the day. The villain wanting to close the open range, rob the free roaming cowboys of their free roaming ways, can't be stopped. Except by superior weaponry. The moral: Those who want to keep an open range, say of mind or commerce, better keep a strong standing army. War is Western. Even a liberal like Mr. Costner can't preserve the poetic freedom and beauty of the open range without ending his film with the most protracted shootout and bloodletting since . . . what is the latest Iraq casualty report?

——◆——

Outtake: . . . as pictured by the spinmeisters and the product pushers.

——◆——

THE BLOGOSPHERE

Blog: www.freemarketanalysis.com

This from Gary Hoppenstand's editorial in the *Journal of Popular Culture* August 2004, "Gone With the Western," a review of Kevin Costner's *Open Range*:

"There were no baby boomers present, only the parents and grandparents of baby boomers. . . . It was then that I was reminded in no uncertain terms that the Western, my beloved Western, simply did not appeal to younger moviegoers. I did not require a sophisticated demographic industry analysis to confirm the plain evidence of my eyes. The major A-list motion picture Western was not in cardiac arrest. It was long dead."

Here's my market analysis: Is there any marketing sense in drawing young people out of a contemporary high-tech product scene where consumer desire can be instilled into the retro-world of the frontier where there are no products to buy?

Blog: www.presidentswardrobe.com

After 9/11 Bush's Image Dept. dove into the wardrobe: Jet Pilot, Harvard MBA, Baseball Regular Guy, Texas Crude, Born-Again, Cowboy on the Ranch, Compassionate Conservative, Family Man, Plaindealer. They took out the cowboy outfit. Henceforth, Dubya would be Matt Dillon telling Osama to get out of Dodge. A huge connect with the post–40-year-olds. Young people's connect could only have been Hans Solo in *Star Wars*, and that was already too old. Anyway, young people were no longer taking required civics courses so they were clean slates and very susceptible to jump cutting, celebrity spin dealers. They had also been primed not to vote because "politics was a dirty business" and the "Federal Government was the enemy" and "all candidates were the same." So they didn't vote. One wag of the old Western Wag was meant to wag the older dogs, get them to line up on the "Good Guy" side of a Range War, I mean, a "holy war." But why was the Western dead to everybody but the oldsters? The writer of "Frontierscape" says it's an analogue/digital divide. The Horse Opera/Oat Burner was too analogue, too linear, no jump cuts, no chance to cell on horseback, no midriffs flaunting tatts, no SUVs, no cyberspace. Kids live in the Now . . . Now . . . Now . . . Visitations for two hours or so to "Old School" is a trip they can't make. What are we selling with these Westerns? Ten-gallon hats, spurs, six-guns, chaps, saddles, horses, lariats, sheriff badges, bows and arrows, feathers? If you spin young people back to pre-auto days who's going to want to buy the Hummer2, or the new Mustang convertible? No, the past is productless. The fashion world does a retro-urban cowboy look for certain red state target areas, but it's a tougher sell to get the urban cowboy to whip out a cell phone or sit in front of a computer playing X-Box games than it is to sell someone who's turned from the past totally as "old, over and adios," as "uncool." The past is not "money" because it's "Old School."

Blog: www.dubyaduke.com

I like the epigram saying President Bush is "The Lone Cowboy" bringing justice in his own way with guns blazing. This fits George W. perfectly. Okay, he's not a "lone cowboy." He's what John Fogarty called "A Fortunate Son," a guy whose brain is a Web site designed by Karl Rove. He does bring about "justice in his own partisan way," doing everything he can to muzzle any dissent regarding either the nature of this justice or the way it's to be realized. And people who wind up "with guns a-blazing" are mostly people who, unlike Vice President Cheney who didn't fight in 'Nam because he had better options than doing push-ups and dodging bullets, don't have any options besides doing push-ups and dodging bullets. How any of this fits in with "American exceptionalism" I don't know, but the Western that most closely connects to this mythology and post-9/11 America is *High Noon*. Bush is Gary Cooper as the Sheriff, standing tall and alone, like America, against a gang of thugs coming to kill him and terrorize the town. Cooper can't muster "a coalition of the willing" but it doesn't make a difference. "A man's got to do what a man's got to do." You can't run and hide; you have to face the threat, take it on, no matter what the odds. The "homeland" is threatened and Cooper/Bush steps out into the main street and walks toward it. You can't ride into an American town and burn it down; you can't put enough fear into a man of the West (*Man of the West*, 1958, another Gary Cooper Western) to make him run. That's the defending mythos. The "Lone Cowboy" bringing justice to "Evildoers," after some evil act has been done. Recall Steve McQueen in *Nevada Smith*, 1966, hunting down the murderers of his mother and father; Gregory Peck in *The Bravados*, 1958, hunting down his wife's murderers, and most especially, The Duke, John Wayne, in *The Searchers*, 1956, on a long search for the murderers of his brother and his family. It's this last film that resonates strongly with Bush's often expressed belief that the search to find and root out the 9/11 terrorists will be long and hard but America will never give it up until every last one is rounded up and brought to justice or justice brought to them. There's a weak-willed coalition in *The Searchers* going along with The Duke, but they turn back and The Duke stubbornly, against all odds, hearing no voice but his own, keeps on searching. There's no doubt in my mind that Bush believes in this picture; Cheney, Wolfowitz, Pearle, Rove, Feith, Rice, and others in his administration are more likely scripting themselves into other, less naïve pictures of the world, but it's hard to think that Bush doesn't see himself as this "lone cowboy with guns a-blazing," as The Duke on a heroic search for evil.

Blog: www.whosthehero.com

I just want to piggyback on that dubyaduke blog where the blogger says President Bush thinks he's John Wayne. From bin Laden's perspective, he's the one who's "the lone cowboy with guns a-blazing" taking on U.S. imperialism and injustice. Look at Lars von Trier's film *Dogville*, 2004. In the end, it's the stranger who comes from someplace else—hence a foreigner—who gets the savage treatment and finally rebels and seeks revenge. Could it be that the town needing cleaning up is the United States? Could it be that Bush is wearing the black hat and isn't riding the white horse? Could it be that the Middle East knows our Hollywood Westerns and projects Bush into the bad-guy role and bin Laden into the good-guy role? It's bin Laden whose stepping out into the street at high noon and taking on overwhelming odds.

Blog: www.capitalistcowboys.com

You can attach the imperialist mission of George W. Bush to the mission of the 7th Calvalry against the Western tribes in the nineteenth century. We've still got the 7th fighting in Iraq, but ironically it was the Iraqis who made a horseback charge in what Rumsfeld called our "Shock and Awe" assault. Michael Medved ("That's Entertainment? Hollywood Contribution to Anti-Americanism Abroad," *The National Interest*, Summer 2002) believes that negativity and anti-Americanism of present-day Hollywood led to a "widespread dismissal of the 'cowboy culture' of Reaganism." Here's how the editors of *Rereading America* (2004), describe this cowboy culture: "Former governor of California and fortieth president of the United States, Ronald Wilson Reagan (b. 1911) was famous for his 'simplistic cowboy style' when dealing with complex issues of foreign affairs." Now look how that "cowboy style" inherited by Bush is still controlling psychology heading us into "the coming wars." I quote Seymour Hirsch on this, who's quoting a former high-level intelligence official:

THE BLOGOSPHERE

"Next, we're going to have the Iranian campaign. We've declared war, and the bad guys, wherever they are, are the enemy. This is the last hurrah—we've got four years, and want to come out of this saying we won the war on terrorism." "The Coming Years," *The New Yorker*, January 17, 2005.

We live in a "wild West" picture of the world, with clear-cut good guys and clear-cut bad guys. But take the American outlaw Jesse James. He robbed the railroad that had robbed him and a lot of other settlers of their land. Read Frank Norris's *The Octopus*. So we created our outlaw, which didn't stop us for the sake of law and order from pursuing him as an outlaw. We did that with Saddam and we're doing that with bin Laden and the 52-card deck of the Most Wanted. But how do you apply that personal cowboy style to a whole culture, a whole religion, an entire region? Obviously, you've got to critique your role in creating the bad guys; generate recuperate policies that will keep the bad guys from recruiting more bad guys to their cause; try through, say, a religious dialogue that the Bush people advocate at their National Prayer Breakfasts to get more Buber-like "I and Thou" into our palaver; and, finally, avoid picturing what's going on within a *Buchanan Rides Again* Hollywood Western scenario. You've got to picture human beings, good and evil, thought and action differently and more deeply than the "cowboy style" allows.

Of course, the United States isn't the first world power to "smack" whole cultures while holding on to the pretensions of noble "exceptionalism." Regardless of the reasons mounted, all empires who issue ultimatums of "Do this or that or we'll whack you!" are notably unexceptional on the pages of history. Imperialists are always "liberating" someone from their bondage and do so with a clear-eyed view of what "freedom" is. Is it so impossible to believe that someone's sense of what "freedom" is could be found in the Koran? Maybe Americans can't be free unless they're free to shop or go to Disneyland, but perhaps Muslims may feel they can't be free if their society is transformed into whatever the pursuit of profit and self-interest makes of it.

Without a doubt, Saddam was a tyrant, hoarding fortune for himself and his own and leaving the mass of people destitute, punishing cruelly and killing those who challenged him. But it wasn't the Koran who created him. We, however, live in a country that puts almost half its wealth in the top 1 percent of the population; and it is not one outlaw whose face we can put on a Wanted poster who has created this miserable state of affairs. It's an economic system tended to by a political ideology that is so incorporated

THE BLOGOSPHERE

THE BLOGOSPHERE

and diffused into the American way of life that we don't know where to find it, what to point a finger at. We can't pursue it in the "cowboy style." In fact, "the cowboy style" is perfectly suited not to recognize, not to search out, what is threatening this democracy once dedicated to egalitarianism, social justice, and the economic well-being of all. Gary Hoppenstand mourns the death of the Hollywood Western; I say its spirit, unfortunately, is alive and well in the White House.

Noirscape

[N]oir is almost entirely a creation of post-modern culture—a belated reading of classic Hollywood that was popularized by cineastes of the French New Wave, appropriated by reviewers, academics, and filmmakers, and then recycled on television.
—James Naremore, *More than Night:*
Film Noir in Its Context, 1998

The film noir hero is the modern social bandit.
—Dennis Broe, "Class, Crime,
and Film Noir," *Social Justice,* 2003

Darkness washed over the Dude—darker'n a black steer's tookus on a moonless prairie night. There was no bottom.
—*The Big Lebowski,* Coen brothers

Opening Cast: Mrs. Phyllis Anklebraceletson, from the film Triple Indemnity; *Linda Florentino, from the film* The Next to the Last Seduction; *Frank O'Bigelow, from the film* Near Dead on Arrival; *Quentin Welles, director of the underground film classic,* Pulp Kane.

———◆———

Script Doctor: Why these characters? Here's the way I see it: You need a character from a classic film noir bumping heads with a character from a postmodern film noir. And you need a director who understands the noir as well as Orson Welles did and a director who understands postmodern sampling and parodying of noir as well as Quentin Tarantino. Voila: Quentin Welles and a parody of Barbara Stanwyck's Mrs. Dietrichson in *Double Indemnity* (1944) and Linda Fiorentino's Bridget Gregory in *The Last Seduction* (1994). Here's your plot hook: Classic film noir is dead, but why? Take a character from a classic film noir film, *D.O.A.* (1950), bring in a parody of the lead character, Edmund O'Brien's Frank Bigelow, who wants to know why film noir died and who did it. Did America have to undergo a drastic change, or did the noir just run out of steam? And what's the link between classic and postmodern film noir? How is film noir dark angst different than post-9/11 dread?

———◆———

Producer: Cut! Let's make sure we get some bloggers posting comments after this. I've got a feeling that whatever film noir is, it didn't die. It's just gone through some changes. Okay. Shoot.

———◆———

Outtake (voice-over sounding amazingly like Michael Moore): America after 9/11 is paranoid and terrorized, but the landscape is not darkened, the mood is not set for film noir. "Get out to the malls, to Disneyland, to NASCAR. Nothing indelible has been written on your soul." Yet the war in Iraq has gone badly with a thousand U.S. soldiers dead and almost seven thousand wounded; twelve thousand Iraqis—civilians, soldiers, "insurgents"—killed. More Americans were glued to *American Idol* than listening to the Democratic presidential candidate, John Kerry, make his acceptance speech. And Americans watch *Survivor* on TV where "real world" reality TV" "real people" compete in an exotic setting to be the "last man [sic] standing," the recipient of a million dollars. This is a picture, and not the world.

———◆———

Voice-over: A picture of Americans after 9/11 shows us that human nature is neither haunted by a primordial sin nor caught in an existential battle between authentic being and bad faith, nor, as in classic film noir, buffeted by the play of chance, driven by desires exceeding rational control and caught in a web of misfortune, corrupted power, past sins and violence that foundationally crack the veneer of a moral, rational social order. In the years 1941–1958, the time when classic film noir flourished, Americans were heading for prosperity but were shadowed by the horrors of war and haunted by not only revelations of the dark side of humanity but their powerlessness in the face of it.

———◆———

Outtake: The picture of the United States today shows us that what was before has now been privatized, commodified, and virtualized and human nature totally territorialized and defined by marketing surveys and profiles. Human nature is not self-examined but viewed on a screen, and what fulfills and satisfies that nature is not projected from within but from without. Those projections from without are market-inspired and -controlled. An American overstimulated by the spectacle of both the media and advertising is cut off and left to his or her own reasoning and imagining resources. The "disaffection" of the underclass is different than the "discontent" of the past in that the former suffer a withdrawal from satisfaction and the means to achieve satisfaction. They are overstimulated by market-driven desires but have no means to fulfill these desires. And the cause of their malaise is utterly unknown to them; they have no perpetrator to target. The "discontent" of the disadvantaged in the past was not felt within this sort of buffer zone of a media and marketing hyperreality. The spectacle-making machinery was either nonexistent or in its infancy and therefore could not draw the "downtrodden" into various domains of seduction, from the rise and fall of the Dow Jones to the fortunes of *Survivor* competitors.

———◆———

Voice-over: Film noir comes out of the darkened dreams of twentieth-century modernism and pictures a sensibility dejected by a world that overspilled that sensibility's power to control or even reliably picture that world.

———◆———

Outtake: Doubtlessly, Americans have been terrorized by 9/11, but we remain "terrorized" within prefabricated political scenarios—that suit a radical neoconservative ideology—as well as social and economic scenarios that continue the repression and seduction strategies of consumer capitalism.

———◆———

Voice-over: Postmodern film noir presents itself as a genre stimulated by classic film noir and yet unable to attach itself to a world behind noir. The only path to the world in the postmodern noir is through the pictures themselves, and in the postmodern world—a world of clashing screenings—every picture is a world that samples other pictures and other worlds. There is, in short, no discernibly self-evident true path to the world. The angst of the classic film noir in the end can only serve a postmodern parodying, a movement between modernist and postmodernist worlds that interrogates both. Multiple realities proliferate beyond the mood of the classic film noir and generate a nostalgic playfulness.

QUENTIN WELLES: Okay. Cut. Cut. Let's try a different angle. We'll use a voice-over this time like in *Murder, My Sweet* (1944). No. Wait. Like in *D.O.A.* But what's dead on arrival is the classic film noir. You sit down over here O'Bigelow and tell us. You're almost dead but not quite. We're all listening.

FRANK O'BIGELOW (begins his narration): I live in a little town called Banning . . .

QUENTIN WELLES: Okay. Cut. You're boring the hell out of me. We need an old guy pontificating. You know, giving us a historical lecture. Get this *D.O.A.* guy out of here and bring in that old guy from *Murder, My Sweet*. What was his name? Graham. Get these women out of here while you're at it. They're going to kill each other in an un-noir way. Soon as Graham shows up roll it.

—— ◆ ——

Script Doctor: Dialogue from *Murder, My Sweet*: "I caught the blackjack right behind my ear. A black pool opened up at my feet. I dived in. It had no bottom." What can you say? The foundation of right reason, moral good, and guaranteed sanity have slipped into a black pool.

—— ◆ ——

MR. GRAHAM (begins his narration): What do you know about jade, Mr. Marlow?

QUENTIN WELLES: Cut. Not jade. Film noir.

MR. GRAHAM: What do you know about film noir, Mr. Marlow?

QUENTIN WELLES: That's it. We don't know a thing. You tell us. We've got all day.

MR. GRAHAM (resumes his narration): The angst of twentieth-century modernism appears in the crack of film noir. When Orson Welles wants to bring film out of naïve realism and Enlightenment optimism, he turns to a dark modernism that film noir will inherit. *Citizen Kane* is our dark, difficult journey out of the sinewy shadows, over hurricane fence barriers between ourselves and reality, wandering from path to path, searching for pieces of a puzzle that we are destined to do again and again because we can't be quite sure we've got all the pieces or whether we're putting them together in the right way. What Welles does is give us a "tragic vision" expressed in film, the tensions and anxieties already expressed in twentieth-century literature, painting, and music. Film noir was then born into a darkened world, a world more twisted and complex than Hollywood naïve realism.

MR. GRAHAM (stops, then says): I'm afraid I'm boring you.

QUENTIN WELLES: Sure. You're analogue time, we're digital. But go on.

MR. GRAHAM: A postmodern slant to film noir samples both naïve realist and late modernist film noir. "Fear and trembling, sickness unto death" is at once in touch with a sly, witty parodying of the mood, a gleeful immersion in dark film noir waters, a rush onto all paths and possibilities without fear of getting back, without an ontological need of finally winding up someplace where there is a bit of light, a place to rest. It's a ride for the hell of it—a ride that we have to take, that we may think we're not taking, but we're taking nonetheless. It's an unraveling, deconstructive journey—a nomadic wandering that has no clear beginning or end. One person's exit is another person's entrance; one person's high is another's low. Who is better than whom, what is better than what, is all in motion. We land someplace; we team up with someone; we pursue a thread of sense. At the same time, we are set in motion again or waiting to take off again. We connect with the extreme precariousness and arbitrariness of connecting. We pursue one thread of sense into another, catch the dialogue, play the parts, construct our answers, develop a style—and parody the sense that comes out of the part we play.

QUENTIN WELLES: Cut. Contrast a postmodern noir like *Romeo Is Bleeding* (1993) with *Out of the Past* (1947).

MR. GRAHAM: You will notice that in *Out of the Past*, Robert Mitchum has tried to escape his past, from what he was, and live in a small town, pump gas, and court a local girl. In *Murder, My Sweet*, Dick Powell just tries to get to the bottom of things as a detective. Both get caught in dark whirlpools that drag them under. Mitchum loses his life and Powell is drugged into the nether regions. The point is clear: We are subject to dark forces not of our own making. The medievalist would cite Satan as the force behind this collapse of the social order and our powerlessness to avoid tragedy. Twentieth-century modernism cites the irrational, contingency, and the unconscious. The power of Enlightenment reason to forestall tragedy, to discipline passion and dominate the emotions, to trump the play of chance is overturned in the classic film noir. In this world, men and women are not distanced, observant, and dominant but ensnared, blind, and haunted.

Jack Grimaldi in *Romeo Is Bleeding* is neither in complete control nor pure victim. He is packaged already into the world. And that world is made up not only of his packagings or cultural adaptations, which appear as self-fabrications, but those of others. All the characters in *Romeo Is Bleeding* live in a high-cycle whirlpool of adopted and adapted cultural constructions. What reality may be outside these constructions is not within Jack's capacity or ours to observe. Jack is a strong player and not just an "unlucky guy" as he says, but an unlucky guy "who fell in love with a hole in the ground." In other words, a guy with a story to spin, a story that spins the guy. And it's not the only story that he concocts or that concocts him. The already culturally fabricated Jack adds to the fabrications that fabricate him. And us.

Mitchum, a modernist film noir protagonist, discovered and reacted to a dark reality that twentieth-century modernism admitted it could no longer calibrate or control, could no longer enlighten. You might say noir was the man on the street's modernist angst, the popularized version of everything from Kafka to Kierkegaard. And because it was the working stiff's angst, it was school of hard knocks and not just existential dread. Noir represented the seamy side of the immigrant's American Dream; it was the nightmare after the Depression and a world war against a maniac who personalized the horrific in human nature. It was deeply personal and deeply social, but it never felt like something we were spinning and weaving out of our own abdomens. It was out there, and maybe it was Fate or Destiny; and the part that was in us, wasn't ours to control either. It was all unexpected and unfathomable, but it was real and not hyperreal.

QUENTIN WELLES: Okay. Cut. Get rid of the old guy. Bring in those grad students writing their dissertations on the Coen brothers. Hi. Don't tell me your names. I'll tell you. You're Arizona. All grown up. And you're Barton Fink. So where's the postmod noir in the Coen brothers? See if you can keep it clearer than the last guy. Here's the scene: I did two courses in a community college and got a degree in video rentals. Okay? Roll'em.

BARTON FINK: *Blood Simple* (1983) seems to be a retelling of *The Postman Always Rings Twice* (1946), a film noir with a Depression-era edge to it. There is the ugly—in every way—husband of Greek descent, the wife fed up with him, and her lover, an employee of the husband, the murder of the husband, and then the drama of fatal miscommunication between the lovers. The angst of twentieth-century modernism appears in the crack of film noir . . .

QUENTIN WELLES: Cut. The old guy said that.

BARTON FINK: I was sampling him. A tragic vision is reconfigured within the classic realist design of Hollywood film while being duly loaded with the tensions and anxieties already expressed in twentieth-century literature, painting, and music.

QUENTIN WELLES: Cut. Too much sampling. Arizona. I want *Blood Simple*. Simple. No sample. Not Blood Sampling. Okay? Roll 'em.

———◆———

Script Doctor: Opening voice-over in *Blood Simple*: "The world is full of complainers. But the fact is, nothing comes with a guarantee. I don't care if you're the Pope of Rome, President of the United States, or Man of the Year, something can all go wrong."

———◆———

ARIZONA: *Blood Simple* does *Postman* all over again—self-consciously, so that *Postman* becomes a reality frame for *Blood Simple*, whereas a dark reality that cannot be illuminated is the outside framing of *Postman*. The ontological mise-en-scène of the modernist noir is this: Darkness swells up out of our own natures, and that opaqueness peers out of a world saturated with either its own darkness or ours or both. Of the postmodernist *noir* it is this: darkness swells up out of the film noir filming of reality and we play into it, into its ins and outs, twists and turns, ups and downs, angles and curves . . . , into a picture of reality that fractures into other pictures of reality.

QUENTIN WELLES: Cut. At this point we run a couple of clips from *The Big Lebowski* (1998), the film noir send-up scenes when the Dude tells Maude that there's a lot of ins and outs, ups and downs, over and unders in this case. A lot to keep in old Dude's head. And then the scene where Brad ushers him into a dark room where the Big Lebowski is sitting in his wheelchair looking into the fire and moaning about his kidnapped wife. That's right out of *The Big Sleep* (1946) when Bogie goes to visit General Sternwood in the greenhouse.

———◆———

Script Doctor: Here's a line sampling the dark pool line of *Murder, My Sweet*: "Darkness washed over the Dude—darker'n a black steer's tookus on a moonless prairies night. There was no bottom."

———◆———

ARIZONA: And the General wants Bogie to go ahead and smoke, because the only way the General can enjoy his vices now is by proxy.

QUENTIN WELLES: But the Dude asks the Big Lebowski if it's alright if he does a jay while Big tells him about the kidnapping. Go ahead with your script. We play into the ins and outs of film noir . . .

ARIZONA: . . . replacing a direct exposure of an ever-darkening reality with a variety of send-ups of both how we hook up with reality and what that reality might be. Our dread is not absolutist, our confrontation not universalist; instead dread is relative to the story this or that character is in, and this or that character's reality-making ways, while riddled by pop culture's stories mostly, have no universalist pretensions. They have no claim on us; we are going along for the ride; what is at stake is not our ability to grasp what is real and true. What is at stake is only what the film noir shows us is at stake within the boundaries of its own fictive world. And the way we extend the boundaries of our own world is only by extending the boundaries of our fictions, our representations. The Coen brothers, therefore, go into the film noir world of *Postman* and do just that. The only price to be paid is what we feel is the price we've paid: the ticket. We can't experience the loss of what we've never had. Nor can we see it in the faces of those on the screen, which is where, in a postmodern age, we look.

QUENTIN WELLES: Cut. It's a wrap. Clear the set, bring in my dogs and set up sitting in a diner just finishing breakfast like at the beginning of *Reservoir Dogs* (1992). We got this guy out of prison to play the part of Lawrence Tierney playing the part of Joe, the gravel-voiced boss of the gang. We're going to be doing aliases like in the movie. I'm Mr. Brown. You're Mr. Orange. You're Mr. White. You're Mr. Blonde. You're Mr. Blue. You're Mr. Pink. Roll 'em.

———◆———

Script Doctor: Mr. Orange: "Nobody tells me what to do."

———◆———

MR. BROWN: So those two guys from *Mulholland Drive* (2001) are sitting in Winky's café. The one guy is telling the other guy about this dream he had about something really bad out back. The other guy listens and then takes his buddy out back where his buddy sees one of David Lynch's nightmares and drops dead.

MR. BLONDE: I'd drop dead too. I don't know about you guys but I'm haunted by all of Lynch's movies but *Mulholland Drive* is over the top.

MR. BROWN: So the friend and the haunted guy go out back to face the guy's nightmare and get all his questions answered—by a guy who looks a lot like Dennis Hopper did in *Blue Velvet* (1986).

MR. PINK: I used to be haunted by Hitchcock's noir, *Spellbound* (1945). But now it's Lynch's *Mulholland Drive*. Those old people laughing and coming out from underneath the door, like rats. It totally freaked me out.

JOE: What are you, an idiot? Don't you see the connection? Diane's got stuff buried in her mind's dark bins. She didn't get discovered in Hollywood.

MR. PINK: You know what this is? The world's smallest violin playing hearts and flowers for every sweetheart of the Midwest who didn't make it in Hollywood.

MR. ORANGE: She came from a small town in Canada where she won a jitterbug contest. Small town probably like Lumberton in *Blue Velvet*. Where at the sound of the tree falling it's always the correct time.

MR. PINK: I bet she couldn't become a lesbian in her home town.

JOE: No. They roll out the red carpet for them. They love lesbians in small towns called Lumberton. What do you think? Of course, she couldn't be a lesbian in her home town. Here's the real deal: career flop, jilted by her lesbian lover, hires a guy to kill her lesbian lover, and then shoots herself. But she botches the job and she's just lying there on her bed dying. And dreaming. She's redoing her whole life in this dream.

MR. BLONDE: Can somebody tell me why?

MR. BROWN: So her life makes sense to her and whoever and whatever is waiting for her when she's dead. She needs to turn all the dark stuff into good stuff.

MR. BLONDE: And that's noir? It sounds like psycho bullshit.

MR. BROWN: Postmod noir. You know why? Because throughout the whole movie we're watching her spin on things. We're caught in her own editing of her own life. Lynch is just making it clear once again that reality is filtered through the stories we're in. In Diane's case, it's one overwhelming story, but we all script and edit, adapt and rewrite, add and leave out what's "out there."

MR. PINK: Was she really bruised? I mean, did bad things happen and her mind got bruised so she got deeper and further away from . . . I mean she got to reason in a twisted way but what else had she to rely on?

JOE: Don't work yourself up, Mr. Pink. She had her choices. You're not her, Mr. Pink.

MR. BROWN: Ha! She had her choices. Wasn't she moral? Wasn't she rational? Isn't that what makes all film noir universal? Is being good just something we fabricate for ourselves the way Diane needs to be someone else and takes the name of the waitress, Betty?

MR. PINK: I'm not going to tip a waitress who isn't tip-worthy just because society says that's what I should do.

JOE: Shoot this guy.

MR. BROWN: Is goodness or badness out there but just something we invent? And if it is out there, it's all muddled up and we can't follow it. Is being rational something we can keep on being even after we're beaten down and tired, pushed around, and flayed by just things that happen for no apparent reason, things that we can't see until it's too late? Or does our reason take a beating, too?

JOE: That's enough out of you, Mr. Brown. We all get the point.

MR. BROWN: *Mulholland Drive* is continuing that classic film noir intensity. The specific feeling of malaise right at the heart of the Hollywood machine.

MR. BLONDE: The world's different than what Frank Capra showed us in *It's a Wonderful Life* (1939). But is the world less noir if we know that humans have been writing their own scripts since the beginning of time, which is a script, too? Or is it less noir to be like Barry Sullivan in *The Gangster* (1947) and think that he made his bad end because he wasn't rotten enough, that he should have met the corruption of the world on its own terms?

MR. PINK: You know what this is? This is the world's tiniest. . . .

JOE: Look, stupids. That gangster wants to live in that one "the world is totally corrupt" story. Meanwhile, Lynch would sample that guy and his story among a lot of other conflicting stories. We're all always sampling stories that are in the culture. I just found this old address book in my jacket and I'm trying to connect names with faces. Wong. Toby Wong. I got the Toby part. But who's Wong?

MR. BROWN: Diane takes the name Betty; she sees a cowboy for two seconds in the distance and then she drags him into her script. What's she doing? She wants a showdown, frontier-style with Adam, the guy who took her girlfriend away. The frontier story comes out of the culture. We all wrote it. Lynch samples the noir style because it's in our cultural vocabulary. It resonates within the whole world of noir that Hollywood has created. It's a cultural shorthand, like the West, like Disney, like soap operas, like Horatio Alger, rebel road movies, Southern crazy, mean streets, Wall Street players, Vegas high rollers . . .

JOE: Who's Horatio Alger?

MR. BLONDE: You know what Tarantino was sampling with the Jules and Vincent hit men in *Pulp Fiction* (1994)?

——◆——

Script Doctor: Jules: "Nobody's gonna hurt anybody. We're gonna be like three Little Fonzies here. And what's Fonzie like? Come on Yolanda. What's Fonzie like?"

———◆———

MR. BROWN: Charles McGraw and William Conrad in *The Killers*. Okay. Cut. That gives me an idea. Clear the set. Everybody cough up a buck each for the tip. Bring in Vincent Le Big Mac and Jules Kung Fu. Okay. You guys are in a car on the way to a hit. Like in *Pulp Fiction*. Roll 'em.

VINCENT LE BIG MAC: Here's the question: Why do all remakes of classic film noir suck?

JULES KUNG FU: I don't know. Why do all remakes of classic film noir suck?

VINCENT LE BIG MAC: *Body Heat* (1981) is this kind of remake of *Double Indemnity* (1944): *Double* couldn't show the sex scenes and in the 1980s they can show the sex scenes. Also it's very hot. Why? To generate a mood in the surround that parallels the characters and plot. In *Double Indemnity* there was no need to make a set for the mood. Why? Because that came out of the contemporary surround. 1944. Post-Depression era. World war. But class too. Walter Neff is an insurance salesman. Fourteen years on the job. The contemporary audience could identify with him. In 1981, he's a loser, not a player, a guy without the right credentials. So he becomes Ned Racine, a not-so-good lawyer. But lawyer nonetheless.

———◆———

Script Doctor: Ned: "I need someone to take care of me, someone to rub my tired muscles, smooth out my sheets." Matty: "Get married." Ned: "I just need it for tonight."

———◆———

JULES KUNG FU: And Mrs. Dietrichson? She was supposed to be kind of old-school hot. But, Vincent, an ankle bracelet is not sexual.

VINCENT LE BIG MAC: It certainly is, Jules. But here's the thing. She was the previous wife's nurse. She was the working girl looking to get what her "betters" had. You meet her again as Mrs. Graham in *Murder, My Sweet* (1944). This time she's a saloon singer who polished up her act and got her chance to live in the "manor house." Class is the surround in these films. In 1981, that has become mystified and obscured; America is now, according to wealthy conservatives, classless; working-class folks are now seen as "losers," wars are remote, "foreign" surgical strikes that even Hollywood can't bring to the screen. There's very little in *Body Heat* that we can share contrasted with *Double Indemnity*. The sex is a spectacle, and the heat makes us glad we have AC. There's nothing memorable in either of these. But the ankle bracelet in *Double* is totally erotic. It trumps the explicit sex scenes of *Body Heat*.

JULES KUNG FU: I liked the 1995 remake of *Kiss of Death* (1947).

VINCENT LE BIG MAC: You would. But I bet you don't know why.

JULES KUNG FU: Sure I do. Nicolas Cage played Junior, and Junior is one mean-ass son of a bitch with an edge of being crazy. Which he wasn't. The man was cool.

VINCENT LE BIG MAC: You got suckered, my friend. The 1995 *Kiss of Death* is supposed to get you out of 1995 when Bill Clinton is driving guys like Newt Gingrich and his reactionary buddies nuts. This film wants to be seen as if it were made in 1947 when all the things that aggravate conservatives in the 1990s didn't exist. Or, if they did exist, they were kept in the closet. So here you have a film that's trying to escape its own times and return to the days before, as Gingrich said, America made "a wrong turn."

JULES KUNG FU: Divine intervention.

VINCENT LE BIG MAC: More like political and cultural suppression. What we get then is a dead kiss. The reason why the noir worked was not because the cameraman was a chiaroscuro artist but because the film twisted itself into the world the viewer was already in. The noir characters and the viewers share nightmares; they are buffeted by the same winds of chance; they see the same abyss.

JULES KUNG FU: Tommy Udo was my hero. Remember Tommy Udo in the 1947 *Kiss of Death*?

VINCENT LE BIG MAC: Tommy's dark. But would a guy sitting in the audience in 1947 connect with him? Or, is he just a psycho freak, a loser that has no connection to anybody?

JULES KUNG FU: Widmark is laughing when he shoves the old lady in the wheelchair down the stairs. He doesn't really have a reason.

VINCENT LE BIG MAC: You're thinking like they want you to think. What's bad is just over there in the "bad neighborhoods" with the "bad" people who do things without cause or reason.

JULES KUNG FU: "Don't go near the Lincoln neighborhood," the spinster aunt tells Jeff in Lynch's *Blue Velvet* (1986). That's the bad part of town. I dig what you're saying.

—— ◆ ——

Script Doctor: Jeff: "Why are there people like Frank?"

VINCENT LE BIG MAC: What I'm saying is that in 1947 the whole world is still reeling from the depression of the 1930s, and they've got a clear picture of the atrocities of Hitler and his boys. This stuff is frightening. How does it square with the hype that we're out of the Dark Ages, that we're civilized, that we're good at heart, that there's an underlying order in the world? Tommy Uddo is pathological, but what are we saying when we say that? That the underbelly of human nature shows itself, that there's a thin veneer of order, sanity, and reason that can crack at any moment. And with the Holocaust it cracked. No, I'm telling you, Jules, we're somehow in that movie. It's scary, but that's what noir does. It makes us complicit; it brings us in.

JULES KUNG FU: I will agree you have a point.

VINCENT LE BIG MAC: And the 1995 *Kiss of Death* keeps us and the world apart because it wants to reassure us, not scare us.

JULES KUNG FU: How scary is it when Vincent Vega in *Pulp Fiction* comes out of the john and gets blown away by Butch? Or when Butch runs into the one guy who's out to kill him, Marcellus, and then both of them accidentally wind up in with those sadists?

VINCENT LE BIG MAC: Junior shows us a pretty frightening mind, but you know what? It doesn't leak out into the world. It doesn't reach us. He's self-contained. He's not us. He's not any part of us. He's so different, so wrongly different, so distanced from us that all we have to do is throw a net on him and put him in jail. Then the audience in 1995 gets involved. They all sigh a sigh of relief and say "Thank God for capital punishment." They're not meant to see connections with their own life. Junior's different, and they know what to do with that kind of difference. Or they should. Only the liberals and the leftists don't know what to do with that kind of difference. Everybody else—real Americans—know he's a nightmare of depravity, a scene from the abyss in human form.

JULES KUNG FU: So you're saying the film is politically tagged.

VINCENT LE BIG MAC: Here's what I'm calling it: It's conservatively revisionist.

JULES KUNG FU: Conservatively revisionist. I like that.

VINCENT LE BIG MAC: We're protected from thinking that the world of the bad guys here seeps into ours. Classic noir is grounded in a common plight that we all share: Chance screws with us, fate makes some men rich and others poor, reason is a slave to our passions, society offers nothing we can adopt as a conscience, and at the heart of our hunger for happiness and a place to rest is discontent, restlessness, and a lingering sense that we are doomed in spite of what we might do. It tags the dark side of the American dream: A lot of people get discarded, by fate or by the dream itself.

JULES KUNG FU: It's true. When I watched the 1947 *Kiss of Death* I felt like it could have all happened to me. I was totally drawn in. But when I watched the 1995 I . . . I felt judgmental.

VINCENT LE BIG MAC: You're put in a position of judging people who have made a mess of their lives. You haven't, but they have. They're the losers. But you know what? Film noir was all about losers, but we were all losers. From the beginning. Somehow. We don't know how. Eve and the apple? I don't think so. Not in noir. You don't ever get the sense that we've got a spiritual side we haven't tuned into. It's got more to do with economics and politics than religion. The rich have the power, but they don't deserve what they've got. Everybody else either bows to the injustice, tries to escape it, or tries to get their piece of the action.

JULES KUNG FU: We'd still be like that today if we weren't surfing porn on the Web or watching Tivo-programmed TV or playing video games or shopping till we dropped or reading about the lives of celebrities or day trading on the Internet.

VINCENT LE BIG MAC: Maybe film noir was the last time Americans expressed a mood of their collective mass psyche. After that we fell into a war of the very few against the anesthetized many. You can't create a common mood out of that. What you can do is what the postmodernists do: Sample the noir, just to recall darker and better days.

QUENTIN WELLES: Cut. It's a wrap on noir. Who wants to run a trailer on private eyes?

———◆———

THE BLOGOSPHERE

Blog: www.socialbandit.com

The voice-over in "Noirscape" totally misses the post-9/11 America connect here, one that Dennis Broe nails in his piece, "Class, Crime, and Film Noir: Labor, the Fugitive Outsider, and the Anti-Authoritarian Tradition," in *Social Justice*, v. 30, 2003. Even Michael Lind admits that Bush's domestic policies are harmful to working-class Americans. A disenfranchised working class is increasingly connected to "crime" and "criminals," an association that suits the present power structure. The Hollywood film noir of the 1940s, however, presented the working class and middle-class as "down-on-their-luck lead characters" who had emerged "directly out of a period of intense class struggle in Hollywood and the nation as a whole and represent certain left attitudes. . . . The films represent a moment of resistance to an increasingly centralized and antilabor state and, later, a critique of a rapacious economic system whose representatives waged a frontal assault on Depression-era collective values of the 1930s and those of the wartime period of the 1940s."

Broe sees the film noir protagonist as a "sympathetic fugitive," one whose "journey outside the law paralleled that of labor as a whole in the postwar period, when unions and wildcat strikers were criminalized first in a massive strike wave and later as victims of leg-islation (the Taft-Hartley Act) and governmental investigations (HUAC) that retroactively outlawed their actions during the strikes."

So the film noir protagonist was a resistance fighter, a "work-ing-class hero" who had enough pluck and hard-edge stubbornness to resist a world that wasn't just existentially dark but dark because of the workings of human greed, corrupt power, craven and depraved instincts, inhuman rapaciousness. Film noir doesn't sur-vive in the present—call it "neo" or "postmodern" or whatever—because we've naturally entered an age of hyperconsciousness lead-ing to ironic parody. That doesn't take into account 9/11, which the writer or the producer or one of the script doctors thinks is a gen-uine factor in why and how America changed and how that change is pictured on the screen. "[T]he almost mystical power of film noir springs from a moment when the crime film was strongly inflected with the struggles of working- and middle-class unionism against corporate America and a state that facilitated corporate consolida-tion. . . . It is especially pertinent to recall this history in light of post-September 11 repression, which is characterized by a strident return in society and in media representation to the order of law. In the history of the genre, such repression is always resisted even-tually by the figure of the working-class–aligned fugitive. The crime film symbolic will not hold; in the dialogic process, dissension lurks just around the corner, or in this case, in the shadows. . . . For example, in the 1980s noir returned in films such as *Blue Velvet*, which directly questioned the prosperity of the Reagan era."

Blog: www.incoherentnoir.com

This chapter in *This Is a Picture and Not the World* begins with a quo-tation from James Naremore suggesting that there really wasn't any "classic film noir" before a postmod sampling of certain film stylistics and characteristics in Hollywood films from the 1940s and 1950s created a "neo-noir" or postmodern noir style. It's a case of a self-reflexive attitude-seeking in past films, a retro-fashion that makes it clear in the postmodern present what the present no longer is and what the past possessed but was not self-reflexively aware of. In other words—and perhaps a clearer picture—a postmodern age needs to sample an identifiable past, and in the case of noir it created that identity from a growing mediascape. "[T]he idea of film noir spreads so widely that it helps to constitute what anthropologist Arjun Appadurai calls our 'mediascape,' which is made up of both the 'capabilities to produce and disseminate information' . . . and the images created through such media" (Naremore, *More than Night: Film Noir in Its Context*, 1998).

The noir chronology in "Noirscape" has classic film noir firmly rooted in twentieth-century modernism, in its dark angst, fear and trembling and so on. But this is descriptive of a great deal of twentieth-century modernist film that exceeds the 317 titles listed in Silver and Ward's *Film Noir Encyclopedia*. It's surprising that someone who introduces himself as a postmodernist fails to follow up on Naremore's very postmodern suggestion that what postmodern noir created was its own "classic" beginnings, a legacy and an influence purely hypertextual. I quote Peter Stanfield in "Film Noir Like You've Never See," *Genre and Contemporary Hollywood*, 2002:

"In academic circles, the concept of noir is still open to debate and, as late as 2000, Steve Neale was arguing that as a 'single phenomenon, noir never existed' and as such is an incoherent critical object."

It must be said, however, that this "Noirscape" chapter is couched among chapters that never existed as any sort of object and film groups that comprise incoherent critical objects, at best leading me to think that there's a certain send-up here of our noir-identifying pursuits.

Blog: www.gaspump.com

The Producer says film noir never died but just went through some changes. I was on a blog that argued we didn't know there was something you could package as a film noir genre until postmodernists began to sample and thereby make perfectly clear and evident film mannerisms of a certain period, in this case 1941 to 1958. So we looked back at a category, a genre, and a time period. Henceforth, films in this certain style in this period are "classic" noir, and then there's a break, and in the late 1970s a postmodern awareness puts out film that samples this "classic" noir and it's called "neo-noir." Now here's what Robert Miklitsch writes ("A Panorama of American Film Noir, 1941–1953," *Film Quarterly*, Summer 2004): "[T]he terminus [of noir] usually set by critics is either 1955, the date of Aldrich's apocalyptic *Kiss Me Deadly*, or 1958, the date of Welles's baroque, south-of-the-border *Touch of Evil* [but] a number of recent films, *Memento* (2000), *Mulholland Drive* (2001), among others, testify . . . that noir as a genre is arguably more robust than ever."

There's no "classic" period in his view if you mean that it was the "golden age of noir." What came after is "more robust than ever" so "classic" is just an historical beginning to a certain . . . what? Does noir represent a deep ontological something or other that can show up in recent films the same way it showed up in the 1940s? I mean, we haven't changed even after 9/11? I think not. Market globalism is the new existentialism. What's the 9/11 hookup? The noir world is in shadows, so this suits a 9/11 mood in a certain way. Things can happen in a noir world that no one can foresee. This all fits the 9/11 mood. But why sample noir if it's not a way to break free of 9/11 trauma? Why not endless animated Pixar escapes like *Finding Nemo*, *Shrek*, and *The Incredibles*?

My answer? Because noir is darkness and angst, dread in anticipation of accidental disaster, couched in a far simpler world of the 1940s and 1950s. Were they far simpler? Hollywood shows us they were, and for the majority of Americans the pictures of those decades Hollywood has put in our heads rules. To return to this far simpler world is a kind of relief. You can become Robert Mitchum at the very beginning of *Out of the Past* hiding out in a small town working in a gas station, escaping some unknown past darkness. When he returns to face the past it's a return you can handle.

We can work through the mystique of noir because it is out of the past, while the present gives us nothing but future projections of those planes flying into the Trade Towers. Maybe we are nostalgic for all of our past, for our lost "magic towns" and "working-class heroes," but noir suits us best. It never died because it never existed before the way we know it now.

THE BLOGOSPHERE

Sneak Preview

Magic Town: America's Heartland

If there is one town that the world would be better off without, it's Dogville.

> —Grace, played by Nicole Kidman, in Lars von Trier's
> *Dogville*, 2004

I never wanted to see Kings Row again but still, I don't know, it's a place I grew up. I used to love to walk around the country and just look at it. If I could do that now. . . . But I'm afraid of meeting ghosts, people I loved, places I remember, stile and pond, the house I lived in . . .

> —Parris, played by Robert Cummings, in *Kings Row*, 1942

All they have to show for their Republican loyalty are lower wages, more dangerous jobs, dirtier air, a new overlord class that comports itself like King Farouk—and, of course, a crap culture whose moral free fall continues without significant interference from the grandstanding Christers whom they send triumphantly back to Washington every couple of years.

> —Thomas Frank, *What's the Matter With Kansas?*, 2004

Which country poses a greater danger to world peace in 2003? With 318,000 votes cast so far, the responses were: North Korea, 7 percent; Iraq, 8 percent; the United States, 84 percent.

> —Norman Mailer, "Only in America," *The New York
> Review of Books*, March 27, 2003

Characters: *Chief Margie Funderson, a filmscape character based on Chief Marge Gunderson played by Frances McDormand in the*

Coen brothers' film, Fargo; *Frank Hopper, a filmscape character based on Dennis Hopper's portrayal of the sociopath Frank Booth in David Lynch's* Blue Velvet; *Johnny, a filmscape character based on the leader of a motorcycle gang played by Marlon Brando in the film* The Wild One; *Agent Dale Coover, a filmscape character based on Agent Dale Cooper in David Lynch's* Twin Peaks; *Dr. Miles Bennell, from the classic* Invasion of the Body Snatchers.

——— ◆ ———

Voice-over: The magic of small-town America is not a film genre; it's a mythos. We didn't know it existed when it existed; we only became aware of it after Hollywood put it up on the screen and Disney enabled us to walk into it as we strolled down Main Street in Disneyland. After 9/11 the Department of Homeland Security was created to protect the American heartland, the imaginary, idyllic locus of Our Town, the locus of our lost origin, the secret heartland of our cultural nostalgia. Any time you wander in the American cultural collective unconscious, you will, like Ishmael trailing funeral processions, wind up walking in Andy Hardy's Carvel; or Cass Timberlaine's Grand Republic; Preston Sturges's Morgan's Creek and Oakridge; George Bailey's Bedford Falls where Jimmy Stewart discovers the actions of one good man make a world of difference; Longfellow Deeds's Mandrake Falls "where the scenery entralls/where no heartbreak befalls"; the Kings Row where Ronald Reagan as the town sparkplug, Drake McHugh, finds love on the "other side of the tracks"; Nathan, the "tired old town" of *To Kill a Mockingbird*," Grandview, the "magic town" whose denizens' views reflect the country as a whole. There is a yearning for the real small town masked by these pictures of small-town life, a yearning that perhaps echoes all of humankind's quest to regain the small but perfect world of Eden, the absent place once briefly present and ours. The best evocation of this foundational dreamscape, a place somehow always back there, in our past, in our beginnings, in our childhood, is Grovers Corners, New Hampshire, the small town of *Our Town* (1940) where "the day's running down like a tired clock." This is the mythic place nowhere but in our souls where like in a dream there is no measurement for the movement of time. This is a town remembered; this is a town from the shadow world of what is no longer here, no longer living, no longer ours. This is the town eternally "as it used to be" and therefore never as it was, never recuperable but as a dreamlike shadow. And this presence, a never-to-be-realized absence, has a magical power over the American psyche.

——— ◆ ———

AGENT DALE COOVER (talking into his minirecorder): Diane . . . 9:15
A.M. . . . up here in Brainerd. On my way to see Chief Marg Funderson. Slept like a log. Air clean. Picturesque town. Have you ever seen
a fifty-foot-high Babe the Blue Ox? Then you should. Hoping for a
slice of cherry pie for lunch. But first, the assignment: Is idyllic small-
town America just a dream I had? Did I see it at the movies? Is there
a magic-town virus blitzing every American's brainpan and sending
each one of them in search of Magic Town? And most relevantly,
Diane, am I really one of those dead people as in the 1940 film *Our
Town*? I don't know, but I think I'll find some answers here in Brainerd. Stay tuned Diane.

——◆——

Script Doctor: Bringing in *Twin Peaks* right away is good. Why?
David Lynch jumps on this American psyche small-town mythos
vibe and blows it apart. Okay, here's how: It's part of the American
Dream, ergo, it's part nightmare. Why? Small-town America is
magic town because it's harmony town; it's where neighbors greet
neighbors in the town square, at the soda fountain, at the church on
the hill, at Baldwin's grocery, at the Sunset movie theater on Main
Street. It's a picture-perfect unified reality. It's a one-peak town,
because everybody shares the same reality, which means they can
communicate with each other. They share the same basic values;
they're on the same page because they live on the same block, in the
same small town; they live in the same reality frame. But if you double the peaks, you double the realities. And if reality can divide like
that, why can't you have four realities? Why can't you have multiple realities living in one small town? All of a sudden, with Lynch,
you have a postmodern small town. It's always been multiple realities, but part of the mythic allure of small-town America has been
the fact that it isn't multiple, that it's the one place you can go to and
find not clashing, crossfire pictures of things, but simple, true, honest, wholesome, authentic being-in-the-world. If you fracture the
mythos of the American Disney small town, you're on your way to
forming international coalitions before you jump to preemptive
attacks. The indivisible isolation and completeness and the self-contained harmony that we invest in our vision of small-town America
is no more than an illusion, a delusion. As long as we hold on to this
illusion that unity beyond all diversity lies at our beginnings—a simplistic, Hollywood created harmony—we will never move within
our imaginations toward any globalism except what global capitalism defines.

——◆——

Setting: *Brainerd*

———— ♦ ————

AGENT DALE COOVER: Good morning, Chief Funderson. I'm FBI Agent Coover. What a beautiful day.

CHIEF MARGIE FUNDERSON: I just don't understand how Mr. Hopper here can't see what a beautiful day it is.

AGENT DALE COOVER: He can't?

FRANK HOPPER: Hi, neighbor.

CHIEF MARGIE FUNDERSON: Frank's been picked up for questioning. Maybe you do things differently in the big city, but here in Brainerd we pick people up for questioning regarding their taste in movies. Frank was just about to explain this fellow David Lynch to me, because, you know, he's a bit strange for our little town of Brainerd.

AGENT DALE COOVER: I'm all ears Frank.

FRANK HOPPER: Yeah, he's far out. He's really far out of Brainerd. But you know, neighbor . . .

CHIEF MARGIE FUNDERSON: Call me Chief.

FRANK HOPPER: Oh, yeah. Sorry. Neighbor. You know in the movie *Fargo* (1996) when the guy lies to Chief Margie about his wife and all that and Chief Margie can't figure out what the hell that's all about?

CHIEF MARGIE FUNDERSON: Now I don't see why you have to use profanity, do you?

FRANK HOPPER: Oh, yeah. Sorry. But you know what I'm saying is that this dude is really outside Fargo. I mean all that stuff about that guy is not in the plot because what that guy is can't be in Fargo. You see what I'm saying? He's outside where they're at. So he can't be in your head. You can't walk with him in dreams, neighbor.

CHIEF MARGIE FUNDERSON: You mean the Chief Margie in the film?

FRANK HOPPER: Right. All I'm saying is that it's like the way Lynch can't be in your head.

CHIEF MARGIE FUNDERSON: Well, I see what you're saying . . .

FRANK HOPPER: But . . . but here's the thing. And it's beautiful, man. I can put him there!

CHIEF MARGIE FUNDERSON: Okay. I see that you want to do that. You want to take me into David Lynch's filmscape of small-town America.

Twin Peaks (1990–1991), *Blue Velvet* (1986), *Wild at Heart* (1990), the little town where Naomi Watts comes from in *Mulholland Drive*. But you're going to jail, Frank.

AGENT DALE COOVER: Alfred Hitchcock put a psycho right at the heart of that small town . . . what was it? In the movie *Shadow of a Doubt* (1943). Uncle Charlie? Remember him? And look at that town in *To Kill a Mockingbird* (1962). Kids playing, neighbor dropping by, swings on the front porch. But hello? It's a racist, lynch crazy town . . .

CHIEF MARGIE FUNDERSON: Uncle Charlie didn't come from Santa Rosa. He came from the big city. And Nathan, the town in *To Kill a Mockingbird* is a depressed town. "A tired old town" is what we hear at the beginning of the movie. "No hurry, for there was nowhere to go and nothing to buy and nothing to buy it with." It's a hurting town, struggling to get out of the Depression. But there are people like Atticus Finch in it. And the neighbor who comes by to pay Atticus with a bag of hickory nuts. There's a simple, innocent good heart at the very center of that town, and it's Bo Radley. Damaged but good. Like slavery had stunned the whole country, shaken its foundations, and racism was the last vestige of that. If that town could shake that racism off, it could be as fine as Atticus Finch and as innocent as Bo Radley.

FRANK HOPPER: A bag of hickory nuts is cool.

CHIEF MARGIE FUNDERSON: You can nearly smell things cooking and feel the night air.

FRANK HOPPER: That's cool too. What's that from?

CHIEF MARGIE FUNDERSON: *Our Town* (1940). Birth, life, death, infinity in a small New Hampshire town. "Something way down deep that's eternal about a human being."

AGENT DALE COOVER: I remember William Holden in that one. But what about that town in the movie *Picnic* (1955). Holden wanders into town and all the ladies are attracted to him. "A town—a stranger—and the things he does to its people! Especially its women!" That was in the trailer for the movie. You could really smell things cooking in that town, Chief. By the way, do you think we could have some donuts?

CHIEF MARGIE FUNDERSON: You FBI agents have excellent memories.

AGENT DALE COOVER: "At the sound of the tree falling, it's 2:25 here in Lumberton where everyone knows how much wood a woodchuck chucks." That's from Lynch's *Blue Velvet* (1986). "Murder, mutilation, and sexual perversion in Middle America." That's what it says in *Halliwell's Film Guide*.

CHIEF MARGIE FUNDERSON: Wouldn't you rather be watching something clean and wholesome like *It's a Wonderful Life*? "Every time you hear a bell ring, it means some angel's just gotten his wings."

FRANK HOPPER: Yeah, but look neighbor, I think Hitchcock had a thing about sexual perverts filling up small towns in the United States, lurking in small motels just outside small towns. Like it's a piece of Americana. Thing is this kid, Jeff, in Lynch's *Blue Velvet*, comes out of the neat side of town and he asks questions like, "Why are there people like Frank Booth in the world?" What kind of question is that, I ask you? Listen up. There's room for guys like Frank and me. What are you looking at? Don't look at me.

AGENT DALE COOVER: I was just thinking that you look a lot like Frank Booth, Frank. Maybe that's why you identify with him. Frank Booth is played by Dennis Hopper and he's a very sick person. He comes from the Lincoln neighborhood, the dark side of town. And young Jeff learns that he can't package everything in this neat story he's in. Things spill over. Like human nature. Like society. Like nature too.

CHIEF MARGIE FUNDERSON: Well, there certainly is hypocrisy here in Brainerd, Agent Coover. But the way I see it is that there's truth that the hypocrisy tries to hide. People who try to stuff other people in wood chippers go to jail. There are moral truths at the bottom of things.

FRANK HOPPER: I think you're crazy, neighbor. At the sound of the tree falling. . . . At the bottom of your Lumberton there's a jingle. What's that? It's like you got Mr. Rogers' Neighborhood in your head, and that means you don't have a chance of coming close to what's really going on.

AGENT DALE COOVER: You know in my personal favorite film, *Wild at Heart*, there's cousin Jingle Dell and they call him that because he wants to always be living in Christmas. But old Jingle is as mad as a hatter, kind of like that guy who thinks when he hears jingle bells an angel is getting his wings. There's some crazy stories out there people got their heads into. That's why in *Blue Velvet* Jeff and his girlfriend Sandy keep repeating to each other "It's a strange world." Yeah, I guess it is pretty strange if you start off thinking, like Sandy does, that when the robins come the world will be filled with love. Or like Jeff lives in this "I'm the 'Master of the Universe' story. I can figure anything out."

FRANK HOPPER: It's what I'm telling you, man. People living in these small towns got more of a chance of having looney tunes in their heads. You know what love is, neighbors, it's a bullet straight to the heart. Posted from the Heartland.

CHIEF MARGIE FUNDERSON: I feel sorry for you, Frank. At least when small-town America grows dark in Hitchcock's *Shadow of a Doubt* (1943) because there's now a man living in town who thinks the world is a foul sty, that the world is hell, he's uncovered and he's destroyed. He's not the heart of that town; he's a dark, evil visitor. But your friend David Lynch thinks the world is wild at heart and even if it wasn't we can't free ourselves of our own illusions long enough to make things better.

FRANK HOPPER: You know why you want someone in charge of reality, neighbor? 'Cause you're the chief of police. You like somebody in charge. Go after the bad guys. Catch them shoving somebody's leg into a wood chipper, pull out your gun, and apprehend them. So you figure what kind of director is David Lynch who can't direct us or himself out of the muddle of a town load of clashing stories. Like in *Twin Peaks*.

CHIEF MARGIE FUNDERSON: If there was an ounce of meaning in two years of that TV series, I never saw it. There's no town like Twin Peaks in America. There couldn't be so much weirdness outside a lunatic asylum.

AGENT DALE COOVER: Okay. Okay. I admit. There's a lot of weirdness for one town. But, jeez, Chief Margie, there's a lot of schlock in Mandrake Falls, too.

CHIEF MARGIE FUNDERSON: Where?

AGENT DALE COOVER: Mandrake Falls. Where Longfellow Deeds lives in Frank Kapra's *Mr. Deeds Goes to Town* (1936). "Mandrake Falls where the scenery enthralls, where no heartbreak befalls." Is this a real town or is it imaginary? All I'm saying, Chief Margie, is that every time a small town shows up on the screen it's just showing us what the folks watching the movie want to see, whether it's their lives right then or their dreams. The way I see it, the way small-town America shows up on the screen is like a reflection of the way Americans are imagining their lives. None of those towns in the movies ever existed; they were imagined. And they're important because somehow from the very beginning they got tied up with the American dream.

CHIEF MARGIE FUNDERSON: You'll find the answer as to why small towns got connected to the American dream in history. The majority of Americans lived in small towns or on farms close to small towns they depended on for store-bought goods and Saturday afternoon movie matinees and church dances and so on.

AGENT DALE COOVER: Okay. Good. But here's the thing, Chief Margie. If what people wanted was to live in small towns or on farms, then how did we wind up with big cities, urban sprawl, and the 'burbs? Bright lights, big cities is the reality; one light on Main Street in some small town is the dream. Here's the way I see it. The mythos swept away whatever small-town America really was. In its place we've got something lodged in our American Dreamworks that suits a growing political conservativism.

CHIEF MARGIE FUNDERSON: And David Lynch's small town . . . what did you call it? Twin Peaks? That doesn't fit the conservative mold?

AGENT DALE COOVER: Capitalism globalizes. Corporations transnationalize. It all suits a market conservative drive to profit by any means necessary. But the expansion beyond provincial borders is also an expansion beyond one reality frame and into another. I mean, if things had stayed little and local, small-town and provincial, it wouldn't have been all that obvious that time and place created the stories people live in. What David Lynch does is show us in Twin Peaks, a kind of microcosm of the planet, that people live within self-fabricated and culturally fabricated stories and everything around them comes to meaning from within those stories.

CHIEF MARGIE FUNDERSON: So there's no idyllic small-town Americana? It's hype? It's what conservative politics needs to put in people's heads to push a family values agenda?

FRANK HOPPER: Hey, there's no threat and no fear if there's nothing sacred that's threatened and nothing perfect you fear losing. You know, neighbors, the story of Main Street, U.S.A., is what old Walt Disney dreamed. Al-Qaeda is threatening Disneyland.

CHIEF MARGIE FUNDERSON: I'm just betting that the picture people have in their heads is what's behind that new "neighborhood mall" they're building right outside Brainerd. You can shop, go to the movies, sit out in cafes, stroll with your friends, and do all the things we do here in Brainerd.

AGENT DALE COOVER: Those kind of simulated small-town atmospheres are designed to put shopping right at the heart of everyday life. So the neighborhood outdoor mall relies on the image of small-town America that Disney and Hollywood have created. It samples all those towns in the old movies that you love. It's a brilliant marketing move. Kids grow up as mall rats; they hang out, fall in love, quarrel, play right in front of—right inside—Gap and Abercrombie.

CHIEF MARGIE FUNDERSON: Okay. Globalized business makes a profit getting everyone to think the world hasn't globalized and that we're still living in small-town America?

AGENT DALE COOVER: It's just another marketing strategy of the global market. To make the consumer think the world hasn't globalized, that all those small-town values and traditions haven't gone extinct. You create a yearning for what never was, while utterly destroying the possibility of it ever existing. The hyperreal small-town neighborhood's success means that we can never have what we yearn for. Marketwise, that's all good because it sets us on a shopping spree. We first try to consume the *faux* world itself, trying desperately to be in that idyllic scene as we imagine it. This is an impossibility, but the hyperreal hamlet offers a never-ending means to possess it: buy it, consume it, possess it—I mean, its wares, endless proliferation of products. Our need for them and their usefulness are not factors, because we are not really buying things: We are buying a dream. Of course, this is a Hollywood dream put on a hyppereal stage constructed by consumer capitalism.

CHIEF MARGIE FUNDERSON: The country's grown more conservative, and at the same time this visionary Americana kicks into high gear.

AGENT DALE COOVER: Yeah, but not at first. Only when the cities turned to wastelands and the 'burbs turned to sprawl 'n mall did the old small-town Americana spin unroll. You could regentrify the city ghettoes and turn the 'burbs into gated communities, but none of that hit the pulse of the American cultural imaginary. But the resurrection of small-town America did. Why? Because Hollywood had put the vision and memory of small-town America in our cultural mindscape. The magic town filmscape is locked in there. All the market had to do was to hit replay. The picture and not the reality was what everyone had in their memory banks.

———◆———

Script Doctor: I would do a whole re-write on this and here's why: We're still talking like there was a real small-town America that corresponds to the Disney mythos we're left with. Nix that. There was never a real small-town America that in any way corresponds to the mythos. Here's what it's like: You can't see a subatomic particle, but you can surmise that it's there because when you hit it with something you can see, this something you can see bounces off what you can't see. So you say there has to be something there. What is it that we can only imagine: small-town America. What is it that we can see: the automobile. The automobile has created the mythos of the open road, of freedom, and has also tied into the mythos of individuality: Your car defines you, it empowers you. We quote this: "But it's not just the individuality a car gives you that's important to Americans—it's freedom as well. The road movie . . . the road songs . . . all romanticize the freedom of hitting the road, of running away from something or running to something in a car—preferably with the top down and your hair whipping around your face in the wind" (Lynn P. Nygaard, "America's Love Affair With the Automobile—a Matter of Dollars and [Lack of] Sense," *www.cicero.vio.no*). What were we running from? What did we have to free ourselves from? So we create Johnny, from *The Wild One* to tell us. He and his motorcycle gang terrorize a small town in the heartland for an entire weekend.

—◆—

CHIEF MARGIE FUNDERSON: I don't understand what you're rebelling against. I don't understand why a motorcycle gang wants to terrorize a town like this.

JOHNNY: What'a ya got? Ya got town laws? You got squares living a square life? Well, that ain't for us. Pedal to the metal. We got out, hit the open road where we're free. You know what a town is? It's a noose around your neck. You know what a chopper is? It's a ticket to ride. As far as you can go, man. With nobody stopping you. We go through towns like yours like paper bags.

AGENT DALE COOVER: Did you ever see the documentary film *Taken For Ride*? Sheriff Margie? It's all about how GM systematically destroyed every kind of public transportation system so that Americans would eventually wind up totally dependent on the auto. The way things shifted from "a man and his horse" to "a man and his car" had to do with a whole chain of associations. The first was easy: The horse linked up with the rugged frontier and that whole mythos. The man on the horse had the whole open range to ride through. But now the horse has become the car, a car faster than a horse, a car with phenomenal "horsepower." So everything has increased in magnitude: The horse is now the car which is superior, and the man in the car can go further and faster than any man on a horse. It's all better. Except for what we know isn't better: We're now aware we've transformed the physiognomy of our wonderful landscape to accommodate the "freeways." We're now aware that we're choking in traffic that leaves us stalled bumper to bumper for half our lives, that we're choking in fumes that are choking to death the natural recuperating rhythms of the planet, that we can't find a loaf of bread or a bottle of milk without getting in our cars, that we're going faster and faster in bigger and bigger cars and we don't know how to stop.

CHIEF MARGIE FUNDERSON: So we go back in our minds to what was before the automobile, what life was like back then, and we wax nostalgic. We fantasize a simpler, more natural, more communal, quiet rocking-on-the-front-porch, nodding-to-your-neighbors-as-they-walk-by-on-the-way-to-a-church-picnic kind of past. I get it.

AGENT DALE COOVER: You take a rebel movie like Johnny's *The Wild One* and you can see the dual carbs at work: The small town is a prison, Squaresville, a place to run from and run through. It's stultifying. If you're young and restless, you need to get out. You can see in a 1984 film like *Footloose*, in a small town called Beaumont, how restrictive small-town life can be. There's no opposing vibe in that movie; it's a production of the Big Three. But in *The Wild One* there's a certain respect paid to the small town. It doesn't deserve to be raped and pillaged by the bikers. There's a tension there between biker rage against a small town, and the enduring qualities of the small town as opposed to weekend biker rage.

FRANK HOPPER: My favorite biker movie is *Easy Rider*. Captain America and Billy. Okay, man, they're on the road for sure. Free men and all for freedom and all. But they're not condoning the world the automobile industry has made. They're not for technology, man. No part of the Corporate State. The bikes are truly the horses that get them out of the world that destroyed the laid-back life of the small towns, the folks doing their own thing in their own time. An Easy Rider is not punching the clock or building roads or making any kind of design on nature, man. It's all about being mellow, man. Being mellow.

JOHNNY: That's where biker gangs wound up? Being mellow?

AGENT DALE COOVER: Well, not really, Johnny. Hell's Angels maintained your 1950s rebel tradition. But the spirit of the 1960s counterculture that you find in *Easy Rider* is definitely not a "rather rule on the road than serve in a small town" spirit. They're quiet rebels, hippy, flower power, searching nomads. The road is within; you just have to project it out into the world. Find your center; find your thing and make it happen out there. There's a trip backward to communal life, and I think that has a certain small-town resonance.

——— ◆ ———

Script Doctor: Interject at the point Johnny says "pedal to the metal" an hommage to Sailor Ripley in David Lynch's *Wild at Heart*. Here's another turn in the road to small-town America. Sailor and his girlfriend Lula head west in the classic road trip from East Coast to West Coast, and they're wild at heart not in Johnny's rebel-without-a-pause style and not in Captain America and Billy's Easy Rider style. Here's what I want to capture: Sailor is sleeping and Lula is behind the wheel surfing radio stations, but all she's picking up are real horror stories. The world all around them is a nightmare filled with sick and sordid news. She screams out in protest, and she and Sailor perform a wild and crazy dance in the desert, a wild exuberant dancing and shouting that crushes the nightmare of the world the radio has reported. Here is a road movie that doesn't send us back to fantasize a small-town world before technology nor into a rebellious attack on small-town America nor into a countercultural mellowness nostalgic for innocent edens. The wildness of Sailor and Lula's hearts trumps the news reports; their wildness is the fertile ground for countering stories to those news reports. Human "wildness" exceeds the wildness of its own creations, of its own representations. And it is here in that wildness of imagination that we dream collectively of small-town America. And its hold on us will last as long as we continue to imagine it. Sailor Ripley is the postmod rebel of the road; he can take a detour into the world of Johnny here, the Wild One, or the mumbling James Dean who has so much within he can't ever get it out, or E, Elvis, who was a kind of rocking the world out of its tired dreams. Sailor lives in endless stories of self.

——◆——

CHIEF MARGIE FUNDERSON: Tell me about this magic town filmscape.

AGENT DALE COOVER: I don't watch a lot of old movies. You tell me about films before, during, and after the second world war. That's when Hollywood implanted the image.

CHIEF MARGIE FUNDERSON: Well, my personal favorites are the Hardy family films. With Mickey Rooney playing young Andy Hardy. MGM put those films out for a decade, 1936 to 1946. And MGM won a special Academy Award in 1942 "for representing the American way of life."

AGENT DALE COOVER: That's the stuff. There you have it. Direct correspondence between movies and the American way of life. Small-town way of life.

CHIEF MARGIE FUNDERSON: The town was called Carvel, and Andy went to Carvel High. Something like Archie going to Riverdale High. Andy Hardy is a rambunctious teenager who's always getting into trouble. But then he has a "man to man" talk with his dad, Judge Hardy, and he learns a little bit more about life and what it is to grow up responsibly.

FRANK HOPPER: Not like the father-and-son chat in Todd Solondz's film *Happiness* (1998), where the dad is a pedophile. And remember the high school in *Pleasantville* (1998)? I don't mean the one in the *Pleasantville* TV show but in the real Pleasantville. Hormonal jungle, I can tell you, neighbors. Like Riverdale High and Carvel High pumped up to surround-sound levels and pushed from analogue to digital speed. Wow!

CHIEF MARGIE FUNDERSON: I saw that film *Pleasantville*. Tobey Maguire wanted a mom like the one in the TV show. Not a divorced mom running to La Costa to take a mud bath with her newest boyfriend. Who wouldn't prefer life in Pleasantville? Reese Witherspoon is just a young tart in the real world. But in Pleasantville she begins to read and develop some character. Of course, the movie winds up mocking Pleasantville. And why? Because they didn't eat, sleep, and drink sex. Because they weren't as sexually liberated as we are. Because Reese Witherspoon's TV mom had no idea what pleasure there was in masturbation. So down with Pleasantville and up with Pleasureville. Let me tell you, small-town America didn't repress or suppress sex. Where do you think all the kids were coming from? They *had* sex; they didn't *shop* for it. Folks in small-town America lived in a world that just shopped for groceries and the seasonal warm coat. They didn't shop for sex the way we do. We shop till we drop, because it's a sublimated sexual activity. Why is it sublimated? Because for all our sexual liberation we're not adult about sexuality. We have to deal with it through products. Advertisers work on that connection, and they do all they can to keep us on an infantalized, sublimating level. Pleasantville isn't unliberated; it's just not had its sexuality commodified.

FRANK HOPPER: Hey, I'm sorry, Chief Margie, but Pleasantville is just stifling, dead, black-and-white, repressed, small-town America by the time this film gets through with it. You know what the biggest problem with Pleasantville is? It's predigital. It's precomputer. It's pre-cell phone, DVD, SUV. . . . You can't surf porn in the privacy of your own home. Consider this, neighbor: Women didn't even know they were supposed to enjoy sex. White men who were breadwinners and macho and held doors for the "gentler sex" and made advances to their secretaries in the office and made sure blacks need not apply didn't even know they were being politically incorrect, racist, sexist . . .

CHIEF MARGIE FUNDERSON: Small-town America as a dream place collapses because it gets linked to all of that?

AGENT DALE COOVER: Hey, it happened before the world went postmod and got its politically correct notions. *Peyton Place* (1957) is a divided *Our Town*. *Our* town is the town on the right side of the tracks. Over on the other side is shack town—*their* town. The poor and ignorant, the trash. It was there in Andy Hardy's Carvel, but the camera didn't focus on it. This is a small town to run away from, like Alison MacKenzie does. It's stifling, hypocritical, full of mean gossip and mean spirited people. "Everybody in this town hides behind plain wrapper," Alison tells a friend. There's a whole lot of trouble in River City is what it is, Chief Margie.

CHIEF MARGIE FUNDERSON: Cities offer anonymity. Small towns offer community. Anonymity is there because the people around you don't really care if you live or die. If you're lying in the gutter in Manhattan, they'll walk over you. Community applies pressure to achieve the kind of conformity of behavior, beliefs, desires, and dreams that it needs in order to be a community. If you're different . . .

FRANK HOPPER: If you're different or want something different or get sick and tired of having to fit in, then small-town life is hell. You know, neighbor, I feel like Edward Scissorhands sometimes. You know, living in that dark castle at the end of that southern California housing tract.

CHIEF MARGIE FUNDERSON: But on top of nobody caring a heck about you in a city, you got to fear for your life . . .

——◆——

Script Doctor: Okay, here's our entre into post-9/11 fear and dread. And the political campaign of fear tied to the 2004 presidential election. You have urban fear and your have small-town America fear; the fear of the blue states and the fear of the red states. The blue states have all those bleeding-heart tax-and-spend liberals who can't do enough for foreigners from all over, druggies, welfare queens, three-time offenders, homeless derelicts, drive-by hoodlums, crackheads, deadbeat dads, work shirkers, and ghetto dwellers. Is crime and fear an endemic part of the urban scene? Yeah. Why would a "security mom" feel secure in any of these blue states, even before 9/11? Security in the urban centers was threatened way before 9/11. You have to go to small-town America if you really want the post-9/11 fear to kick in, even though al-Qaeda probably has no designs on Mumford, Indiana, or South Park, Kansas. If you're running a presidential campaign on your rapid response to terrorism, you have to keep the spirit of terrorism alive, just like Castro tried to keep the spirit of his revolution alive. And to keep that spirit alive you need to hone in on who and what is terrorized. You call in Dustin Hoffman, the producer from Wag the Dog (aka Karl Rove, the Architect of America), and he produces a small-town America scene for you. What are we tapping into here? We bring in Dr. Miles Bennell, played by Kevin McCarthy, in the first, the 1956 Don Siegel version of *Invasion of the Body Snatchers*. A small town named Santa Mira is comfortable and secure, and then an awareness of alien enmity slowly dawns . . .

———◆———

DR. MILES BENNELL: Wake up! They're here! They're here!

AGENT DALE COOVER: We know they're here. That's why we need to strengthen the Patriot Act so we in the FBI can have an easier job of separating patriots from terrorists. The nineteen behind the Trade Towers attack were all living in this country.

CHIEF MARGIE FUNDERSON: They would have stood out in small towns.

DR. MILES BENNELL: Not if they looked like everybody else. Not if everyone in that town had their appearance simulated by pods. Not if real people were then left as just so much dry dust and the simulations went around as if they were real people. You couldn't see they were aliens but inside they were. They are. Aliens.

FRANK HOPPER: Man, that's far out but I dig what you're saying. It's like one day you wake up and you're not you. Somebody has taken over your whole identity. And you don't know that person anymore. You like stayed on the job too long. You paid too many dues. Punched the clock too long. Too much lawn mowing, man. Small towns will do that to you. Suck the juices right out. One day you're cool and the next day you're a pod.

DR. MILES BENNELL: You don't understand. I'm talking about real pods.

FRANK HOPPER: Yeah, I met some real pods, man. They're, like, all over the place. Smaller the town, bigger the pod. More of them, too.

AGENT DALE COOVER: I saw the film you were in, Doctor. *Invasion of the Body Snatchers*. You know what I thought? It wasn't the aliens that invaded that town. It was what snatched their bodies and minds. Fear. The only thing you had to fear was fear itself.

FRANK HOPPER: Are you saying the pods weren't real?

AGENT DALE COOVER: If you put a pod near us while we're sleeping, it will invade us. Okay, what happened on 9/11 was destruction of life and property, of our homeland, but it was also an invasion of our sense of security, our psychic home base. Al-Qaeda put a pod near us. How it continues to affect us now is by insinuating itself into our frame of seeing and feeling, our framing of the future. Bin Laden's been painting the picture of the world we're now living in. What the future holds may be yet another attack, a more vicious attack. But that will be, like 9/11, limited to time and place, and will once again leave a trail we can follow to the perpetrators. But there is no rush to this next havoc, because the pod of fear is now lying beside the American mass psyche and doing its work.

CHIEF MARGIE FUNDERSON: I can't believe that something so insidious has been relied upon to form the basis of a political campaign.

AGENT DALE COOVER: And it's effective, Sheriff Margie, because as long as there's a small-town America vision of a womblike safety and security, of endless well-being, we have within our mass psyche a vulnerability, certainly to the kind of dramatic, sudden and inexplicable attack that was 9/11. If we had been less in Disneyland in our imaginations, less in bubbles of all sorts, we might not have psychically needed a "war of terror," a preemptive strike against a country with no 9/11 connection. We might be paying closer attention to what a politics of fear may be spinning us away from. We have to break out of our bubble, not fortify it.

———◆———

Spin Doctor: We'll lose Whitehouse access so drop this and pick up with what Sheriff Margie was saying about big cities.

———◆———

CHIEF MARGIE FUNDERSON: . . . You could easily be a victim. Maybe somebody hates you because they think you hate them. Maybe it's because of the color of their skin or their foreign accent or who they worship. So you run from the violence and racial hatred and fear and go to the 'burbs. If you can afford it. And out there in the 'burbs they build neighborhood malls that make you think you're living in a quaint, picturesque Americana village.

FRANK HOPPER: I hear you, neighbor. The 'burbs are like a safe zone between the rural outback where your car can break down, like in the 1997 flick *Breakdown*, and the degenerate locals can start messing with you. . . . Between that and a megalopolis like L.A. where you go berserk like Michael Douglas in *Falling Down* (1993) 'cause you can't take the pace of city life anymore.

CHIEF MARGIE FUNDERSON: You're wrong. The allure of the 'burbs is over. You spend forty years trimming and "Rounding-up" your lawn and then someone drives you to a three-tiered retirement home where someone else trims and "Rounds-up" the lawn while you play bridge until the Grim Reaper calls your hand. The young leave the 'burbs and never come back. We've got a whole generation now that looks back to the 'burbs where they grew up and they see nothing but a car, gassed up and ready to go. Then they either rush to the city or to Main Street, Disneyland.

FRANK HOPPER: Let's face it, neighbors. Why do you think Tim Burton does films like *Edward Scissorhands* (1990) and *Ed Wood* (1994)? Marginal lives. Marginal communities. A sociopath like me is just as liable to flourish in Fargo as in the Big Apple.

AGENT DALE COOVER: I have to agree. America doesn't offer any real community at all. Not in the cities, not in the small town, not in the 'burbs. *Boogie Nights* (1997). Paul Thomas Anderson's film. Burt Reynolds makes porno flicks, but he's surrounded by community. They're making porno flicks; actors, actresses, directors, producers, cameramen . . . the whole works. They're outside Hollywood mainstream. They deviate from the norm. But what's the norm? Hollywood? It's like, not only doesn't this country foster real community but to find it on your own you've got to go underground, break the rules, search for the margins where the American norms and values can't find you.

CHIEF MARGIE FUNDERSON: Is that the magictown filmscape?

AGENT DALE COOVER: *Magic Town* (1947) was a Frank Capra kind of movie directed by William Wellman. Fast-talking, big-city pollster finds a town, Grandview, that thinks exactly the same as the country does. So he goes there to poll, pretending to be in the insurance business. He's exposed; the town gets flooded with people who want to live there and this sudden fame wreaks havoc on the town. It's no longer representative of the country; its opinions become disconnected. They're not representing reality any longer.

CHIEF MARGIE FUNDERSON: I could see that happening to Brainerd if we let the Paul Bunyan and Babe the Blue Ox connection get out of hand. We'd be just another phoneyville like Vegas.

AGENT DALE COOVER: But Rip Smith—that's Jimmy Stewart, the pollster—convinces the town to pick itself up by its own bootstraps and show the whole country that this small town can't be defeated, that its citizens can pitch right in and build the new civic center with their own hands because they have all those values and virtues their pioneer forebears had. So the small town is resurrected.

CHIEF MARGIE FUNDERSON: So the movie is really a call to 1947 America to put the war behind them, dip into what makes America great, and rebuild the war-torn American dream?

AGENT DALE COOVER: Sure. We're magic. We're a magical people. America is us. We're special. It never means Central or South America. It's just us. We can rebuild Grandview. But now in our postmodern America, we can't. Not only because we've deconstructed that small-town mythos and can't put it back together again but because we've lost sight of where it fit into the American dream in the first place. All we can build are Disneylands, plastic towns, hyperreal Europe in the new Las Vegas. Towns lose their authenticity and become picture postcards. New Orleans is the last holdout.

CHIEF MARGIE FUNDERSON: I thought you said the magictown filmscape represents a fundamental yearning that's somehow connected with the American dream?

AGENT DALE COOVER: That's right. It's a beam of light passing through a strip of film, an image projected on our cultural imaginary. It represents a yearning that exceeds what it's yearning for. It's desire detached from its object. It's a nostalgia for a place only ever seen on a screen in a movie theatre. Why keep it alive? Because it's a yearning that every newly launched product and service promises to satisfy. Sex is the most useful marketwise. But the yearning for a safe zone, a community of mutual aid and compassion and understanding, for a wonderful life in our town in a world whose commercial energies have overwhelmed our simplicity loving souls . . . this will prove to be our most vulnerable yearning.

FRANK HOPPER: I don't know about you, man, but I'm heading for Nawleans.

———◆———

THE BLOGOSPHERE

Blog: www.greenzone.com

The yearning for an idyllic small-town America is a yearning for the womb, for some archetypal safe zone. I look at it this way: America was a vast open *terra incognita*. Pioneers built cabins in the midst of wilderness. They nestled in. They kept out the darkness, the wilderness, the beasts. It's all in the film *The Village* (2004), where folks escape the modern world and take try to live in the past, in a "village." Get into the twentieth century and you find in almost every American an irrational hunger for "home ownership." No house is ever big enough. It's always being "added on to," remodeled, expanded. We're marking our territory, private personal safe space. But there's always a threatening "outside." There has to be. You can't mark a safe zone, a green zone, without at the same time marking an unsafe zone, a black zone. If we Americans were comfortable in the world—rather like Aborigines who sing their land into their lives—we wouldn't be caught up in this conflict of a safe inside/threatening outside, of secure womb (whether it be our IKEA homes or the parlor-like interiors of six-ton SUVs) and a terrorist-lurking surround. What I think Hollywood small-town America evokes is what the French (!) call fraternity and we call neighborliness. Home ownership, or any kind of ownership, a protected, gated community, an electronic home protection system and so on marks our secure, private, personal space. We guard against the intrusions of those around us, convinced in our deeply divided Two Americas—Ownership America and Wages America—that the "losers" mean us harm. After 9/11 we extended that category from the underclass losers of our derelict inner cities, trailer parks, and foreclosed farms to the whole Middle East. The winners have been trying for twenty years to find a protected "green zone" where not only will threats from the losers be eliminated but the losers themselves will vanish from the picture.

But what's the harm in this? It's Homeland Security. What lengths do we go in order to protect our insulated cocoon? An "Axis of Evil" is "out there" and may have already infiltrated our "green zone." In order to preserve our safety—well, we have to follow former Bush Press Secretary Ari Fleischer's advice: "These are reminders to all Americans that they need to watch what they say, watch what they do, and this is not a time for remarks like that." He was referring to a remark by Bill Maher on *Politically Incorrect*. Maher was subsequently fired.

I don't think anyone behind this *This Is a Picture and Not the World* project fully realizes that "small-town America" is just code for something really dark, not just a marketing scheme or a political campaign tactic. It's code for the same thing Germany got wrapped up in with the Third Reich. "Homeland" is not a Disney word in human history; it's a frightening word, or should be. Maybe it isn't because we have become the United States of Amnesia, as Gore Vidal suggests. How else to explain Defense Secretary Rumsfeld's amnesiac use of the phrase "shock and awe" to describe our initial assault on Iraq?

Blog: www.bigdog.com

If you want to see how "magical" America looks to a European, watch the Danish director Lars von Trier's *Dogville*. It's a post-9/11 movie but I doubt von Trier's view of America pre-9/11 would be

THE BLOGOSPHERE

much different. The American reaction to the film is certainly caught up in a defensive post-9/11 attitude. What would you expect? David Denby in the article "The Quick and the Dead" (*The New Yorker*, January 16, 2005), writes: "We're in the dead zone of schematic abstraction and didactic moral fable . . . what Lars von Trier has achieved is avant-gardism for idiots." J. Hoberman in *The Voice* takes the bait and steps up and writes: "For passion, originality, and sustained chutzpah, this austere allegory of failed Christian charity and Old Testament payback is von Trier's strongest movie—a masterpiece, in fact, almost a contribution to American literature."

Where precisely in American literature? Perhaps the really dark side of *Our Town*, which is really only dark because death is dark for Americans and growing darker. No, I look to film and specifically to the forbidden "Lincoln" neighborhood in David Lynch's film *Blue Velvet* that Jeff's aunt warns him away from. Dogville is Lynch's Lumberton with this difference—everyone in Dogville is a secret Frank Booth, the sicko played to perfection by Dennis Hopper in Lynch's American film masterpiece. In *Dogville* we have a female Christ—Nicole Kidman—brutalized, raped, chained, made to drag a heavy iron wheel. She's a fugitive seeking asylum in Dogville, and she winds up being savaged by every member of this "magic town." But as Denby says, "This female Jesus seeks revenge." Is this the revenge that bin Laden sought on 9/11, a revenge against the Dogville that America had become? Is it George W. Bush's revenge against bin Laden and the savagery of 9/11? Is this Christ figure rising up and smoting the townspeople a premonition of what yet awaits America? "If there's a town that the world would be better off without, it's Dogville." Not a very magical end for the magical kingdom.

Blog: www.nothollywood.com

There's a fundamental problem in "Magic Town": small-town America is being economically transformed—I mean, destroyed—and while Thomas Frank in his *What's the Matter With Kansas?* describes the culprit, the writer of this screenplay has to work to it through film. Hello? Hollywood isn't running after the culprits so there's no film representation of what Frank describes.

Here's what popular film is complicit with and can't expose:

"Deregulated capitalism is what has allowed Wal-Mart to crush local businesses across Kansas and, even more important, what has driven agriculture, the state's *raison d'etre*, to a state of near collapse."

Every "magic town" is now vulnerable to a resident corporation deciding to "outsource," so that "hosting some multinational's plant is less an achievement today than it is a gun pointed at your head, a constant reminder that some executive has the power to turn your town into an instant Flint [MI]. . . ." Rather than learning from Flint—and what Michael Moore documents in his 1991 film *Roger and Me*, which attempts to question a corporation's responsibility to its workers and a city which depends upon it—we have put our "magic towns" in even greater jeopardy by adopting policies that hurt family farms, the "magic towns" those farms created, salaried workers, consumers, and the environment.

There are reasons why in the post-2004 presidential electoral season we saw documentaries with very specific targets come to the fore. First, the issues themselves, seen as essentially political, have economic roots, which, in short, means that this new globalized capitalism is the tail wagging the dog of our democracy. Along with "class" and "cancer," "capitalism" is an unspoken "C" word. Second, the issues require a certain dedicated attention span; they demand a patience with historical background, a willingness to learn how transnationals operate, an ability to decipher promotional spins. We have two angered populations at the moment in this country, each highly critical of the other, without the assistance of any critical reasoning. People have already made up their minds on any issue. Why is this? "Out here the gravity of discontent pulls in only one direction," Frank writes, "to the right, to the right, farther to the right." It will take countless historians of the future—if we have one, which is doubtful if anybody accepts the "Futurescape" chapter—to explicate this mystery. The fact remains, however, that those most at risk in our present right-sponsored, deregulated global capitalism are least willing to attend to any critique made of the right.

Rather than take on this fight to reach the minds and hearts of Americans, popular film has followed the money and offered the most mindless of escapist fare: Pixar animated productions, comic book heroes, "Brad and Angelina"-like romance, video games brought to the screen, recycled stuff that was fluff the first time around, cyberspace adventures, psychic thrillers, police procedurals, and high production Broadway musicals brought to the screen as high production dramas. I don't doubt that something linked to post-9/11 America can be found if you turn loose a doctoral student looking for a thesis. You can, for instance, see parallels between Colin Farrell's *Alexander the Great* and George W. Bush in that both were rabid to turn democracy into empire; or, see Mr. Incredible as a return of the Nietzschean *ubermensch*; or see the new *Manchurian Candidate*'s transnational corporation as the villain and not the original film's Soviet Union.

THE BLOGOSPHERE

Novelists are once again saying the novel as a form of imaginative expression is dead—this time not because someone like James Joyce took it to its limit, but because few in the new generations can either extend the sort of imagination the printed page requires or has the patience to follow a text longer than an e-mail. Instant messaging collapses, not exercises, the imagination. Mass-market bestselling novels follow strict genre rules and certainly do not take on what's happened, for example, to our "magic towns." Popular film has always been quite limited in being able to reflect real issues, although I do think that Hollywood has always dipped into hot issues in order to draw a contemporary audience. The problem is that, until the film *Flight 193*, we existed in a climate in which no one was going to the movies to see pictures of what they didn't want to think about, namely, 9/11 and its aftermath. We are also in the sort of political climate in which hot issues have to be more cleverly wrapped in order to defuse a very volatile political climate. That sort of cleverness requires equal unwrapping cleverness, which, sadly, is a disappearing facility.

Let's hypothesize: Why Joe Sixpack in his cozy digs is doomed in this ever-growing plutocracy requires deep penetration and lots of detail; a very complex picture has to be drawn. Connections have to be made; incremental progression is the order of the day. However, Americans measure everything by the click of a computer mouse or the flip of a TV remote. Doubtlessly, the ethos of conservatism is growing more and more powerful as it makes its case with a few simple slogans, like "Big Government Is Bad," "Taxes Are Bad," "Liberals Are Traitors," "You Can Spend Your Own Money Better Than Washington Can," "Liberals Want To Reward Bad Behavior," "Liberals Want To Leave The Defense Of the U.S. to the U.N.," and so on. A movie industry that wants to maximize its profits with box office blockbusters has to appeal to this growing majority of the country. And the more the imaginations of such an audience are fueled by such an ethos, the more difficult it will be for challenging views to find a distributor and, therefore, an audience. This is where we are at already. The folks behind "Magic Town" think not; otherwise they would have looked elsewhere than popular film, in the past or in the present, to find answers to what happened to "Magic Town."

Blog: www.cupcakeland.com

Magic Town? I don't know where that fits in. From what I see, there are two types of town in the United States today. You've got the

Flint, Michigan-type, the corpse-like remains of a town after "the Factory" closes down, and then you've got Cupcake Land. To quote Thomas Frank: "Cupcake Land is a metropolis built entirely according to the developer's plan, without the interference of angry proles or ethnic pols. . . . Cupcake Land encourages no culture but that which increases property values; supports no learning but that which burnishes the brand; hears no opinion but those that will further fatten the Cupcake elite; tolerates no rebellion but that expressed in haircuts and piercings and alternative rock. You know what it's like even though you haven't been there. Smooth jazz. Hallmark cards. Applebees. Corporate Woods. Its greatest civic holiday is the turning on of the Christmas lights at a nearby shopping center—an event so inspirational to the Cupcake mind that the mall thus illuminated has been rendered in paint by none other than Thomas Kinkade" (Thomas Frank, *What's the Matter with Kansas?*, p. 50).

A picture by Thomas Kinkade, you know, *is* the world.

Blog: www.nailer.com

Two points to nail down that this screenplay leaves flapping:

First: Soccer Moms easily morphed into Security Moms. Why? Because the psyche of the Soccer Mom is a control psyche, the kind of psyche that schedules every minute of the day for *her dependents*. She can't bring genocide in Africa to ground, or the Palestinian–Israeli conflict, or health care to 45 million Americans, and so on, but she can bring order to her family's life. Her psyche is set up for a Karl Rove invasion after 9/11; it doesn't take much to morph her into a Security Mom where "just do something even if it's attacking those who didn't attack" us is what we do. Threatening her secure order is something al-Qaeda should never have done.

Two: Family values. Mentioned and dropped. But they're at the heart of magic-town security; they're what dysfunctional families don't have, and they don't have them because economic woes are like hurricanes ripping through marriage and child-rearing. But no, this economic view is too crass; family values are existential, ontological, ineffable, inside and not outside, moral compasses possessed and not money to pay the rent. You can't tax and spend in order to build family values; how to build them will, in the view of the Christian Coalition, remain a deeply spiritual matter, severed from governmental intrusion. The magic-town middle class is not expected to do anything for the dysfunctional poor, certainly not vote to raise taxes. Of course, the presence of "family values" among the top twenty percent of the population is never pictured, because no attention is drawn here, although we get daily glimpses of what values this upper class does possess.

Middle-class Americans were in lockdown, Orange Alert in regard to the working class (read the underclass) *before 9/11*; it was a relatively simple matter to extend the threat to Magic Town from the underclass and illegal Aliens to the whole Islamic world. I would also note that there was no symbolic attack on this American dysfunctional Underclass, this class remiss in these mystical "family values," on September 11, the symbolic attack being clearly against Money and Power. One always remarks that bin Laden's is a religious cause and his recruiting power among the young is purely religious. Perhaps it is also a global class struggle he is mounting against those who have only hypocritical values and on behalf of those who are the victims of this hypocrisy.

There is no inherent moral worth in security: The Third Reich had it and the Jews didn't; the Roman Empire had it even during the reigns of Caligula and Nero, and the White Man had it and the Red and Black Man didn't. Putin's Russia sees its own security threatened by the Chechnyans, but at the heart of Putin's Russia is the Russian mafia, and at the heart of the Chechnyan battle is what Americans sought in their own revolution.

You need Walt Disney and Hollywood and Madison Avenue and political spinmeisters to spin security into the American dream—and put it right there on Main Street in small-town America. Nothing magical, just a spin, a picture, and not the world.

There's no security when you go all the way down: Anyone can die at any moment.

THE BLOGOSPHERE

Documentary

The Short-Term Memory Detective

He could reconstruct all his dreams, all his fancies. Two or three times he had reconstructed an entire day. He told me: "I have more memories in myself alone than all men have had since the world was a world." And again: "My dreams are like your vigils." And again, toward dawn: "My memory, sir, is like a garbage disposal."

—Jorge Luis Borges, "Funes, the Memorious"

Well, isn't it pretty clear that the dictatorship is in place? We're not supposed to know certain things and we're not going to know them. They're doing everything to remove our history, to damage the Freedom of Information Act. Bush managed to have a number of Presidential papers, including those of his father, put out of the reach of historians, or anybody, for a great length of time, during which they will probably be shredded, so they won't be available. What I have always called jokingly the United States of Amnesia will be worse than an amnesiac. It will have suffered a lobotomy; there will be no functioning historical memory of our history.

—Gore Vidal, in an interview with
Amy Goodman, May 13, 2003

History did not begin on September 11.

—Mark Hertsgaard, "The Oblivious Empire"

What kind of profound amnesia had overtaken us? How had it taken hold, come to prevent the laying down of not only political but cultural long-term memory? Could we no longer

hold a thought long enough to connect it to the events we
were seeing and hearing and reading about?
—Joan Didion, "Politics in the 'New Normal' America,"
The New York Review of Books, October 21, 2004

Voice-over: The United States of Amnesia is what Gore Vidal calls the
U.S.A. We are in a market-induced or market-spun cultural amnesia.
The ideal in this market-driven technoworld is the homo sapien of fifteen-minute memory. A short-term memory, a memory that locks onto
the present, consumes it, and then loses it and stands ready to lock onto
a totally new present.

Imagine the marketing delerium over this state of affairs. We fall in
love with the newest new, purchase it, and then in fifteen minutes can't
recognize it, or our desire for it. Obsolescence on a fifteen-minute cycle!
We're out shopping again. Endgame consumer capitalism. Imagine such
a brave new world, such a society, where continuity in thought, word,
and action is rendered meaningless. Coherence would vanish, as nothing
from the past would need to be tied to the present and everything said
would need to meet—or not—the requirements of a fifteen-minute intel-
ligibility. Identity would also need only meet the requirements of a fifteen-minute present and would, therefore, be free to "remake" itself
continually. No one would need a psychiatrist, because no one would be
trying to find a true self—a unified, coherent, continuous self. Authenticity of self is a fifteen-minute achievement. Welcome to the United
States of Alzheimer's.

Have we come close to describing the present generation of primary-
school students? Perhaps the latest computer software programs will dissolve fragmented and fractured attentiveness, and the market will, thereby,
resolve the problem it creates by the very means it created the problem.
Only a fifteen-minute memory span would, of course, believe this.

Christopher Nolan, the director of *Memento* (2001), is not as given
to absolutely ludicrous scenarios. His detective, Leonard Shelby, is the
only one suffering from a short-term memory loss that makes it impossible for him to form new memories. But he still possesses memories
formed before his accident. Note that it takes an accident, not a Madison Avenue marketing campaign, to produce this new creation. And the
world and everyone in it still possesses the normal memory span. They
know who they are, because they recall who they were. They can tie
thoughts, actions, and words together beyond the fifteen-minute time
limit. There's no cultural amnesia.

But then again a question is raised—a question already raised by the
new millennium American culture. Did we forget that Gore Vidal refers

to this as the United States of Amnesia? And within the last fifteen days didn't Studs Terkel go on the *News Hour* and say that we suffer from a cultural amnesia causing us to forget our working-class heroes, our devotion to the common man, to the poor and downtrodden, the homeless and oppressed, the immigrant, farmers, factory workers, union organizers, rebels and radicals, iconoclasts and freedom fighters, poets and dreamers, ordinary lives, suffering souls, our fellow men and women, Americans all? Perhaps we talk about cultural amnesia because we fear we have it. Perhaps our memories have always been culturally produced with only the more traumatic personal experiences trumping the cultural prescriptions.

It is not difficult to see how September 11, 2001 has been established as our culture's new temporal demarcation. *Before and After 9/11.* Is this demarcation enduring because an America threatened by nonstate terrorism began then and continues now? Or is it enduring and the threat still felt because it fits and serves a market-sponsored neoconservative reality frame? You may say perhaps both, but let's investigate the first possibility. When a beginning is established is not a neutral matter. A beginning, you might say, has to wait until ensuing events and words mark it as a beginning. It may prove, for instance, to have been a consequence rather than a beginning. George W. took certain actions that required 9/11 to be a point of origin, of inception, of cause, of ground zero. 9/11 had to be enfolded within a story in which it was the beginning, otherwise regardless of how monumentally memorable the event was, it would have faced the same market-shaped, consumer memory span as greeted every other headline event. We Americans are now packaged with short-term memories. The idea of a continued terrorist fear would also have had a short tenure if it too had not been enfolded within a narrative of the future, a threatened future. Something that doesn't happen but is said to continue to exist needs some assistance in that continuance. It needs to be stoked, like a fire. For instance, there's a real threat that an asteroid or meteor may crash into the planet and upset our delicate planetary balance. No one stokes that fear or sees any reason to enfold it within a narrative of beginning, middle, and end. If there were a market or a political reason to stoke it, it would be stoked. But right now the idea that our lives are precariously held, that death in any form awaits our mortal selves, that time runs out for each of us, that no amount of shopping or toys or cars in the garage or stocks amount to much in that last second review of our lives, serves corporate capitalism, *not at all.* But 9/11 does.

It is not by chance that the theme of memory appears in *Memento* and sets us off in many and various philosophical meanderings. This is a culture that in many and various ways is haunted by what it can remember and what it can't. Some tap into the past as a reservoir of memories counter to the present order of things. The memories of others are outfitted by the latest episode of *Survivor*, by MTV's week's top ten videos, and the latest distraction from *Fox News*. What if we were in the same predicament as Guy Pearce's Leonard Shelby and suffering from anterograde amnesia and had set ourselves to the task of finding our wife's killer? Immediately we see that it's the memory predicament that's our case, that's the mystery we have to deal with. We have to deal with the consciousness that is brought to bear on the world. We have to be hyperconsciously aware. So the film becomes self-reflexively aware of what it's about, what it's showing and telling us. Narrating and representation—the means by which we can follow Shelby as he pursues his investigation—have to constantly be halted and brought up for investigation. We're investigating the way we investigate. Maybe Shelby should start investigating himself. Maybe we should start investigating ourselves.

One of the stories told about postmodernity says that it's not just another belief but it's about how we believe. *Memento* is not just another detective yarn; it's about how we detect. In this case, how dependent are we on memory? Let's just postulate and say we're all private investigators, each and every day. What are we investigating and who's hired us? We open our eyes in the morning and consider the room. We examine the floor for our slippers. We search for the toothpaste. It goes on until bedtime and then we investigate our dreamworks. And we know that we're ultimately self-hired to investigate ourselves, although if we do have cultural amnesia we may have forgotten this. So what does Shelby ponder and what does he discover? It seems that he starts out with a neoconservative disdain for memory.

Neoconservative disdain? Why and wherefore? Because cultural memory digs up a whole lot of stories that challenge the casino logic of market conservatism. Why are books burnt in *Fahrenheit 451* (1966)? Why elect twice as president a man who has no cultural or historical memory and who sees this absence as an asset he wants to hold on to? Memory is the key that opens the past, and the past is a threat to a present that wants to be conscious of no other values but market values. Memory is a threat to a political regime that wants to re-begin American history on September 11, 2001.

Shelby opposes memory with facts. In his view, memory distorts. "Memory can change the shape of a room. It's just an interpretation." On the other hand, he thinks a Polaroid snapshot doesn't require interpretation. He thinks it's unmediated truth, pure fact. So if he can gather up the snapshots, tattoo the facts on his body, and keep all his notes, they can provide the factual background he needs as he reemerges every fifteen minutes with memory banks that closed . . . how long ago we don't know. In our new millennial, global market world, turnover of everything is instantaneous, faster than a mouse click with a new computer screen. All new info overwrites the old info. Shelby doesn't have to delete; he's on AMD—automatic memory delete.

But that's Shelby; not us. We get a chance to observe someone who thinks he has an identity even though he doesn't know if what he's doing now is identical to what he's done or said or thought fifteen minutes ago. We observe that he's seriously mistaken when he says "There are things you know for sure." We don't know anything for sure in this movie. We turn out to be lousy investigators. Or is it that in this postmodern world investigation is endemically lousy because we only always know things from a certain perspective? Because we remember things from the perspective of the present, we reason and come to conclusions within memory frames that are personally idiosyncratic and culturally bound. It's not a showstopper for Shelby when he turns over one snapshot with the note "Do not trust her" written on it and then turns over another snapshot with the note "Do not believe him" on it. He has just been told by the "him" (Teddy) that the "her" (Natalie) is not be trusted. So much for factual accounts. Inevitable perspective inevitably leads us to the Spanish Prisoner paradox.

For Shelby to get to the point when he can say "Someone is fucking with me, trying to get me to kill the wrong guy" he has to upgrade his valuation of memory. He has a fifteen-minute memory span: He's vulnerable. He's a sitting duck; he can be victimized, exploited, spun, manipulated, seduced, socially and personally engineered by anyone he runs into. The motel clerk, Burt, seems like a nice enough guy, but once he knows Shelby's memory problem he rents Shelby another room every time Shelby shows up. Shelby thinks Natalie is helping him because she has pity on him, but it remains unclear whether Natalie used Shelby to kill Teddy after Teddy used Shelby to kill her boyfriend, the drug dealer, Jimmy.

And we're manipulated and seduced as well. We think the beginning is the beginning. We think Shelby finally kills the man who killed his wife. We think that we were following this one investigation. We think Shelby is slowly learning what a tough bind he's really in and how incapable he is of doing what he wants to do: Find his wife's murderer. We even think his wife was murdered. We believe all this until all this is confounded in one way or another. What we become aware of is that there's been unknown rounds of investigation already.

Shelby has found his wife's murderer any number of times. What's special about this cycle of investigation is that Teddy, a cop who has been using Shelby as a hit man, loses his temper and gives Shelby some more "facts." Shelby's wife was attacked but survived and was subsequently given an overdose of insulin by Shelby. The story about Sammy Jankis, a man suffering from short-term memory loss who gives his wife an overdose of insulin because he can't remember having already given her previous shots and she goes along with it to find out if he really can't remember, is really a story about Shelby himself. Shelby's own memory of his wife refutes this. He doesn't remember her being diabetic. He has a visual memory of not giving her an insulin injection but just pinching her leg. Is Teddy's story a lie? Further manipulation? We have only Shelby's word that his memory before the accident is intact. Perhaps that memory is also subjected to a fifteen-minute rewrite. Shelby writes down Teddy's license plate number and makes a note to himself that the man who owns this car killed his wife. And thus when he reawakens to a new cycle of memory he will read that note and pursue Teddy. The film opens with the murder of Teddy. With this manipulator gone, are Shelby's problems over? Or will he be manipulated by the next person he runs into? Or will he wind up in the asylum that his memory has put the possibly fictitious Sammy Jankis in?

Look how different *Angel Heart*'s (1987) Mickey Rourke's Harry Angel's memory problems are when compared to Pearce's Shelby's. Harry Angel is a detective hired to find a man named Johnny Favorite who has disappeared. When we go from *Angel Heart* to *Memento* we've only traveled from 1987 to 2001 but we've actually gone from an immersion in certain familiar stories to a hyperconscious treatment of how we storify. Harry Angel's memory loss has roots in depth psychology: As the singer Johnny Favorite he's made a pact with the Devil (Lewis Cypher) in a voodoo rite, but after an accident and plastic surgery he's become Harry Angel, detective, a man who has no conscious memory of his earlier self. Hired by Cypher to find himself, Harry sets out in full investigative pursuit. At least it's his conscious self's investigation. But his buried self shadows the investigation and murders whoever has information to offer Harry. The Devil's bargain can't be settled until Harry is brought to a full awareness of who he really is. His memory loss fits a psychological urgency. It's a protective defense mechanism. There's no scrutiny and pondering of what memory is in the way Hamlet holds out Yorrick's skull and thinks on death. Harry's deal with memory can be found within modern depth psychology's plot of what memory is. Harry's caught in a late modernist frame, although one that treats rational investigation as reliable as voodoo belief. We're not repressing the irrational in the name of the rational. Every story, of devils or detectives, can generate its own need for repression, its own therapy and its own recuperation. It's all mythos, and no mythos is more reliable than any other in leading us to the truth of, for example, memory.

There's no narrative of memory that Lenny Shelby's deal with memory falls within. He's just a man with an impaired memory, a man who has no continuous memory of his thoughts or actions beyond fifteen-minute intervals. If Harry Angel is having an identity crisis, Lenny Shelby is discovering what it takes to bring the word "identity" to any kind of meaning. If Harry is unconsciously trying to escape a punishment he deserves, Lenny's detached from both the capacity to choose and the assumption of personal responsibility. If Harry is the self-deceived detective brought back to investigate his wrecked self, Lenny is the detective who reminds us that we, too, are following snapshots and tattooed facts toward conclusions and endings fantasized or not our own.

Are we correct in seeing *Angel Heart* as an allegory of the America Reagan began to create, a country hiding and repressing its dark beginnings in genocide, slavery, and the use of weapons of mass destruction on innocent civilians? Is Shelby's plight in *Memento*—his short-term memory loss—our best escape from our own history, our own cultural memory? Or is it a reminder of how a market-driven need for instant obsolescence now controls our access to our own cultural memory? There's a political faction that at some unconscious level feels a bargain made at the beginning . . . this brave new world that has such people in it . . . has to be remembered and fulfilled, that the only honor we can accrue derives from the persistence of what is best in our cultural memory. There is also a political faction that would preemptively strike out against those who question and jeopardize the honor we grant ourselves within a present fifteen-minute sound byte produced by Wall Street and Madison Avenue. When amnesia vanquishes the former faction while serving the latter, we become Leonard Shelby listening to a tale told by an idiot counseled by a wizard behind a curtain.

———◆———

THE BLOGOSPHERE

Blog: www.spinning.com

I think the point here is the content of our memories as much as the duration of our memories. A great recall facility scanning a mental repertoire of sports statistics is like a Lamborghini jacked up and spinning its wheels. It doesn't make any difference how much you rev it up, it's going no place. Leonard Shelby's problem is that he can't store new memories. Whatever he experiences has a fifteen-minute run and then it's gone. If he had been born with that kind of memory, he'd not have accumulated long-term memory. In the film, however, Shelby has a storehouse of long-term memory. Now, if it's beneficial for marketers to have consumers living in the veneer of today's fads and fashions and not yesterday's, then it seems that short-term amnesia would be a target. With short-term memory loss you could charge Shelby for a new motel room every time he shows up. Long-term memory loss suits an administration that wants to replace the Bill of Rights with September 11, 2001. However, if the newest generation of Americans starts off with a market-induced short-term amnesia, they will, of course, wind up with no historical memory. They will have an almost biological thirst for the newest new (which will keep them shopping). They will also have a total incapacity to summon from historical cultural memory any challenge to any political campaign that seems not to disturb their shopping.

Blog: www.cockrobin.com

"There are things you know for sure." Such as whether Saddam had WMDs? Were Saddam and bin Laden in a "the enemy of my enemy is my friend" kind of relationship, or not? Or right at this minute whether Iran is developing WMDs? How about whether Senator John Kerry was a Vietnam hero or a sham? Or whether George W. Bush did fulfill his national guard service or not? Did America's preemptive attack on Iraq lessen the al-Qaeda threat or strengthen it? Who killed Cock Robin? Who knows? How do you find out, regardless of whether you have a fifteen-minute memory or a one-hundred-year memory? Whatever retention period you have, what you do is establish facts, get them down, and then go on from that point in your next memory cycle to establish more facts, get those down, and go on from that point . . . until you get The Big Picture. This is a film about the scientific method, which for me has real connections with 9/11 and everything thereafter. We've ditched the scientific method and hired Karl Rove and his band of spin magicians. What's the pop-culture connection? Take a look at TV: sixty-five different versions of crime scene investigation, shows where somebody reminds us that "the physical evidence speaks for itself." Just like it did when Marcia Clark presented it at the O. J. Simpson trial. Just like Colin Powell presented it before the United Nations. Just at the moment when we are, post-9/11, deep into a return to the "superstitious rot and nonsense" that Bertrand Russell railed against, we're pushing our rational and empirical methodologies. Our CIA is feeding us empirically validated intell. NOT. We're planning to export our democracy and freedom all over the world even if we have to preemptively attack every country in the Middle East. And we're doing it all rationally, with facts and evidence, with indisputable proof, with rigorous review of all alternatives and so on. NOT!

There are things you know for sure, such as what "freedom" is, beyond not being in jail, and what "democracy" means, beyond one person/one vote. And for those who have forgotten, tune in to *Fox News*.

Blog: www.historybegins.com

Both history and death challenge the mission of the market, which is to maximize profit by creating new "needs." History is a warehouse of events and ideas that refer to very different missions. Death is an inevitability whose contemplation provokes a re-examination of earthly "needs." Mr. Bush wants history, everyone's history it seems, to begin on September 11, 2001. No challenge to the market there. But he also wants Americans to remain continuously terrorized, for political reasons, only one of which I will cite: Polls show that a majority of Americans believe Republicans will handle terrorism better than Democrats. This is historically not validated, but, nonetheless, it is the picture Americans have in their heads. Now an aspect of fear is death; it's our deaths we fear. Dirty bombs, poisons in our water, poisons in our food, Anthrax blowing in the breezes, and so on. But a populace saturated in fear and envisioning death may begin to question whether in the grand scheme of things comfort and speed and quantity and convenience were the aims of their lives, and perhaps whether or not they ever really did anything that needed to be done, or, for that matter, bought anything they really needed. They might even question whether they might have done something that would leave the world a better place than when they entered it. Perhaps they might ponder whether they voted for those who would do something for so many in the world in such great need. I believe it's a most dangerous game that Mr. Bush & Co. is playing: Putting death's head at our feet for our contemplation while hoping the consequences of that contemplation will not move this country from a pursuit of self-interest to a concern for humanity. But, of course, Mr. Bush & Co. have their faith to see them beyond the portal of death. This is not the first faith-based inhumanity in human history, but to *recall* this one would have to possess a memory of human history.

Blog: www.blowjobsandnotempire.com

I get it: There's more profit to shareholders if consumers can't remember things. It's a Republican victory when voters don't

THE BLOGOSPHERE

remember things. Facts either get forgotten, spun any which way, or don't connect with anything. We elected George W. Bush twice because he's like us: He lives in a fifteen-minute present and feels good about it. And, finally, we can't really remember what we did last Tuesday so what the hell kind of investigators of anything could we be, including our own lives? That being said, I want to say this: I can remember that we went through an impeachment of Bill Clinton for a blow job, and I can remember that George W. Bush joined Genghis Khan, Attila the Hun, Hitler, and Hirohito in preemptively attacking another country and did so based on a pack of lies. Am I going to come to the wrong conclusion here?

Shortscape

Never Far from Melodrama

> He would forget his fine disgusts, cease to rage against the tyranny of money—cease to be aware of it, even—cease to squirm at the ads for Bovex and Breakfast Crisps. He would sell his soul so utterly that he would forget it had even been his.
>
> —George Orwell, *Keep the Aspidistra Flying*

Characters: Rick Casablanca, owner of Rick's Café Norteamericano, the model for Rick's Café Americain in the film Casablanca; *Captain Louie: model for Captain Louis Renault played by Claude Rains in* Casablanca; *Major Strasser: the original Major Strasser of the Third Reich, killed by Rick in* Casablanca.

———◆———

Voice-over: Here's what you have to delete from the personal imaginary to make melodrama work in a postmodern age: self-reflexivity, irony, overstimulation, hyperconsciousness, self-interest, greed.

Here's what you'd have to remove from the cultural imaginary: Disneyland, instant messaging, credit cards, porn surfing, Oprah and Dr. Phil, day trading, Monday night football, hyperreality, cell phoning, bling bling, cyberspace, neighborhood shopping malls, celebrities, support groups, XBox and PlayStation, Tivo, reality TV, iPods.

Here's what you'd have to re-introduce into the personal imaginary: all of Dickens's novels, diaries, two years at Walden Pond, long walks on the moor, meditation, dreams and nightmares, afternoon naps, lunch boxes, sketch pads, epistolary novels, goldfish, bowling teams, nostalgia, heart. And into the cultural imaginary: meaningless rituals, a nineteenth-century rail system, poetry readings, Irish wakes, reel mowers, B-movies, family dinners, soda jerks and egg creams, Sundays in the park, ballroom dancing, radio dramas.

———◆———

Script Doctor: Delete this voice-over. The melodrama right up to Douglas Sirk in the 1950s is all of one piece: a hard-working working-class spends their dime on all the stuff they know but intensified and condensed in ways unavailable to them. Sometimes life is so hard they want to cry, or take to drink, or murder someone, or just rebel. But they aren't given the latitude to do any of that. They can't take anything to extreme levels; to stay alive they can't indulge in theatricality, in histrionics. They're understimulated, not overstimulated. There's no time for emotive outpourings given on the clock you punch every day. But it all lurks beneath the surface. Then you go to the pictures where you just don't get your own life thrown back at you, because who wants that factory life? What you get is what you know of life brought to cathartic emotive highs and lows so your imagination is vindicated, your emotions are allowed release, and your senses swell. Try it again.

———◆———

Voice-over: We no longer value an emotional or an imaginative life, and our senses have degraded into a purely passive, receptive mode. Everything is reduced to exchange value. What profit is there in our emotions? In our imagination? Our intellects are not sharp surgical instruments but blunted gatekeepers of Boolean bytes, of the endless deferment of e-mail messages and replies. Just as the peptic billionaire John D. Rockefeller envied the digestive system of a humble worker on his estate, we now envy the power of classic Hollywood melodrama to exercise the emotions, imaginations, and senses of its audience.

———◆———

Script Doctor: Use Captain Louie from *Casablanca* to point out the futile attempts in our postmodern age to recapture the power of melodrama.

———◆———

CAPTAIN LOUIE: My dear Rick, in the 1993 soapy melodrama *Sleepless in Seattle*, Tom Hanks refers to the 1957 soapy melodrama *An Affair to Remember* as a "chick's movie." *Sleepless* has been sampling *An Affair* throughout: We watch the characters in *Sleepless* watching *An Affair* on video: "I've watched this movie too many times," Meg Ryan's character, Annie, says at one point. The movie is threatening her very ordinary engagement to a very ordinary guy. The movie is kicking love up to High Romantic Melodrama levels.

RICK CÁSABLANCA: If you say so, Louie, but I think maybe she loves this guy the way she's already seen it in one of those melodramas.

CAPTAIN LOUIE: She resists that; but she can't. What's going on between the two films? Simply this: *Sleepless* wants to capture and exude the same melodramatic magic that made *An Affair* an unforgettable movie. The Hanks/Ryan movie wants to piggyback on the magic of the Grant/Kerr movie; the 1990s movie wants to jump out of the pastiche and parody mode of the 1990s and back to the unselfconscious naivete of the 1950s. The 1990s are saturated with a politics of suspicion. It's a far from sentiment atmosphere. Romantic love is a passé thing, a puritanical camouflage, a cheesy remnant of a time when sex was feared and repressed. The 1950s—whatever they were "in reality"—are in the 1990s assumed to be what Douglas Sirk shows them to be in his melodramas. And yet the 1950s *An Affair to Remember* has what the 1990s *Sleepless in Seattle* wants. How to steal the romantic fire of the 1950s movie without setting yourself up for the mockery the 1990s holds for melodramas?

RICK CÁSABLANCA: I think you're forgetting, Louie, that Sirk's melodramas are already panning the melodramas of the 1930s and 1940s. You see, Louie, the way I see it . . . and I'm just a saloon keeper . . . by the 1950s it was pretty clear that it was the Hollywood dream machine working the tear glands, just like they had a rainfall machine. It wasn't real; it wasn't life; it was all a Hollywood imitation of life. Sirk was pushing that machinery as far as it would go so you'd come out the other side and see you'd be taken for a ride. I'm not saying, of course, that it wasn't a ride he really enjoyed. Think of it this way, Louie. Here's a guy that can work up the hype from baroque to rococo and he likes to let you know that he knows it's hype. Nobody could do a melo like Sirk, but he's always telling you that this a Hollywood picture and not the world.

CAPTAIN LOUIE: Follow along, Rickie. We want that old-time romantic magic that pours out of Cary Grant and Deborah Kerr, but we don't want to face the cheesiness charge that naturally emerges in the hyperconscious, postmodern 1990s. The way *Sleepless* solves the dilemma is to take the offensive. It doesn't wait for the viewer to think *this is a cheesy chick's movie*. *Sleepless* attacks *An Affair to Remember* ("This is a chick's movie," Hanks says, as we watch the female characters weep over a viewing of the video of *An Affair*) and thereby distances itself from the overwrought melodrama of the earlier melodrama. *Sleepless* shows its 1990s mockery credentials; the movie is too hip to fall into such romantic schmaltz. But, of course, at the same time, *Sleepless is* a high-schmaltz movie, like *An Affair*, except for this: No one will be watching a video of *Sleepless* fifty years from now.

RICK CÁSABLANCA: Yeah, but that Bogart melo, *Casablanca*, is timeless.

CAPTAIN LOUIE: I don't know, Rickie. If you sampled *Casablanca* right now, say in some kind of parody of real and fantastical film genres would the twentysomethings pick up on it?

RICK CÁSABLANCA: Times change, Louie.

CAPTAIN LOUIE: But more importantly, Rickie, our sense of time changes. We can't do a timeless classic now; we can't give anything a permanent place in time. Think of it like memorializing a computer screen you surf onto. It's not in the cards. In *Sleepless* I think maybe it's because for all the sampling of Cary Grant's charisma, Tom Hanks is so obviously *not* Cary Grant. That's perhaps the most vulnerable aspect of sampling the earlier film: When one thinks of the earlier movie, one realizes sadly that the magic that *Sleepless* tries to reinstall in romance is absent from this movie but present in the earlier movie. Cary Grant was a cultural construction; a persona of a cultural imaginary that Hollywood had shaped; romance was inflected by music (melos) and a heightened sense of drama. The 1993 movie has a double-edged, parodying soundtrack. Jimmy Durante "unsings" "As Time Goes By" at the movie's beginning. This isn't Sam tickling the keyboard and singing "As Time Goes By" at Rick's Café Americain. This is Durante's croak of a love song. The dramatic plot of the 1993 movie also draws back from the heights and does so mostly through Hanks' puncturing comic repartee, directed at self as well as the world. The picture is too obviously a picture of a melodrama; Hanks and Ryan are too flip to be serious and soap.

RICK CÁSABLANCA: *Sleepless* wants to recapture the magic of *An Affair* but the more it tries, the worse it is. Look, Louie, melodrama was a contrived, soapy, cheap shot at reality and the audiences who were swept away and wept real tears were incredulous, unsophisticated saps. They didn't get enough hype in their real lives so they had to rush off to the flicks.

CAPTAIN LOUIE: That's right, Rickie. They would seriously rush to see a film with a title like *All That Heaven Allows* or *Magnificent Obsession* and not expect a send-up, a clever deconstruction of heaven and hell, a multilayering of clashing stories in search of a center. They would expect to see their emotions and desires, their fears and anxieties modeled for them on the screen, unmediated by anything more than the charismatic inflections of Cary Grant's speech or Joan Crawford's eyes. This direct hook-up with reality, especially the reality of love, is like a thing lost to the world that *Sleepless* comes out of. Lost but still sought, my dear Rick.

RICK CÁSABLANCA: I stick my neck out for nobody, Louie, but the way I see it, this Douglas Sirk guy touched a hot spot in that film of his. One you mention: *All That Heaven Allows*. Now when you see the 2002 Todd Haynes parody, *Far from Heaven*, it's slick alright. I mean, the way he does a hats off to Sirk and mocks him at the same time. Thinks he's dealing with stuff Sirk wouldn't or couldn't touch.

CAPTAIN LOUIE: And you think he doesn't, Rick?

RICK CÁSABLANCA: It's pretty clear that *All That Heaven Allows* is using the love story between an upper-middle-class widow and her younger gardener as a front. For what? For exposing the class elitism and class division in a country that turned its back on European elitism and stood up for what they called back in them days "the common man."

CAPTAIN LOUIE: And woman, Rick. You want to be politically correct in the new millennium.

RICK CÁSABLANCA: Women don't want to be called common, Louie. Thing is, in Sirk's film both the guy and the gal take it on the chin. She traffics down below the country club line so she has to see the error of her ways and hope they'll welcome her back in the fold. You know that fold, Louie, it folds the right people in and the wrong people out.

CAPTAIN LOUIE: Yes, but Rick, you're missing all the delightful mischief in Hayne's detailed portraiture of that repressed and suppressed 1950s world.

RICK CÁSABLANCA: You trying to tell me, Louie, that fifty years from now some post-postmod director won't bring the dawn of the third millennium to the screen in what you call a delightfully mischievous way? Don't kid yourself, Louie, Haynes is backing off. Thing is, he's backing off from what Sirk took on. Class warfare. And why is he backing off? Because conservatives have managed to outlaw the use of what they call the "class warfare card." They were using the race card as late as the 1988 presidential election when Bush Sr. ran the Willy Horton spots on TV. You couldn't run on a war of Haves and Have-Nots in 1988. Why? Cause the Have-Nots couldn't say they were

Have-Nots without labeling themselves "Losers." It was a real bind. Conservative social engineering at its finest, Louie, its very finest.

CAPTAIN LOUIE: My dear Rick, Haynes runs his fingers across the fine façade of 1950s respectability and then rips it off and exposes the hypocrisy underneath. Of course, as I've already said, Sirk wove that fine façade grandiloquently enough for us to see it. Here's another Hollywood fabrication with a caveat emptor reminder.

RICK CÁSABLANCA: You know, Louie, all you've got to do in our new millennium to get high marks in the serious social criticism game in the liberals' playbook is tweak the cultural constructiveness of gender, sexual preference, race, and ethnicity. You leave the class divide and the wealth gap alone. They don't exist. Then the conservatives refer to stuff like moral values, family values, choice, personal responsibility, equal opportunity, democracy, like we all naturally and inherently went along with their spins on all of these.

CAPTAIN LOUIE: Rick, this is Major Heinrich Strasser of the Third Reich.

MAJOR STRASSER: Are you one of those people, Mr. Rick, who can't imagine a man with a German accent as governor of California?

RICK CÁSABLANCA: Life imitates art, Major. Or haven't you heard? Now let me ask you one. Two versions of the same melodrama: *Imitation of Life*. One's done in 1934 and the other in 1959. I'm partial to the 1934. Don't get me wrong. It's trying to jerk my emotions around, but generally I'm partial to the movies of the 1930s and 1940s. Closer to the bone. Less glitz. More working-class heroes. More guys and gals down on their luck. War brought us together like we had one national mood. Fifties. Tight box always coming apart. Sixties. The explosion. Seventies. Short road to Reagan.

CAPTAIN LOUIE: Rick's a hopeless romantic, Major. He comes right out of a movie like *Casablanca*. The jaded hero who makes the noble gesture in the end. And tells his friend Major Renault that this is the beginning of a beautiful friendship.

MAJOR STRASSER: Why would you think, Mr. Rick, that emotions run truer in bad times than in good times? Or do you think the older and mustier a film looks, the closer it is to truth and reality? Are you going to tell me that civilization and progress have dulled our capacity to feel and to imagine? Or, are we now just too wise, too aware, too sensitized to be manipulated by melodramatic love and tragedy?

RICK CÁSABLANCA: Seen too much or heard too much, maybe, Major. All I know is what I see in the movies. And I remember that scene in *A*

Clockwork Orange where they keep this juvenile delinquent's eyelids open, tie him to a chair, and stuff him full of moving pictures and noise. Overstimulation is like a narcotic, Major. It desensitizes. Modern and postmodern advertising and marketing campaigns rub out any space for the kind of imagination you need to narrate the world and respond to narrations about the world.

MAJOR STRASSER: Do you lament the fact that the world has become a more interesting place, Mr. Rick? Free of what you call overstimulation, what does the human mind do but build castles out of air? And without a rich mental palette of human experiences we are susceptible to the excesses and falsification, the exaggerations of melodramas. We are too alert to such misrepresentations now. And why? Because we live in an age of spectacle and, therefore, we are Magister Ludi of spectacle. We cannot easily be deceived, at least no longer by the bathos of an over-sentimentalized movie like *Imitation of Life*.

RICK CÁSABLANCA: You'll have to excuse me, Major, my business is running a saloon. But I've got this theory about movie melodramas that goes like this: The 1934 *Imitation of Life* was an unapologetic tugging at the heartstrings that had something to do with the first signs of a post-Depression upbeat mood in the country. So the rags-to-riches story in the 1934 film has a broad cultural context. At the same time the film takes on a deeper depression that darkens the cultural psyche: race. Here's an American birth defect that's not rebounding like the stock market. Fortune doesn't mean a thing to Delilah, because her daughter's black, looks white, and wants to pass for white. Maybe the film wants all blacks to stop trying to be white, stop trying to be equal with whites and settle for what God has made them. Delilah has accepted her lot; it was her pancake recipe that made the fortune, but it's the white woman who can live a fortunate life. If God's hand were behind this setup, Delilah's wish to die would be an act of rebellion. She does die, willfully, and it's pretty clear she wants to be rid of a world in which there is no justice for blacks—and that injustice is not God's creation but man's.

CAPTAIN LOUIE: So I suppose the Americans went back twenty-five years later and did the movie again because their conscience was still plagued by what you call the birth defect of slavery and racism?

RICK CÁSABLANCA: They went back to do it better, Louie. It wasn't that the 1934 film was too cheesy. It was a repackaging of the cheese in a new and modern wrap. What brought tears to your eyes in the 1934 film was the fact that you could imagine yourself in that rags-to-riches story. America was experiencing a "New Deal," a come back after being knocked down. The 1959 film is loaded only with Hollywood's presumption that it could reflect just Hollywood and *that* was American culture; it could just put a Lana Turner in full Technicolor on the screen and trigger Hollywood's success story. Which was what? Lana Turner was seen in a tight sweater in a Hollywood drugstore and immediately put under contract. The 1959 *Imitation* imitates that Lana Turner success story, her rise to stardom. Lana's own daughter had killed Lana's gangster boyfriend. Her picture was her life and her life was the American dream. Glitz and glamour. And the dark side of the dream, violence and death, were there, too. And the race issue? The 1934 Peola is now Sarah Jane, and what Sarah Jane wants is to be a saloon stripper and singer; she wants to pass for white so she can get to Hollywood.

CAPTAIN LOUIE: I get it, Rick. Viewers in 1934 have their heartstrings plucked because the melodrama comes out of the world they're in. They know in ways similar to the ways characters on the screen know the world they're in. Viewers in 1959 go to the movies to have their heartstrings plucked by a Hollywood melodrama that comes out of Hollywood's version of the world—which they accept because it's both seductive and repressive. They wanted their reality "Sirked" up, if you will. They didn't want a clear reflection of their own lives.

MAJOR STRASSER: You say repressive. In what way, Capitain Louie?

RICK CÁSABLANCA: Hollywood always helps us repress what might burst the balloon, right Louie?

CAPTAIN LOUIE: Exactly, Rickie.

RICK CÁSABLANCA: Let's say you learn to substitute the emotions on the screen for your own. It's the very beginning of a total simulation of emotional response. Which takes us back to Todd Haynes's *Far from Heaven* and Nora Ephron's *Sleepless in Seattle*. You see, Major, both those films want to distance themselves from the mawkishness and hearts-and-flowers of melodramas like the 1934 *Imitation of Life* and the 1957 *An Affair to Remember*. Audiences are no longer sponges waiting to sop up all the sappy stuff. But they also want to distance themselves from melodrama remakes like the 1959 *Imitation of Life*, a film that stylizes and glitzes reality to the point of embarrassment.

CAPTAIN LOUIE: Which was where Sirk wanted to take us. And now in the postmodern age, the new millennial awareness, films like *Far from Heaven* and *Sleepless in Seattle* can only cast a skeptical eye on Hollywood modelings of reality. They're busy unraveling the legerdemain of moviemaking and exposing bedrock reality. Or so they think. I personally think that for all their flippant sampling of classic melodrama they are pathetically aware of their inferiority.

———◆———

Script Doctor: Okay. What are we saying here? Really. Classic melodramas of the 1930s and 1940s connect somehow with a real-world surround. They play out issues like race, class, and poverty. You get to Sirk's films in the 1950s, and the Hollywood style now replaces any real-world connection. Sirk makes us aware through the very extravagance of his production and direction that this is a picture and not the world at the same time as he seduces us by means of that same extravagance of production and direction. We get up to the present moment, and melodramas don't play at all except in pastiche or parody, both of which reveal an elemental loss of attachment with reality and a suspicion of all representations. There's modernist angst lurking there, an ontological quest for true being in the world and all of that. Do a voice-over that takes us from this sort of modernist psychology to a postmodernist one. Go back to what Major Strasser began . . .

———◆———

Voice-over: Psychologically, moviegoers of the classic melodramas were in need of a Saturday night B-movie melodrama and its heightened, histrionic, overcharged display of emotions. They needed to pump up their flat, nine-to-five factory lives with huge rushes of on-screen drama that were denied them everywhere else. Let's say everyday life overwhelmed them, but emotionally and imaginatively and sensuously they were understimulated. By the 1950s, attention must be paid to the dream factory itself—Hollywood. What ordinary life denied the many could be transmitted by Hollywood. The lives of Hollywood stars as well as the transformative magic of Hollywood glossed the plots of every melodrama. Moviegoers of the past—unassaulted by the myriad varieties of telecom links into private lives faced by those in the new millennium—were set up for all that Hollywood could offer. Switch to the present: Rather than being understimulated, present moviegoers are overstimulated by the aggressive offensive launched by marketers and politicians who are so aggressive because folks today are already jacked into cyberspace or iPods, interfacing with XBox video games, poking at Palm Pilots and Gameboys, endlessly receiving or making cell phone calls, or staring at MTV, or pretending in a post-9/11 world that they are "survivors." Whether their emotional, imaginative, or sensuous lives have been pulverized by such an assault, or totally fulfilled by the same, is open to debate. What is clear is that melodramas of the past both display what the present cannot receive and demand what the present cannot give. A hyperreality that only Hollywood could lay claim to is now an ordinary feature of everyday life. A hunger for life at histrionic levels is now replaced by a hunger for raw, unhyped, unspun, undramatized, unproduced productions. Reality TV situates "real" people within "real" settings and proceeds without a script. That all this is a picture of "real" people, etc., and not really "Real" people, etc., is, as always, what must be concealed. Already emotionally and imaginatively drained, viewers have no inclination to accept more stimulation. That's the kind portrayal. What may actually be going on is a degradation of viewers' capacity to extend imaginatively and emotionally into a melodrama. There may be no need of catharsis, because there is no need for emotional release if emotions are vestigial, and there may be no identification with the characters of melodrama because there is no projective imagination tying the viewer to the viewed. Therefore it's not a postmodern hyperconsciousness that distances us from melodrama but a loss of affective response.

———◆———

RICK CÁSABLANCA: To complete the tale I'm telling here, Major, and not the one you've just heard, we go from total credulousness to presumptuous manipulation to endless deconstruction. What's ironic is that the only way to deconstruct is to set up a construction—a patsy you then slap down.

CAPTAIN LOUIE: And what's even more ironic, Rick, is this setting up and tearing down, these parodies exposing the hypocrisy and gullibility of the past, wind up exposing what the present lacks in relation to what the past possessed.

RICK CÁSABLANCA: You said a mouthful, Louie. They wanted to ditch the hyppereality of the 1959 *Imitation of Life*, but they wanted somehow to re-tap the wellsprings of genuine emotion that was there in some of those old melodramas, like a pearl in an oyster.

CAPTAIN LOUIE: Did you ever see *The Champ*, Rick? The 1931 not the 1979. A real weepie, but there's something bedrock authentic about the feelings it creates.

RICK CÁSABLANCA: I'm partial to "Jerry, we have the stars. Let's not ask for the moon."

MAJOR STRASSER: *Now, Voyager*. Bette Davis. But don't you choke up more in the final scene of Miss Davis's *Dark Victory*?

CAPTAIN LOUIE: Why, Major, you surprise me. Next you'll be saying *Little Lord Fauntleroy* brings tears to your eyes.

RICK CÁSABLANCA: That's right, Major. Better watch it. What will the Third Reich think? Next you'll be weeping over dog movies like *Lassie, Come Home*, and *Old Yeller*. I'd have figured you'd have more sympathy for the hound than the fox, Major. Disney animation like *Bambi* and *Dumbo* will steal your heart away.

CAPTAIN LOUIE: But what about the theory, Rick, that our emotional response has been short-circuited by our market-driven barrage of advertising spectacle? And that assault has made us so wary that we're virtually affectless. Am I right?

RICK CÁSABLANCA: Overgeneralized, Louie. You need somebody to lay out the detail. Look at it this way, Louie. We're supersaturated with appeals to go out there and shop. But what makes you shop? Desire. What's the biggest player in the desire game? Sex. So sexual desire has to be attached to everything. That's a market manipulation. Meanwhile, sympathy and compassion, which kick in at higher levels of imaginative projection than sex, don't figure in. They're left to die on the vine, if you see what I mean.

MAJOR STRASSER: And why is that, Mr. Rick?

RICK CÁSABLANCA: Because if you exercise your imagination enough you'll realize that it doesn't take much to see that the problems of three little people don't amount to a hill of beans in this crazy world. Someday you'll understand that.

CAPTAIN LOUIE: Round up the usual suspects. But not the film.

———◆———

THE BLOGOSPHERE

Blog: www.premodernnow.com

I don't agree that post-9/11 Americans can't follow a melodrama script. Sure they can. What do I mean by melodrama? It's *sayonara* to rationality. It happens when you get so emotionally lost in a concocted narrative that you go pre-Enlightenment. It's Garry Will's lament on November 4, 2004 in the *New York Times* Op-Ed page. That 2004 Presidential vote was the Day the Enlightenment Went Out. And this from Joan Didion: "This was a year in which it would come to seem as if we had been plunged at one fell stroke into a pre-modern world. The possibilities of the Enlightenment vanished" ("Fixed Ideas," *The New York Review of Books*, January 16, 2003). We're obviously living at a time when we can be swayed as we were by those old Hollywood melodramas. And the Dubya people know how to script a melodrama.

"This White House is famously secretive and on-message, but its skills go beyond that. It knows the power of narrative, especially a single narrative with clean-cut heroes and evildoers, and it knows how to drown out any distracting subplots before they dominate the main story" (Frank Rich, Preface to Didion's *Fixed Ideas: America Since 9.11*).

We're not overstimulated by Madison Avenue to the point that we have no emotional response. The opposite is true: September 11 has traumatized us in a way that has brought all our irrational ways of responding to the world to the forefront while at the same time enervating our "cool rationality." How else to explain a twice-elected president who never ever appeals to reason but always to melodramas and cowboy justice, of Axis of Evil, and Wanted Dead or Alive? Here's a twice-elected president who preemptively attacks another country based on "instinctual response," a president who in the twenty-first century in a secular democracy looks to "faith-based policies" as rational policies.

Melodrama is alive and well.

Blog: www.doorofimagination.com

I want to speak up on behalf of art, the most innovative art form of the twentieth century—film. Mr. Natoli's thesis is, in brief, that Americans' capacity to respond on any affective level has been worn out by aggressive advertising, by an overstimulation of our souls. This steady barrage of directives to shop, to lose weight, to take a "mystery cruise," to botox, to color the gray, to Viagra, to call E. F. Hutton, to pimp your ride, to catalog, to go on-line, to save the Sudan, and on and on and on, overstimulates their receptive neural networks and eventually puts them on "automatic." Their sensitivity to the finer edges of life is worn down. If the average American could manage to be stranded on a distant island—like Tom Hanks in *Castaway*—his or her imagination could be regenerated, like a liver can be regenerated. And that imagination would re-enkindle a rich emotional life while living close to nature would re-enkindle one's senses.

So the story told here goes.

But the average American isn't lucky enough to be stranded on a deserted island. So what then gives us passage to our own affective being? Art. Film, for instance. I've just seen a film that actually makes this transforming process of art its subject. The film is *The Door in the Floor*—the film's title but also the title of a children's book written by Ted, played by Jeff Bridges. A student who has written a twenty-eight-page paper on this children's book states categorically that the child's desire to go through the door in the floor is an archetypal desire to return to the womb.

The whole film, however, is about how one tells a story (for example, Ted teaching his summer intern, Eddie, how to be a writer) and, therefore, I suggest that the "door" is art, namely Ted's fictionalizing and his painting of nudes, and the director's, Todd Williams', film. The "floor" then is this "real world" we walk upon. The film imaginatively represents and reshapes and transforms the world, even the media and marketing overloaded world of the present that Tom Vanderbilt calls "the advertised life." The "advertised life" is "an emerging mode of being in which advertising not only occupies every last negotiable public terrain, but in which it penetrates the cognitive process, invading consciousness to such a point that one expects and looks for advertising, learns to lead life as an ad, to think like an advertiser, and even to anticipate and insert oneself in successful strategies of marketing" (Baffler #6, in *Commodify Your Dissent: Salvos from the Baffler*, Thomas Frank and Matt Weiland, eds., W.W. Norton, 1997).

The Door in the Floor leads us slowly from a floor of reality so shadowed and haunted by some unrevealed past tragedy that there seems to be no order to it. Eddie, the young intern, enters a divided world, husband and wife separated but also trying to hold together a center for their daughter who is imaginatively bound to a tableau of photographs from the past. She wakes looking for this or that photograph, a representation of a past she never knew but yet is somehow reassuring to her in the present. We, the viewers, the audience of this film are lost in this fractured world; we can't find the door into it or out of it. This is indeed a world in which people have separated from any emotional attachment to others or anything around them. They are not the Dead-in-Life for the reasons presented in "Never Far From Melodrama" but they are Dead-in-Life and will therefore stand for the "affect-less" described in this essay.

Halfway through the film, Ted critiques Eddie's writing and we realize that we, like Eddie, have been interns. We are given a lesson on how to find the door in the floor. We also realize that the scenes we have been watching are Eddie's creation, his narrative, his point of view, his representation. The scenes generate no sense of anticipation, no interest on our part, no surprises, no sense of imaginative transformation, because Eddie doesn't have the art to transform, doesn't know how to find the door of transformative art in the floor of disparate reality.

Eddie's probing into the past leaves Marion, Ted's wife, catatonic. Eddie can't find the door to her emotional being, because he remains on the level of a reality she is trying to escape. Ted, however, is the *Magister Ludi* here, the Magus; he tells Eddie a story of an auto tragedy in which both their sons died. And in telling the story, Ted uses all the tools at the disposal of the artist—pain, betrayal, death—that he has instructed Eddie are the tools of fiction, of all art, tools that Eddie lacks. Like a painter—or filmmaker—Ted uses all the colors on his palette. And we understand at this moment that the film we have been watching is the door of art that leads us through and ultimately out of the floor of a tragic reality.

Art has the capacity to do that for "the advertised life," "the overstimulated life," even the life severed by personal tragedy. The question arises, however, whether Ted's art of narration—Tod Williams' directorial art/John Irving's narrative art—has led us to an imaginative entrance into the order and meaning of reality, or has it led us to a transformative place where art and imagination slip through a door in the floor of reality into a fabricated world of their own making?

In a penultimate scene, as Eddie leaves, Ted tells him the brand name of a shoe that one of his sons was wearing on the day of the fatal accident. The shoe is important because his wife, Marion, had gone to pick it up and discovered that it was attached to her son's severed leg. "Specific details, Eddie," Ted tells him. "Specific details." The specific details that Ted has told Eddie are essential to fiction have also been essential to his account of the "real" accident. Has this film employed its art as a tool to bring us to some emotional/imaginative/sensuous grasp of reality, or has it been a door through which we can escape that reality to another place, to a world within a photograph that somehow mysteriously dispels our nightmares?

In the last scene of the film, Ted is on his racquetball court building up a sweat. He collapses to the floor, reaches over and opens up a hidden door in the floor that he disappears into. If there has been any doubt that he is the Magus and therefore the artificer of what we have seen, the revealer of the door of the imagination, it is here dispelled.

In the end, in his treatment of melodrama, the writer of "Never Far From Melodrama," like Eddie, stays on the outside, on a media-saturated floor, for sure, but he fails to seek the door that all art, including film, possesses. This is a failure of all discussion that treats any form of art as a function or a mirror of the surround, whether it be a traumatized post-9/11 America, or a cold war America, or a Disneyland America. Melodrama, however, is a flagrant expression of art's adding music to life, of offering us through its own expressive means an imaginative door into the landscape of America—and you cannot pass through that door unless you set out to find it.

THE BLOGOSPHERE

Trailer

The Jesus Genre

It was now possible "to believe" in one proposition or another on the basis of no evidence that it was so. . . . [F]ew elected officials are anxious to go on the line against faith.
—Joan Didion, "Politics in the 'New Normal' America,"
The New York Review of Books, October 21, 2004

Is the United States turning into the Republic of Gilead? That was the name of the theocratic Christian America that Margaret Atwood imagined in her novel *The Handmaid's Tale*. Following the November election in the United States, a map circulating on the internet showed the blue states of the east and west coast annexed to Canada, with the red-state portions of the country that had voted Republican labeled "Jesusland."
—Michael Lind, "Red-state Sneer," *Prospect*, January, 2005

Film as a fictional medium might appear a poor substitute for effective political agency; nevertheless, it has an important role to play in mythologizing and framing current cultural debate.
—David Henninger, "Wonderland: Blue Democrats Lost Red America Back in 1965,"
Wall Street Journal, November 5, 2004

The Passion I think is junk, but at least it's not trivial, cynical junk in the usual style of postmodernist pop—the gleeful rooting around in the scrap heap of discarded illusion, Kill Bill-ism for nonbelievers. No, *The Passion* is medievalist junk, a literal, blood-and-bone rendering of agony and death, and, for the audience coming to it with the right emotional wiring, seeing is believing.

—David Denby, "The Quick and the Dead,"
The New Yorker, January 16, 2005

Script Doctor: Here's the motivation: We fear we're into a Holy War, we're back to the Crusades. Where's the dog-wagging here? In one shot, a Holy War summons fear and resolve. We fear the whole Middle East, every Arab who is really an Arab, and everybody else who we think is an Arab, including Sikhs. The resolve comes in because it's a "holy" war not just, God forbid, a war over oil or a DoD contract. Americans are standing up for Christ, just as he stood up for us. We're threatened, but we're dedicated to winning. Enter the George W. Bush team on offense. And defense. Run this with a guy who doesn't see any good in Christianity, a parody of Bill Maher, and bring up Mel Gibson's *The Passion of the Christ.* Roll it.

——◆——

BILL MARRED: Thank you. You're too kind. Are we in post-9/11 fear gear in this country so anything that comes down the pike gets greeted by the fear factor? Yeah, I'm talking about the presidential election. Let me tell you folks we can be gotten. And it's easy now. All anybody has to do is say "bin Laden." Or 9/11. Or al-Qaeda. Here to talk to us tonight is a Liberal Security Mom; Assistant Secretary of Defense, Paul Wolfish; pop singer Brittney Fears; filmmaker Michael Lessismore; and Anarcho-syndicalist, Chum Chimpsky. *The Others* (2001). Is the fear evoked in this film a first run at exploiting 9/11 fear?

SECURITY MOM: There were no Arabs in this movie, so I don't see the 9/11 connection, but I will tell you that I identified with the mother. With Nicole Kidman. Her husband is off fighting in Iraq and she's doing everything she can to hold the family together, to protect her children. In this country we are, unfortunately, surrounded by disaffected people who want to enter our homes and destroy our families. I thought this was a strong family values movie . . .

BILL MARRED: Come on now. You identified with the mom? She's dead. She's haunting the house she's living in. The good guys are the ones she thinks are the bad guys. I mean, isn't this the kind of role reversal you get if you go anyplace in the Middle East and ask them, *who are the bad guys here?* I know we think we're the good guys. And the whole family values thing is just as shaky. I mean the cozy family we become part of is a family of dead people. We assumed they were haunted, but instead they were doing the haunting.

WOLFISH: We didn't attack Afghanistan or Iraq until after we were attacked, Bill. We're not haunting the Middle East. They've gotten into our household and are doing everything they can to keep us fearful.

LESSISMORE: I think oil has forced us into every household in the Middle East for a very long time, Mr. Secretary.

BILL MARRED: Okay. Let's get back on track. Is Hollywood playing to the post 9/11 fear? We know it worked in the election.

SECURITY MOM: Moral issues were what people were concerned with.

BILL MARRED: Give me a break. That's a code word for Bush's people having issues with gays getting married.

WOLFISH: There's real fear there, Bill.

BILL MARRED: Yeah, but it's not 9/11 fear. Are you telling me fear of gays trumped fear of bin Laden?

SECURITY MOM: 9/11 was more of a New York thing. What red-state America fears is a seeping moral decay instigated by Hollywood.

LESSISMORE: I know what moral decay means. Twelve-year-old girls wanting to be Brittney Spears showing her midriff or Janet Jackson showing her tit.

BILL MARRED: And don't leave out the idea that blow jobs are not a sex thing. I mean who's launching the sex campaign? The Democratic Party or Madison Avenue? Without repressed, infantilized sexuality in the United States, Madison Avenue wouldn't be able to push product.

WOLFISH: We're not Islamic about sex, Bill. You know that. I know that. But we are facing a declared jihad against Americans and we're not sure why.

BILL MARRED: Maybe it's because Bush has been following a road map to jihad instead of to peace in Palestine. Fact is, Wolfish, that folks in Indiana are worried about a kid being adopted by gays and not worried about a terrorist on a plane to Disneyland.

CHUM: I don't think Bush won in 2004 because a campaign of fear was waged or a campaign of moral issues. I think a foundation of hate was laid that trumped fear. You don't fear for four years; at some point in there your fear turns to hatred. And war follows on the heels of hatred, and that war, regardless of how stupidly it's waged, and how many people die, is a child of hatred, which means we never think of disowning it. It's off the table and no longer under consideration. Only liberals and those in various places on the left were still considering it. The rest of the country, which turned out to be enough for a Bush victory, were free to be seduced and spun in other directions. The gay marriage issue, like 9/11 itself, fell in the neocon's lap.

WOLFISH: An awful lot of hatred has to be behind an "anybody but Bush" campaign.

CHUM: I'm referring to one movie.

BILL MARRED: I know you're talking about *The Passion of the Christ* (2004). Tell me you're not going to try to link *The Passion* with . . . I mean, it's not a thriller. It's not a movie that makes its audience cringe in fear.

LESSIMORE: I think the idea here is that it's a film that made us hate more than fear. We got a chance to rally around Christ while getting a good look at his killers. I mean, why would the average American in Nebraska watching that movie hook up the dark, foreign-speaking murderers of Christ with Jews? Most of red America has never even seen a Jew. But at the moment they're watching the film, we are in a war on terror; we are fighting radical, Islamic fundamentalists. The villains of that movie are not the Israelis living in the Middle East but the Arabs.

BILL MARRED: So when folks are saying Michael Moore's *Fahrenheit 9/11* (2004) preached hate and would be the reason Kerry won the election, if he did win, you're saying Bush did actually win the election and Mel Gibson's *The Passion of The Christ* had a lot to do with it.

CHUM: It reached into the mass psyche and settled Iraq and the war on terror in Bush's favor. After all, he was the man in the White House who had waged these wars. Bush already had their hearts on this. Once the most important issues of the campaign were no longer issues, all that was needed was to distract them from their economic woes: enter "moral issues."

BILL MARRED: Yeah, and that one was built on fear and hate, too. What do men fear in the reptilian part of their brains? That they're gay. Come on now. What's all the macho posturing about if it isn't supposed to prove you're not gay?

WOLFISH: I think we fight to survive, Bill, not prove we're not gay.

BILL MARRED: We went into survivor mode pretty quick. One attack on home soil and everybody is watching a bunch of idiots on TV who couldn't survive without a cell phone.

CHUM: You've deciphered the gay code that the Bush people used?

BILL MARRED: Okay. Guys fear they might be gay. That fear turns to hatred of gays. The image of two men together disgusts them. You know why? Because deep down their reptilian brain is interested and that subconscious whatever-it-is disgusts them. Karl Rove marketed that hate to a victory for Bush.

WOLFISH: I think you're letting your reptilian brain, as you call it, take over your rationality, Bill. I thought we were talking about *The Passion of the Christ*?

BRITTNEY FEARS: I saw that movie.

BILL MARRED: Yeah, Britt, give us your impressions.

BRITTNEY: There was a lot of background stuff missing.

BILL MARRED: Like, how could one guy get himself into so much trouble with the authorities?

BRITTNEY: Yeah, like that. It sort of starts at the end like *Pulp Fiction* (1994). I know it was a star vehicle for Jim whatever but you still, like, you know, need a plot or a story people, like, know. You know what I mean?

BILL MARRED: It's called the Bible, Brit.

LESSISMORE: It's a hate movie. Jesus is a good guy who gets his ass kicked, gets tortured like he was at Abu Ghraib, but that's just the first part of the movie. That was the Empire doing its dirty deed. But then there's a return of the Jedi. The Jesus.

BRITTNEY: I saw that movie. Jesus wasn't in it.

BILL MARRED: You know it reminds me of the way Mel Gibson gets fired up in all his movies. *The Patriot* (2000). First he's a peacenik because he's seen too much war but then one of his sons is killed by this British sadist and . . .

LESSISMORE: He sits in the tomb with a purposeful look on his face, then gets up and walks out of that tomb with some "we're going to triumph" miltaristic music on the soundtrack. This is the Hollywood here's-your-hero, here's-your-hero-getting-thrashed-by-the-bad-guys, here's-the-moment-when-you-can't-figure-out-how-your-hero-is-going-to-make-a-comeback.

BILL MARRED: It's your typical Hollywood naïve realist format. Gibson took the four Gospels, which really parallel more of a David Lynch script than the script to Gibson's *We Were Soldiers* (2002), and goes Hollywood on them.

LESSISMORE: The good guy is brought to the edge of death and then bounces back and kicks butt. But here we've got a topper. The good guy actually dies. If you figure the intensity of the hero's retribution is proportional to the intensity of the villain's evil, then you can't top actually killing the hero.

CHUM: The closest to that is *The Count of Monte Cristo* (2002). Remember, a man is wrongly imprisoned and suffers greatly but then escapes by sewing himself into a dead man's shroud? He subsequently has revenge on his tormentors.

LESSISMORE: Jim Caviezel was the Count. Same guy who played Jesus in Gibson's movie. If you make that transference at the end of *The Passion* you know Jim's going out there, like Gibson has done in some many of his movies, and he is going to even the score.

WOLFISH: Is there anything wrong with us evening the score in Iraq?

BILL MARRED: Hey, we're not the only ones with a warrior religion. Bring the Holy War on. But leave the rest of us out of it. Call us secularists, call us the blue states. But just don't call us to fight your wars.

LESSISMORE: The warrior was never going to be Kerry even though he had the Silver Star. The Warrior was Jesus. Gibson brought that home in his film. Jesus goes through 9/11, is killed, and then he rises up and struts out in a glorious return. And Dubya? The guy who didn't go to 'Nam, who didn't get a Silver Star? He's a born-again. He's a warrior in Jesus's army. Kerry wasn't running against Dubya. He was running against Jesus.

BILL MARRED: Look, you know why Jesus monopolizes morality? Because he's been packaged in this country away from any surrounding political or social issues. I mean, you can do nothing to help anybody but yourself and still be a good Christian because you went to church, voted against gay marriage, give your old clothes to St. Vincent de Paul, and don't use the "F word." Meanwhile, the poor will always be with us, and anyway, God helps the have-nots who learn how to fish and don't expect the haves to be sharing their fish with them.

CHUM: Capitalism invests in an ethics that can't be traced back to it.

BILL MARRED: You'll have to explain that, Chum.

CHUM: Put simply, evidence that capitalism savages most people's lives is not admitted into the courtroom of moral judgment. Are the Seven Deadly Sins sins of purely personal commission and omission, or, are they fed by the capitalist will to turn all worth, including human, to coin?

BILL MARRED: I don't know if I can recall all of those, Doc. Pride, lust, envy, wrath, gluttony, sloth, deceit?

CHUM: Covetousness, not deceit. Deceit is one of my seven though, along with arrogance, selfishness, indifference, exploitation, megalomania, and greed.

LESSISMORE: There's two of the seven out there to protect property and keep the rich safe. Don't envy the rich guy's privilege and don't covet his goods. I can see the defense all morality builds for capitalism right there.

BILL MARRED: Yeah, and don't get angry if you're being exploited, downsized, outsourced, or robbed by a CEO who absconds with your retirement money. What's the connect with lust, Doc?

CHUM: It's a reminder in case you missed the sex in advertising bombarding you every three seconds. Lust is the grease that keeps capitalism's machinery working. Sloth is what Welfare Queens are guilty of; also workers on the assembly line who work below projected production levels. Gluttony is also a reminder that you aren't poor or exploited because you can eat as much fast food as you want any time you want.

LESSISMORE: Watch out for pride, because it might lead you to speak up and defend yourself. The meek and humble will finish first, especially in the capitalist competitive arena. If you believe that, maybe I can convince you that less is more.

BILL MARRED: Yeah, and what satisfaction in knowing you're not cocky like Donald Trump, or petulant like Bill Gates, or pushy like Rupert Murdoch. And your seven, Doc, can all be traced back to capitalism.

CHUM: There's nothing moral in a war of all against all. You also can't expect a moral result from a market crapshoot, but you can expect that the few winners won't escape the notice of the multitudes of losers forever. Enter "moral concerns," which are, of course, a concern of the privileged few, their concern being whether they can instill a numbing set of such concerns in the minds of the multitudes before these same multitudes can track their misfortune to our capitalism—I mean, our democracy and freedom.

———◆———

THE BLOGOSPHERE

Blog: www.postmodpit.com

There's a great social moral tone in all the Frank Capra films, my favorite being *Meet John Doe* (1941) when Gary Cooper reads that manifesto of find-your-own-peace-and-happiness-in-helping-your-neighbor. Coop puts that neighborliness in action in the film *Good Sam* (1948) but my all-time favorite is *Grapes of Wrath* (1940) where Tom Joad promises his Ma that wherever there's a man in need or in trouble, he'll be there to help. Chaplin's *Modern Times* (1936) captures, I think, humanity's heart when it was still beating for something more than money. But, I'm afraid, in our postmodern age there's something very naïve and hokey in these sorts of film, and I suppose that's because their certitude and solemnity are Hollywood packaged to warm the cockles of our hearts. Reality doesn't multiplex in these films, offering us competing narratives that deconstruct each other and enable us to conclude that moral notions are just part of the staging of the hyperreal. *The Passion of the Christ* isn't really a film, more like a pageant before Mass; it certainly doesn't create characters whose experience we can imaginatively project ourselves into to the degree that we can take baby steps out of the box of self-interest. That being said, I must also say that I can think of no postmodern film that displays a moral view inextricably tied up with the social and political. Charles Kaufmann's films *Being John Malkovich* (1999) and *Adaptation* (2002) portray the difficulties the artist has in capturing any sense of reality, including a moral sense, that isn't culturally "scripted." But his films are like a call for help from the pit of postmodernity not evocations of what a social morality is in a postmodern age. I remain depressed.

Blog: www.reciprocalmoral.com

I think I can come to the aid of postmodpit blogger. Take a look at two 2004 films: Martin Scorsese's *The Aviator*, and Terry George's *Hotel Rwanda*. *The Aviator* employs the life of eccentric tycoon Howard Hughes to show us how, for instance, we moved from the world of *Meet John Doe* to our post-9/11 world. Here's "the aviator" who didn't fly into the Trade Towers but rather exemplified the will to fly wherever he wanted, no matter how high, how fast, or how big the plane. What Hughes symbolizes is the very beginnings of a will that seeks to control both images of desire and desire itself. The reward is fame and fortune, money and power; but the cost is a self thrown into that self-created whirlpool of will, desire, and hype. "Wave of the future . . . wave of the future . . . wave of the future . . ." is the phrase Hughes cannot stop himself from saying at the film's end. He is indeed the wave of the future: the self-willed fabricator of a selfhood that has no center, no stability; the pure capitalist nightmare personified, a neurotic, uncontrolled will, desires brought to the screen but not into reality. Here's the aviator who inspired the 9/11 aviators.

I recall reading this in Terry Eagleton's *After Theory*:

"What is immortal in the United States, what refuses to lie down and die, is precisely the will. Like desire, there's always more will where that came from. But whereas desire is hard to dominate, the will is domination itself. It is a terrifyingly uncompromising drive, one which knows no faltering or bridling, irony or self-doubt. It is so greedy for the world that it is at risk of pounding it to pieces in its sublime fury, cramming it into its insatiable maw. The will is apparently in love with all it sees, but is secretly in love with itself. It is not surprising that it often enough takes on a military form, since the death drive lurks within it. Its virile vigour conceals a panic-stricken disavowal of death. It has the hubris of all claims to self-sufficiency" (Eagleton, *After Theory*, 2004).

Juxtaposed to this frightening depiction of neurotic will totally devoid of any moral dimension is Paul, played by Don Cheadle in the film *Hotel Rwanda* (2004). For a hundred days in 1994 the Hutu tribe slaughtered an estimated 800,000 Tutsis, an atrocity inspired, the film reveals, by a Belgian classification of Rwandans into Hutu and Tutsis based on physical appearance. The Belgians had placed the Tutsi minority in power, but upon their departure the Hutus sought vengeance, their weapons supplied by the French. The American government has no appetite for another African encounter after their humiliating disaster in Somalia where eighteen American soldiers were killed, a disaster for the military superpower brought to the screen with more technical bravado than critique in the film *Black Hawk Down* (2001). At the moment the American public is responding to all "reality" as if it were a reality TV show; for the young a new video of machete-wielding mayhem gets a video-game response and nothing more. "If people see this footage," says a cameraman who has just taken a video of bloody mayhem, "they'll say 'Oh my God, that's terrible' and then they'll go on eating their dinners." The United Nations is present in a ridiculously small contingent under orders not to fire their weapons. They await support from the United States and Europe, which comes only for European and American passport holders.

What I'm trying to point out is that there is a context to this atrocity, a certain staging that is not morally innocent. One reviewer remarked that the event was media-inspired, referring to the "Squash the Tutsi cockroach" radio broadcasts of Hutu Power Radio. Incendiary speech transmitted over the radio can't be reasonably added on to our "Reasons to Hate the Media" list. Drums

THE BLOGOSPHERE

would probably have been equally incendiary. But our American media is culpable not because its very reportage may alter and/or augment an event but because it fails to report what exceeds the interests and concerns, the compassion and imagination of post-Reaganite Americans. And after 9/11 the situation has grown worse as Americans have been led to turn off Europe as "anti-American," the United Nations as feckless and corrupt, the Middle East as an al-Qaeda camp, and Africa as a "bottomless pit" into which no amount of money or tears will help. A simpler scheme separates the world into short-term investment opportunities, long-term investment slogs, and no possible return on investments. You will see very little interest on Mr. Bush's part in bringing "democracy and freedom" to any country in Africa.

The moral dimensions of *Hotel Rwanda* then, are not personal but international and transnational. How does one man, Paul Rusesabagina, the manager of a Belgian-owned hotel, the Hotel Des Mille Collines, navigate a moral path through this nightmare world? When we first meet him he is the consummate concierge, the thoroughly efficient and courteous fellow for all hotel emergencies. He puts the rich and powerful at ease with single-malt Scotch and Cuban cigars; he anticipates everyone's desires. He's in fact "networking" and pursuing "self-interest" very thoroughly and very cleverly. When a neighbor is taken out and beaten and Paul's wife wants him to intervene, he tells her there's nothing they can do. He will spend the capital he has accrued with the powerful only on family, not on a neighbor. When Paul discovers a young son covered in blood, he and his wife are hysterical with concern, which is quickly abated when someone says it is not the boy's blood. One person then asks "Who's blood is it?" This is not a question whose answer Paul cares about. Paul is very far from seeing his well-being and safety in terms of the well-being and safety of his neighbors. At the film's beginning, he is as far from seeing this as are the Americans who turn back from the news video of the genocide to their dinner.

With the news that his sister-in-law and brother-in-law have probably been killed and their daughters are somewhere in the most dangerous part of Kigali, both Paul and his wife become determined to find them. In looking for them, Paul finds other children needing refuge from the massacring Hutus. He takes them into the hotel. And from that moment on, he finds a place for everyone who seeks refuge. He begins to use up the goodwill capital he has accrued in order to keep his hotel "guests" from being slaughtered. He uses all the skills he has developed in dealing with the selfish and powerful; he knows when to flatter and when to threaten. He uses that adaptive agility that the serving class develops in dealing with the oblivious but dangerous. He plays them not to his own interests but to the interests of the others he is determined to save. Finally, he reaches a moral stage where he cannot be safe, he cannot surive, he cannot flourish through his own efforts; it all now is interdependent; he will survive because the others survive. Morality becomes a reciprocal arrangement.

In the final scene when he once again halts his own flight to freedom to go back for others, he is told that there is no more room on that freedom bus. Paul says simply, "There's always more room." Provided, of course, others make room.

"There's always more room" are the last words in *The Hotel Rwanda*. "Wave of the future . . . wave of the future . . ." are the last words in *The Aviator*. A morality based on reciprocal self-realization; a morality based on an insatiable will to dominate. Neither American politics at this moment nor America's version of Christianity is serving *The Hotel Rwanda* ethic but clearly the furious insanity of *The Aviator*.

THE BLOGOSPHERE

This Genre Does Not Exist

Once we become a twenty-first century embodiment of the Old Roman Empire, moral reform can stride right back into the picture.

—Norman Mailer, "Only in America,"
The New York Review of Books, March 27, 2003

Voice or no voice, the people can always be brought to the bidding of the leaders. That is easy. All you have to do is tell them they are being attacked and denounce the pacificists for lack of patriotism and exposing the country to greater danger. It works the same way in any country.

—Herman Goering, at the Nuremberg Trial

The idea of fulfilling your nature is inimical to the capitalist success ethic. Everything in capitalist society must have its point and purpose. If you act well, then you expect a reward. For Aristotle, by contrast, acting well was a reward in itself.

—Terry Eagleton, *After Theory*, 2003

Voice-over: Nobody includes political films as a defined film genre. Maybe it's because we think everything is political, or we think only films about election campaigns are political and there aren't enough of them to establish a genre. Maybe they get subsumed within other genres that don't exist like Espionage or Utopian Shangri-La or Mafioso or Jim Crow. Maybe it's because politics is a dirty word and it's a dirty word because it refers to a dirty business, namely, the business of government. Ironically, those associations are very much tied to a sea change in American politics. You can witness it in the extinction of our sense of an "egalitarian" democracy as well as our communitarian reverence for the "common man," in our lost respect for the more politically correct "working-class hero," in our hostility toward unionization, our demonization of the underclass, our transference of the constitutional rights of citizenship to the rights of corporations and shareholders, our adoption of the corporate view of taxes although taxes serve the public good, our readiness to accept profit as the bottom line in education, health, penal systems, war, natural disasters, and retirement, our adoption of "creative destruction" in regard to nature, our willingness to accept the largest wealth gap of all industrialized nations, our planned attack on contingency-based lawsuits called "tort reform," our attacks on the free press by fining and imprisoning journalists for refusing to reveal their sources, our ridiculing of the UN . . .

—— ◆ ——

Script Doctor: Delete that last rant and get back to the intro.

—— ◆ ——

Voice-over: "The age of Big Government is over," a Democratic president, Bill Clinton, declared in 1996, a pronouncement reassuring to Big Business and unsettling to "Old" (read FDR) Democrats. The atmosphere since Reagan has not been conducive to creating and marketing with any success a "political" genre, even if we could be "proactive" and not merely reactive about such a matter as film genre. All that said, it remains that we are a politically divided nation—red and blue states—but less equally divided in 2004 than we were in 2000. In 2000 the liberal candidate actually received more votes than the conservative candidate, but that same conservative candidate, now recruited into the neoconservative faction, was elected in 2004 by receiving some 3.5 million more votes than his liberal opponent. Is this indication that the country is growing more politically conservative? Or, does the fact that more voters cited "moral issues" as their voting prompt indicate that a winning number of Americans are socially conservative and align themselves politically with a candidate who also seems socially conservative? If this is the case, the country has not become more politically conservative but rather an already socially conservative population decided to vote in this political election.

—— ◆ ——

Script Doctor: "Okay, here we desperately need to get back to defining the genre. If you put aside the explicitly political films, like say, Robert Redford's 1972 *The Candidate*, or, the 2000 film *The Contender*, or, the real 1976 box office megahit, *All the President's*

Men—all of which can isolate and focus on the political, because politics still remains unsubsumed by global economics or by conservative morality—what do you get? Go.

———◆———

Voice-over: Corporate-based consumer capitalism is the tail that wags American politics. American Protestantism has, as Tawney pointed out long ago, always been compatible with capitalism, but here spiritual life spills over into worldly success and is not shaped or driven by such success. From the corporate side there has been very little interest in religion. When in recent history—and why—does that interest start? Most decisively it starts with Roe vs. Wade and the Democratic Liberals, the party of governmental regulations and entitlements, fixing their political star to pro-choice. The Corporate Republicans turn their gaze to this Christian Coalition formed against Roe vs. Wade and find that many of the problems initiated by an aggressive supply-side economics against the working class could be attached to a "moral politics." For instance, what a market-driven politics discovered was that so-called losers didn't just become extinct but rather became disaffected, frustrated, angry, and more violent and criminal than the "winners."

"Family values" was the phrase that described both the cause and the remedy. And it was a phrase the moral fundamentalists would incorporate. Prisoners, formerly linked to a liberal ethos of rehabilitation, were easily translated by Corporate Republicans into sinners who needed to accept moral responsibility and suffer a just punishment. Doubtlessly, Bush 41's 1988 Willie Horton campaign appealed to racists, but it also appealed to those who felt a liberal parole strategy muddled the line between good and evil, between just punishment and arbitrary reward.

Euthanasia was just as easily attached to suicide, the self-slaughter prohibited in the Bible. The homeless, the unmarried pregnant, the unemployed, and those on welfare could never be facing hard times because the Goddess Fortuna had spun the wheel against them but always because they had chosen evil over good. The last thing a good Christian would do was "reward bad behavior," which in moral terms means interfering with God's plan for personal redemption.

The Corporate Conservatives had gay marriage thrown in their laps in the 2004 campaign. There was no finessing needed to make it an issue that the moral fundamentalists would adopt. And strangely and paradoxically, bin Laden's jihad against the presumptuous intrusions of American capitalism, his Holy War, has also been a gift to Corporate Conservatives. Not only are we in a war over the moral soul of America but we are fighting a moral war globally. And we have a president who is championing that fight and will not give up, regardless of what sophistry the press, or U.N. inspectors, or apostates of the party concoct. The Conservative Economic-Political-Moral complex is working both nationally and internationally.

In this fashion, a conservative politics—itself driven by global market, transnational capitalism—made a bitch of conservative morality. Why would an ideology in the service of the Invisible Hand of the Market and not the Invisible Hand of God have any connection with religious fundamentalism except to use it to win elections and keep bleeding-heart liberals out of the White House and Congress? Moral issues that have a social face—such as a preemptive attack propelled by lies, killing thousands; an attack on the environment made on behalf of corporate profits; a disenfranchisement and disentitlement of the poorest; and a depletion of the Treasury to fight an unneeded war simply to declare the Social Security fund bankrupt and ultimately privatize and put at risk the retirement of the many—remain unconnected to the personalized moral code of the moral fundamentalists.

The peculiarly personalized, sex-fixated American version of Protestant conscience is overwhelmingly absorbed in the blow jobs Bill Clinton received in the White House and not at all concerned as a matter of conscience with presidential lies, imperialistic war, or the resulting deaths. So deftly have the Corporate Conservatives won over conservative moralists that the precipitating event of this new America—the attack on the World Trade Towers on September 11—has been exploited politically and economically without protest from the conservative moralists. Perhaps the response to evil is to turn the other cheek or seek an eye for an eye. Our response has fulfilled neither of those Christian protocols. This remains unnoticed by the moral conservatives. There is a mind-numbing immorality also in pursuing imperialistic goals that increasingly place Americans in harm's way, both at home and abroad. This also remains unnoticed by the moral conservatives. These do not rise to the level of moral concern within a conscience so fixated on two gay men or two gay women kissing on the steps of the city hall in San Francisco.

———◆———

Script Doctor: The abortion issue has enough moral force to trump every other issue, but I'm thinking, why didn't that keep Clinton from getting elected for two terms? Moral synergy at work in 2004: Upcoming Supreme Court appointments and a chance to overturn Roe vs. Wade, the war on terror, and lastly, the gays. Find a way to get this in. So what do we expect in a political genre? Mixture of money, morality, and politics. We know what corporations are all about, and we know that morality in the United States is personal and not social, but what good can we say about politics? Not now but ideally, theoretically. If there's a moral dimension to politics that isn't a simple bending of the political to fundamentalist beliefs, what is it? We picture the American dream as mo' money and even mo' money, not to *everybody* but to the winners. We also picture ourselves dreaming on a perfectly flat mattress, a level playing field. If this is a picture and not the world—and we know this is so—then who's holding up a better picture? Do we have pictures that show us a different American dream?

This genre does not exist so we can't be wrong about it. Characters: Grab a spinmeister, a working-class radical, and three nimrods. Shoot.

———◆———

Characters: Pitt Bull, a character parody of Brad Pitt's Tyler Burden in Fight Club; *Spin Vitti, a character parody of Robert De Niro's Conrad Bream, spin doctor, in* Wag the Dog (1997), *and Frank Vitti, mobster, in* Analyze This, *and the sequel,* Analyze That; *Forrest Chump, a character parody of Tom Hank's Forrest Gump in the movie* Forrest Gump; *Ray I. Savant, a character parody of Dustin Hoffman's idiot savant in the movie* Rain Man (1988); *Trance Gardiner, a character parody of Peter Sellers' Chance the gardener in the movie,* Being There (1979).

———◆———

PITT BULL: The first rule of *Flight Club* in the 2's is that there is no politics. Only share holders and shopping.

FORREST CHUMP: My mammy always said that politics is like a box of chocolates . . .

SPIN VITTI: Never mind what your mammy said. The president wants a blockbuster movie that makes the Iraqis look happy. They're shopping in malls. They're voting. And the women are getting makeovers on Iraqi Oprah. You. You want to make the hero an investment banker like this guy says, or you want an old-fashioned *Mr. Smith Goes to Washington?* You. Come on. We're brainstorming here. You. Ray. The *idiot savant.* It says here you're an idiot when it comes to everything but Aristotle.

RAY I. SAVANT: Aristotle says people fulfill their basic humanity through civic life. And the role of government is to promote the good life. His teacher Plato saw the ideal state as a moral unity that covered a citizen's whole life and should guide him toward a good life.

SPIN VITTI: Okay. What I'm hearing is we got to show the new, redeemed Iraq as an ideal state with moral unity. That'll make the prez look good.

PIT BULL: Listen up. Second rule of politics in the 2's is that market principles are better than governmental intervention. Third rule of politics in the 2's is that market rule leads to the good life. Fourth rule of politics in the 2's is that market values define the good life as having stuff, from an Ikea duvet to a trophy wife.

RAY I. SAVANT: That's not what Aristotle means by the good life. The highest good in life for anything is in discovering what its specific nature is and fulfilling that. For people it's our rationality. For a frog it's jumping. Well-being for Aristotle is not living well but living to the fullest potential of what's special about your being. He calls it *eudaemonia*. And that's not hedonism, which is what you're talking about.

PIT BULL: The frog can't know what it is, Ray. Instinct makes it jump. The frog doesn't work on its jumping. It just jumps. Do you hear what I'm saying, Ray? The frog just jumps.

SPIN VITTI: Hey, he's right, Ray. There's no self awareness in a frog. A frog can't have a sense of well-being. You're an idiot when it comes to frogs, Ray. Stick to Aristotle. And you know something? I'm sick of hearing about Aristotle. Did Aristotle make a movie? Did he ever go to a movie? I'm asking you. You. Trance. I'm talking to you.

TRANCE GARDINER: In the spring the water level in the garden rises. A frog is instinctually driven to self-preservation so it jumps, snaps flies, procreates. In the summer the plants reach their lushest growth. The whole garden is filled with life achieving its seasonal high. In the autumn . . .

SPIN VITTI: There's not enough water to turn Iraq into a garden so forget about that. But the idiot savant here gave me an idea. What if producing oil is what the Iraqis have to do to fulfill what's unique about them? That would make the oil companies synonymous with the government. You know, multinational oil companies with Iraqis as the front men.

RAY I. SAVANT: Not oil. No, not oil. Not what makes people different from plants and animals. Definitely not oil. Definitely not oil. Definitely not oil.

PIT BULL: Calm down, Ray. We are trying to create a political film genre in a post-9/11 age . . .

SPIN VITTI: Which is a problem, Ray, because a political film genre doesn't exist. What you've got are a lot of Hollywood leftist films like *Meet John Doe, Sullivan's Travels, The Grapes of Wrath, Norma Rae,* and agitprop documentaries like *Fahrenheit 9/11, Outfoxed, Uncovered . . .*

PIT BULL: And remember, Ray, the oil you own winds up owning you.

RAY I. SAVANT: We have brains not oil. Not oil. We're thinking, thinking, thinking . . .

PIT BULL: Alright, Ray. We heard you. You want to do a movie with people thinking. How is that going to help the president, Ray? No. Just answer that, Ray. How the hell . . .

SPIN VITTI: Hey, take it easy. What he's trying to say here, Ray, is that, sure, we're rational and nobody else on the planet is. But that ain't the end of it. We use the brain to think about things. And what it turns out people mostly think about is having a little bit of pleasure here, a little bit of fun there, and that's what it's all about. The Iraqis want some good times. So they got to think about oil because oil means money and money is what makes the world go round. See what I'm saying, Ray?

PIT BULL: And free markets are pleasures' best delivery system. I might not like that, and Aristotle might not like that, and you might not like that, but that's the way it is, Ray. Do you understand, Ray?

RAY I. SAVANT: Yeah, but Aristotle doesn't like hedonism. Virtue is in observing the mean. Observing the mean. You have to observe the mean. I want to observe the mean.

SPIN VITTI: Hey, Ray, he made it up. It's his prerogative. Observe the mean. What's that? How are you going to deliver that, Ray? How are you going to package that? I'm thinking it's like being lukewarm. Virtue is in being lukewarm? And you know what Jesus said about being lukewarm? There you go. Virtue now is in shopping.

RAY I. SAVANT: Yeah, but going out shopping is not exercising our thinking. You have to exercise thinking. Thinking is the thing that separates us from frogs. Not shopping.

SPIN VITTI: Ever see a frog go shopping? There you go.

FORREST CHUMP: My mammy didn't like it when I was sitting around thinking all the time. She would say don't you see that people think about something? They just don't think without thinking about something. So you just start thinking about something and then Bubba was always thinking about shrimping so I got a shrimp boat that the bank had fore-closed on. And I made a whole lot of money.

TRANCE GARDINER: I understand, Chump. You got a shrimp boat and made a whole lot of money.

PIT BULL: And what they think about in the 2's is shopping at the mall, shopping on-line, on their cell phones, through catalogs. Shopping their asses off. Work is what they do so they can shop. They don't work so they can sit around observing the mean.

SPIN VITTI: It's easier if you let the corporations. . . . Look, one of the ser-vices corporations provide is doing all the background thinking for you. Bingo! The results of product research and development are on the shelves. Or in the showroom. At the Web site. Wherever. All you have to do is choose.

FORREST CHUMP: I know that's the plum part. Choosing. We're all here free to choose. My mammy said she didn't want to spend all her time thinking about what goes into all those cereals in the cereal aisle at Piggy Wiggy. She chose the box with the most colors.

TRANCE GARDINER: I understand, Chump. She chose the box with the most colors.

SPIN VITTI: You know why the Green Party will never be big in the 2's in the United States? They want you to think about the dirt you're going to be buried in, the birds shitting on your deck, the trees you gotta cut down to build a garage big enough for your Hummer, the oceans that it takes so goddamn long to fly over. . . . You know what nature is, Ray? Resources. And out of resources you make stuff. Why? So people like you and me can buy stuff.

RAY I. SAVANT: I go to K-Mart to get BVDs. I need to go to K-Mart to buy BVDs.

SPIN VITTI: Let me ask you something. Do you think drugs in this coun-try is the multi-billion-dollar business it is because, one, people take drugs so they can think better, or, two, people take drugs so they *don't* have to think about things. One or two?

TRANCE GARDINER: The old man took drugs. Ben took a lot of drugs. When you're old and sick you have to take a lot of drugs.

SPIN VITTI: When you take drugs, anything from pot and hash to coke and ecstasy, you're on a long pilgrimage to getting to where you don't have to think about things. You don't have to observe the mean any-more; it's all sweet.

TRANCE GARDINER: I understand, Spin.

PIT BULL: The second rule of Flight Club is to avoid escapists. That includes druggies, born-agains, sports fans, and fools maxing the pleasure quotient.

SPIN VITTI: What makes us unique on the planet is that we can pursue our own pleasure. We can plan, organize, control, buy. Pleasure. We could use our brains to read Aristotle. But find me a twentysomething who's reading Aristotle. You know why he's not? In the pleasure game, Aristotle has been knocked out of the box. Look at the prez. He's been elected twice because he doesn't read. Today smart people rather play with their Gameboy or watch a Knicks game. But you're choosing. Freedom to choose is a unique possession of humans.

TRANCE GARDINER: The old man gave me a TV. I like to watch. I watch and play with my gameboy.

RAY I. SAVANT: Yeah. Aristotle. Not Gameboy. I like Aristotle.

SPIN VITTI: Aristotle feeds your mind. So you go out and feed your mind some more. You keep reading and thinking. Thinking and reading. You're on a pleasure kick. You're pursuing self-interest. You're thinking that thinking is the end result of thinking. Your thinking leads you to believe that thinking is the highest good. But you know what I think? I think thinking is a tool you use to get what you want.

RAY I. SAVANT: Aristotle says man is a political being and he satisfies that part of himself by getting involved in civic functions. We're not hermits but we're social and society needs governance and it's part of what we are to be part of that governance. We're not supposed to be just thinking about ourselves. We use our brains to promote the common good, the well-being of not one but many.

PIT BULL: You think government promotes our well-being, Ray? Is that what you think? So, government promotes our well being, which lies in contemplation, and when we contemplate we come up with the thought that it's government that promotes our contemplation. What if I promoted my well-being by thinking that government is a necessary evil, Ray, and the most rational thing I could come up with, Ray, was to go out there and promote my own self-interest and try my darndest to keep the government out of my life? What then, Ray?

RAY I. SAVANT: Aristotle wouldn't like that.

PIT BULL: Improper use of reason? In Aristotle's view? But then again maybe he meant something else.

SPIN VITTI: Hey, let's face it. Reason is a strumpet. She'll do what you pay her to do. Aristotle wanted people observing the mean; capitalism wants them shopping to the max. Which is more reasonable? It's a matter of persuasion. It's seduction, Ray. Pure and simple. Which kind of reasoning are you going to buy? Which kind of reasoning . . .

TRANCE GARDINER: Ben said he'd like to meet a reasonable man for a change.

PIT BULL: Didn't you ever see the movie, *Wag the Dog* Ray? What people think is a production, Ray. It has to be produced. So you need a producer. A Hollywood producer. Lay out your goals, your market, your timeframe, and your resources, and a good producer goes to work. That's why the third rule of Flight Club is avoid Hollywood producers.

SPIN VITTI: When he says goals, he means a script. Sometimes you need an original script. Say, like you want to tie an unknown Arkansas presidential candidate to a couple of American political mythologies. Abe Lincoln reading by candlelight in a backwoods cabin. Clinton becomes "the man from Hope." JFK legacy. Photo of a young Bill Clinton shaking hands with JFK. Passing-on-the-mantle-of-greatness spin.

FORREST CHUMP: I shook hands with JFK also. He was a nice man. I saw that movie *JFK*. Back and to the left. Or was it to the right?

SPIN VITTI: Or you need a script doctor. That's when the headlines are already running a story you want to detour in your direction. George W. Bush can't identify any of the world's political leaders nor does he seem to know where any of their countries are. Script doctor steps in: George W. Bush is not a beltway wonk or a liberal elite. He's not a politician whose head is filled with the nasty and dirty business of politics. He's a regular guy like you and me. He doesn't know crap about who's running France or Khartoum because *you* don't know who's running those places either. He's Mr. Smith going to Washington. He's pure, innocent, honest, and uncorrupted by Big Government. He's the little guy who's going to stand up for the little guy.

PIT BULL: Meanwhile the guy is what he is: ignorant. But with a new twist: This guy is willfully ignorant. He knows he doesn't know and he doesn't care and he doesn't care that you know he doesn't know because he knows you don't care because you don't know anything either.

TRANCE GARDINER: I understand, Bull. The president doesn't know anything except you don't know anything either, so that's why he doesn't care that he doesn't know anything.

PIT BULL: Guys like Spin Vitti here can put a vote-getting twist to it.

FORREST CHUMP: My mammy said never underestimate the American people. They're not naïve and they're not morons.

PIT BULL: You're a moron, Chump. Listen, Ray, people are not thinking in Aristotle's vacuum. They're someplace when they're thinking. It's sometime. Not timeless. And how do the dream makers and the spin-meisters have them positioned? They're positioned over there on the far right where government is bad because it can't turn a profit the way the private sector can. It can just spend. And what does it spend? Your good money to keep some low lives drugged up and unemployed.

TRANCE GARDINER: I understand, Bull. They spend good money to keep some lowlifes drugged up and unemployed.

PIT BULL: Corporations are good because they provide jobs, profit share-holders, and give you all the product choices you want. Government tries to regulate them on the behalf of the environment, workers' rights, consumer protection, and democratic principles of social justice.

TRANCE GARDINER: I don't think so, Bull.

PIT BULL: What do you mean, you don't think so? That's all been spin-doctored. One: Environment is a guy out of work because a spotted owl is threatened. It's a crazy woman living in a tree for a year to save it. Workers' rights: Jerry Springer crowd joining together in Mafia-run cor-rupt unions, which want a lot of benes and freebies for doing nothing. Consumer protection? Hey, assume personal responsibility: You're stu-pid enough to spill hot coffee on yourself and drive around in an unsafe car, face the consequences. Democratic principles of social justice? If I'm working, you should be too. If you want some justice, get out there and compete. Don't be waiting in bed for the government to give you a hand-out. Social justice is a two-way street.

TRANCE GARDINER: I heard a man named Spuds Turtle on the TV the other night. He said people think the way they do about the government because they have amnesia. They forget what FDR did for this country after the corporations had run everything into the ground because of greed. The old man had amnesia. Louise gave it to him.

PIT BULL: Sure they got amnesia. What's amnesia? Come out of the blue? Or is it a production number with a script? Getting a guy to forget what you don't want him to remember. For instance, you don't want anybody to remember their grandparents except that they had nothing. No cell phones. No TIVO. No Internet. No SUVs. No instant messenger. Grandpa worked for the railroad for forty years and retired with a gold watch that wasn't a Rolex. No stock portfolio. No time-share. Nothing.

A real loser. Died without a toy, and you know the guy with the most toys in the end wins. And grandma? Let's not begin to talk about what choices she never had. Washing a dish or changing a diaper. Another loser. Hard lives. Then a little voice in your head says, yeah, but I think they were happy. They didn't take a pill for depression. No South Beach diet. No trading on the Web. Hey, no Internet hookup! No e-mail! But then you look at these photos here. And you remember. They had something.

SPIN VITTI: A good Hollywood producer would wipe out that memory. They had nothing. In fact, there's nothing worthwhile in the past. It's a predigital time. It's like, when the Enlightenment occurred did anybody sit around crying about those good old Dark Ages? Everything written, said, done in the past doesn't apply now, because the past is just what was before all the good stuff was invented. It's a technology dead zone.

FORREST CHUMP: Is that another rule of Flight Club, 'cause I want to join.

PIT BULL: If you remember whatever the past has to say, you're predigi-tal. And you'll want to join our Flight Club. You know what I'm say-ing? The script doctors and the scam producers work for the power elite. Top 20 percent of the country. The professional class. And that profes-sional class serves the top 1 percent of the population. Everybody born since Reagan's day has been fed a steady diet of market casino logic. That's when you allow the free play of the stock market, which repre-sents the flow of capitalism, to handle all the needs of your democracy. You can't think of anything this market logic leaves out or destroys.

TRANCE GARDINER: When the garden is flooded, Bull, you have to stay and suck the water out. You can't run away, Bull.

PIT BULL: Ask Moses why he took off from Egypt. Anyway, who's to fight? Bottom 20 percent have been liberated from the welfare roles, which means they no longer statistically exist. How do they manage to exist if they do exist? Theory is they got jobs and portfolios. Fact is, they're too busy hunting and gathering to look up and vote. Next 20 per-cent are anesthetized with sports, video games, surfing porn, and listen-ing to smashmouth radio. They sponge up the spins against gay marriage, potheads, peaceniks, gun control, feminazis, pro-abortionists, liberals, Greens, the City of Angels, the Big Apple, Muslim fundamentalists, the United Nations, class warriors, unions, leftist academics, socialized med-icine, public schools, social security, government regulations, welfare, affirmative action, Bill Clinton, Old Europe, especially the French, illegal aliens, and on and on. Meanwhile, they're the working poor, paying off credit card interest that would make a loanshark blush. Trick is to keep them seduced while they're being raped. The next 40 percent pretend to themselves they're middle-class or better and doing well. They might just see how their democracy has turned into an oligarchy if it wasn't for the fact that they expect any day to become members of the oligarchy. They'd really be pissed at Lizzie Grubman and her Hampton elites if they weren't thinking they were a stone's throw from that kind of life themselves. So they identify with the folks at the top who are sucking their blood. So, I say, who's around to fight? Thus the creation of the Flight Club.

TRANCE GARDINER: I understand, Bull. Lizzie Grubman and the Hampton elites suck blood.

—◆—

Script Doctor: Okay. Now we move in closer to what we would label as a "political" film. But it's not just a trip down history lane; the present is pressing on our lens. How so? Post-9/11 al-Qaeda fears, 2000 Bush "victory," red and blue divide, Afghanistan, Iraq, Abu Ghraib, 2004 "moral issue" sweep. Fear and conservatism. We see every political film of the past through those lenses.

We need fresh characters. Sully from Preston Sturgis's *Sullivan's Travels* (1941), the Colonel from *Meet John Doe* (1941), Raymond's mother from *The Manchurian Candidate* (2004), Bob Roberts from *Bob Roberts* (1992).

—◆—

BOB ROBERTS: You can see the red and blue state divide in the two versions of *The Manchurian Candidate*. In the 1962 John Frankenheimer version there's a clear sense of who the bad guys are and who the good guys are. Evil is not us; evil is out there. Call that the red state version. Now, friends, if the evildoers in this film had won—and they didn't— they would have made the 2004 *Manchurian Candidate*. I say that because this film takes our attention away from the evildoers out there— and I'm talking about the bad actors in the Middle East—and directs us to technology and corporations as the evildoers. This is the blue state view. And in the 2004 presidential election, that view lost.

THE COLONEL: That's a helot view. *Manchurian Candidate* (1962). Feller brainwashed by the Commies and controlled by his neocon mom is in Washington to kill a left-leaning senator. What could becloud the mind more? What's the goal? Keep Americans paronoiac and xenophobic. Us against them. They want to steal our minds. That's what helots want to do.

RAYMOND'S MOM: Just what is a helot, Colonel?

THE COLONEL: A helot calls you any time day or night to sell you something. A helot will scare the bejeezus out of you to get your vote. A helot will divide the whole country right down the middle just to pump up the Dow Jones. A helot will ask you to give up your life fighting a war for oil. A helot will tell you what to do because God told him what to do. A helot will turn your whole life into profits for shareholders which you ain't one of. That's what a helot is.

RAYMOND'S MOM: Politics is something upper-middle-class Manhattan liberals do. It's Woody Allen–land. And you know how well Woody Allen plays in the Heartland, what Bob here calls the red states. They are, I can tell you, not amused. How much liberal, blue state biases are in films like *The Candidate* (1972), *The Best Man* (1964), *Advise and Consent* (1962), *Last Hurrah* (1958), *Mr. Smith Goes to Washington, Meet John Doe, Alias Nick Beal* (1949), *All the King's Men* (1949). . . . They reek of union propaganda. Working-class heroes and common John Does on the march. Against what, I ask you? Against a system that allows them to compete freely and reach for the ring? Fear of failure makes them underachievers and attaches them to the propaganda of underachievement. It's un-American, I tell you.

BOB ROBERTS: Colonel, today if you're a self-interested player, you're not interested in politics. You know why? Because government won't make you millions, and pursuing its inefficiencies has no purpose. On the other hand, pursuing self-interest can have compounding returns.

SULLY: I always thought the government was by the people, for the people. But now politics is economics. I mean, sure, we had a real tragedy on September 11 but what we want to do and should do is hijacked by the corporations. They want Iraq, not bin Laden. You can get oil out of Iraq and a political victory out of having bin Laden around. I tell you, I protest the state of civilization. I stand behind FDR's second Bill of Rights in which he declared "the one supreme objective for the future" was security: physical, economic, social, and moral.

BOB ROBERTS: And higher taxes extracted from the winners and given to the losers was the delivery system? With government lining its own pockets in the process?

RAYMOND'S MOM: You have to admit, Sully, that government doesn't grow the economy. Rather, it's a deterrent to economic growth. Only business can grow the economy. Freedom is grounded in prosperity, not dreams of prosperity engineered by government.

BOB ROBERTS: Precisely. Did you see the film *Dave* (1993). A guy who knows nothing about politics but looks like the president steps in for the president. And he turns to an accountant buddy of his to straighten out the national budget. That guy says legislators are only good at spending money, not saving it, or making it. The smaller government is, the better off we'll all be.

THE COLONEL: I saw that film. What's going on there? Setup for a know-nothing like George W. to become the real president. Dumps heavily on elected representatives of government. They're liberal tax-and-spend guys. But I say at least they're the helots who have been elected. I never heard of any elections for the three helots who now have more wealth than the bottom quintile of the population.

SULLY: Well, if Dubya is a corporate president, you voted for him, Colonel.

———◆———

Script Doctor: This is a draw. Get into religion.

———◆———

BOB ROBERTS: I saw the movie *Forrest Gump*. I thought Forrest shone with an inner light of goodness and innocence and wisdom. It was a message to all the socialists in the audience: One individual, if his heart is pure and true, can achieve personal salvation in a world where men seek to marry men, where babies are killed by legal degree, where a man's gun will be forcibly taken from him by the United Nations, where corporations working to make a better world for all of us are traduced, where the weak want to legalize their addictions, where the lazy and depraved are given welfare payments, where the criminal are coddled . . .

THE COLONEL: I saw that movie. Idiots don't get a free pass from the helots. A guy like Forrest Gump would be the most victimizied in our Winner Take All democracy. He'd drown in the vicious competitiveness of the entrepreneurial arena. Guys like him would have no identity, because he's not a player. He's not a helot himself. It's pretty cynical showing a guy like that standing above it all, making his way, and even making sense of all the horrors of recent American history. That was a film written by a helot to help other helots get fools like Gump to vote for them.

BOB ROBERTS: You have to admit, Colonel, that Gump is good and he's innocent, untainted by the crazy 1960s, uncorrupted by liberals and left-ists, by Washington politics. His girlfriend Jenny takes the wrong path, like so many radicals and free lovers of the 1960s who succumbed to drugs, sex, rock 'n roll. And AIDS. But Forrest is drug-free, no sex, and an entrepreneurial success. He's the link Newt Gingrich wanted to make between America before the radical degenerate 1960s and the neocon America brought into being by Reagan.

THE COLONEL: Reagan? There's a helot for you.

SULLY: Here's what FDR included in his bill of economic security: "The right to a useful and remunerative job in the industries or shops or farms or mines of the Nation; The right to earn enough to provide adequate food and clothing and recreation."

BOB ROBERTS: I think you might find those rights in the Soviet Constitution, not our own. Besides it's not up to government to secure economic well-being of its citizens. It's the give-and-take of a free market that will create our economic security.

THE COLONEL: You know what I like about that film *Jerry Maguire* (1996)? There are no politics in *Jerry Maguire*. No politics. No. There's no politics in *Jerry Maguire*. He's a helot trying not to be a helot and he almost makes it.

RAYMOND'S MOM: Oh, there are very leftist politics in that film, Colonel. Jerry says he wants to cut back on wanting to get it all. He wants to downsize his own profits. Who but a leftist in 1996 with the Dow Jones skyrocketing would choose to give up the desire to be rich? Why, the whole country is talking about winners and losers and every young person is anxious that they might fall on the losing side. So Jerry's conversion doesn't make sense according to the cultural value scheme. Winning is going to be transformed to a different kind of winning. Translation: He's putting aside self-interest and deciding to be a loser.

BOB ROBERTS: Jerry writes a mission statement, but we never get a chance to know what's in that mission statement. You know why, Colonel? Because no one in America knows what that new winning mission might be. Not Jerry, not the filmmakers, not the audience, not the critics. It just looks like Jerry lost the will to be rich, which is what happens to losers.

RAYMOND'S MOM: But the filmmakers pull off a classic Hollywood trick: Love trumps and conquers all. Jerry's less of a winner than he was at the beginning of the movie and what he's converted to as a higher plane of winning, we don't know. But in the end he wasn't a man challenging capitalism. He was just a guy with love problems. And he got the girl in the end. That's what you liked, Colonel. He got the girl in the end. Happy ending. Now everyone in the audience can go out and go for the money and the girl. Winning under the same-old same-old rules of the game. You see, Colonel, you can't escape to any level of existence in this world where money doesn't matter.

SULLY: Is that a moral statement?

BOB ROBERTS: I think when Donald Trump says "You're fired!" on his TV show we're a lot closer to the truth than we are in those Hollywood films. But let's face it. Who's identifying with the Norton character in *Fight Club*? What kind of hero is he? He blows up credit card company buildings. And Lester winds up dead. He's been in a nosedive to Loserville since the film started. The Giancarlo Esposito character in *Bob Roberts* (1992) is a voice crying in the wilderness. He's a wild-eyed radical, and like the big Lebowski says to the Dude in *The Big Lebowski* (1998), "The sixties are over. You lost."

THE COLONEL: That's because a bunch of Helots have buried every kind of opposition. The Soviet Union and communism, which means every form of leftism to Americans, went off the air, were canceled, the way a TV show gets cancelled. And history books are like old copies of *TV Guide*. They refer to dead stuff, obsolete, out-of-fashion extinct stuff. What's important is the newest new. Not dead stuff. The essence of politics in the United States in this new millennium is that all criticism of capitalism is radical and everything radical—the thought, the people, the history—is dead and without meaning.

RAYMOND'S MOM: You mean the political strife of the past is dead and without meaning.

THE COLONEL: Top screwball theory of the twentieth century: Reagan's "Voodoo economics."

BOB ROBERTS: No way. The top screwball theory of the twentieth century was Marxism. Everybody knows that.

———◆———

Script Doctor: Contrast respect and worship of power to empathy with losers.

———◆———

SULLY: What do you think of *American Heart* (1993), Bob? Jeff Bridges playing Jack Kelson, ex-con and reluctant Dad who finally does all he can to save his son from being a loser like him.

BOB ROBERTS: I didn't see it.

SULLY: A movie that got totally overlooked. Even if you went to see it, you didn't see it. Why? Because it focuses on a loser, and we live in a culture that doesn't want to focus on losers. They're invisible. They've been "creatively destroyed." No one wants to take the time to hear about them or see them in the movies. We've been through that. Now we let market forces take care of them.

BOB ROBERTS: No surprise then why this film didn't get on anybody's radar screen. Hello? We've already done welfare reform.

SULLY: Just like we've done Roe vs. Wade but it's still haunting half the country. We may have automatically written off a guy like Jack Kelson but we're still haunted by him. And others like him. That's the beginning of doing something. Legislatively. And the conservatives don't want to do anything legislatively about the losers. You know why?

RAYMOND'S MOM: "The Lord helps those who help themselves" is a good place to start.

THE COLONEL: Yeah, and the helots keep helping themselves until somebody arrests them.

BOB ROBERTS: The conservatives don't want to do anything to help the losers because they think the losers have *chosen* to be losers. They're free to choose, which means they've got free will and can be held personally responsible for their fate. Helping them just makes things worse. It rewards their losing behavior. They can chose not to win, not to be rich, and still get a handout from the government. And when they piss and moan about how bad their lives are, they're just hoping some bleeding liberal will legislate another Great Society package and send them a monthly check.

SULLY: There's a dangerous political message in *American Heart* and it's this: Jack Kelson is an ex-con, has no skills, has no value in today's marketplace, was a deadbeat dad, and he has no future, but he grows in this movie. He moves up on the Richter scale of moral awareness; he climbs up several points on the Dow Jones of respect. He doesn't get to Mother Theresa levels but he makes progress as a human being. Something rehabilitates his soul, and grace and self-sacrifice enter his life. The smallest seed, the thinnest ray of light. But you see it by the end of the movie.

THE COLONEL: I'd love to see a thin ray of light by the end of any movie.

SULLY: That enkindled ember could be fanned to a new life. He doesn't need a check every month from the government. And he doesn't need neglect. He doesn't need a government that will nurture him from birth to death. And he doesn't need a government that will stand back and let the social Darwinism of global capitalism decide his fate. Like all humans, he is never free to choose but always constrained by a prevailing order of things, by the priorities of power in place at that time. Some, like President George W. Bush, are born into a Harvard legacy and all that means. Others are born into a legacy of poverty and crime and all that that means. The true value of a social order and a culture lies in the capacity of any individual to trump those congenital legacies and fulfill his or her potential. Chance, talent, a surround that rewards that talent, and our own actions are all factors that affect that fulfillment.

———◆———

Script Doctor: Too much *Mr. Smith Goes to Washington*. Sounds like we're heading for *Grapes of Wrath* Tom Joad's promise to be there for every little guy who's being oppressed. That's after he gets two nickels to rub together. Let's counter with some power politics from Raymond's old lady in *The Manchurian Candidate*.

———◆———

RAYMOND'S MOM: You assume the innate potential of humanity to be fulfilled isn't selfish and corrupt. And you talk about power as a constraint but power can both leash and unleash corruption and selfishness. We live, unfortunately, in a world in which heart and compassion can be crushed by individuals realizing what you call their human potential. You want to assign even more rights to individuals, the right to economic security, to a good education, to a decent living, and so on. A second Bill of Rights. You want to build a wall between us and what's inherently nasty in us. We are the only schizophrenic creatures on the planet, Sully. Your government is like Dr. Jekyll trying to keep Hyde hidden.

SULLY: There's something wrong with that?

RAYMOND'S MOTHER: Declaring this a right and that a right doesn't do the trick. Power does. When it's time to slap back a corrupt power that threatens our own corrupt power. . . . Do I surprise you? Should I have said when the forces of Justice and Goodness slap back the forces of Injustice and Evil? You know, Sully, when it's all going our way we can afford to act as if morality and perfectability were our causes. But we've no time for such delusions after September 11. We're an incredibly self-centered, selfish, ravaging, polluting, arrogantly ignorant, ersatz, apathetic culture which has had the means to supersize and broadcast those virtues all over the world. We are surrounded by cultures that, had they equal means, would follow the same path. You might say it's in our species's genes. We are today surrounded by augmenting potentiality. And we might not be the ones with the leisure time to talk about "rights" if, say, for instance al-Qaeda fulfills its mission—I mean, its potentiality. Politics is a series of power plays—call it diplomacy—but survival politics is not play but action, and winning survival politics is a matter of acting while your self-interest can be fulfilled, while your neighbors have only the potential for fulfillment.

THE COLONEL: That's what people are, just a crowd of helots. And as for politics, I know the world's being shaved by a drunken barber and I don't have to read about it.

SULLY: I don't buy that picture of the world or the people in it.

—— ♦ ——

Script Doctor: Okay. Now we hit them with this new neocon genre. *Mystic River* (2003).

—— ♦ ——

BOB ROBERTS: Did you ever see the film *Mystic River* (2003)? Sean Penn won an Oscar for Best Actor. He plays a tough Irish street guy— Jimmy—who runs the neighborhood grocery store but is really the power force in the neighborhood. His daughter is brutally murdered and Penn and his goons go looking for the killer. He winds up killing the wrong guy, a guy he grew up with, and he's feeling some remorse. His wife doesn't want him to feel like he did anything bad. Here's a paraphrase of what she tells him: "I told your daughters that they would never have to worry because their Daddy would do whatever he had to for those he loved. It would never be wrong. No matter what their Daddy had to do. I told them that their Daddy is a king, and a king knows what to do and does it. Even when it's hard. And their Daddy will do whatever he has to for those he loves and that's all that matters. Everyone is weak, Jimmy. Everyone but us. And you. You could rule this town."

SULLY: Jeez, that sounds like what Eva Braun might have told Hitler when he was feeling a little down about his Final Solution. We Americans are the daughters living in fear and President George W. Bush is Daddy who knows what to do and can never be wrong, even when things are hard. And it's Daddy's duty to rule us like a king because we're weak and he's the only one that can do what has to be done.

BOB ROBERTS: Don't forget the fact that we're also the wife who's urging him to act like a king and go ahead and do what has to be done. I'm referring to the mandate Bush received in the 2004 election.

—— ♦ ——

Script Doctor: Okay. Now a film in this nonexistent genre that allegorizes the world of fear we've created for ourselves and is so carefully maintained: *The Village* (2004).

—— ♦ ——

THE COLONEL: Helots don't always vote for a King Helot. Seen the movie *The Village*? Supposed to take place in rural Pennsylvania in 1897. So in my mind it's an end-of-the-century film. Close to home. About sixty helots are living in a little village surrounded by woods inhabited by mythical creatures that the villagers don't refer to as helots but as "Those We Don't Name." The villagers can't go into the woods, but in the end a blind girl does so she can get some medicine. She runs into one of the mythical helots who's really tall, thin and covered by a cloak and hood. Turns out that this is just a costume the village leaders have been putting on to keep the villagers from wandering off.

RAYMOND'S MOM: So the boogey man in the woods is bin Laden?

THE COLONEL: Looked just like him. And I figure the village ain't nothing more than the U.S. of A. separating itself from the rest of the world and living in its own little preserve of paranoia. Which of course works to keep Dubya and his neocons in power.

RAYMOND'S MOM: But bin Laden is real not a myth in a mask. 9/11 was only too real. And if we've assumed a protective posture we've got ample reason.

SULLY: I think the point of that film is that people in power have created the monsters who are surrounding and threatening them. We didn't attack ourselves on 9/11 but we set the stage for the attack and helped recruit the attackers. And afterward, a winning politics was developed by keeping that fear alive. We've done almost everything we can to add fuel to the conflict and nothing to dissolve its root causes.

THE COLONEL: 9/11 was an opportunity for a bunch of helots to do what they've been trying to do for a long time: get in a dominating strategic position in the Middle East to ensure our oil supply, protect Israel, a nuclear armed ally in a region otherwise hostile to the United States, and get military bases closer to China.

SULLY: I'm thinking that tax rebates to the rich wasn't enough to wipe out the surplus left over from the Clinton administration. There was a real need to deplete the Treasury if any successful move to privatize Social Security and public education was ever to happen. Besides, war means destruction, and destruction means construction, which means a lot of lucrative government contracts. There's profit to shareholders in the rebuilding of Iraq.

RAYMOND'S MOM: It's like positioning yourself strategically on a chessboard, gentlemen. On the domestic front, we've got to get ourselves in global fighting shape and right now we're hampered by a legacy of

Liberal regulation and entitlements, the last gasps of the unions, increasingly marginalized peaceniks and leftists, environmentalists, contingency-fee lawsuits against corporations, minimum wage laws, and the last notes of drivel regarding social and economic rights.

SULLY: I protest against the state of civilization. I want to talk about the average guy. The character of a country is the sum total of the character of its little punks. I'm paraphrasing from Frank Capra's *Meet John Doe*.

RAYMOND'S MOM: My, isn't that over with. The average guy. No American today thinks of himself or herself as average. We're all unique, ten seconds away from winning the lottery, starting a business, earning a million. We're all future celebrities; we're two steps away from being on *Survivor* or *Elimidate* or *The Bachelor* or *Who Wants to Be a Millionaire*. The character of this country is expressed in the Dow Jones. And you know why there is no politics genre in American film? It's because greed and power are dispersed across every genre.

SULLY: We need teamwork. Your teammate is the guy next door to you. Your neighbor. He's a terribly important guy. You're going to need him and he's going to need you. If he's sick, call on him. If he's hungry, feed him. If he's out of a job find him one. To most of you, your neighbor is a stranger. The meek can only inherit the earth when one John Doe starts loving their neighbor. That's what I remember from *Meet John Doe*, and I believe it.

RAYMOND'S MOM: One inherits after someone dies. I think Christ meant after the world dies the meek will inherit. Meanwhile . . .

THE COLONEL: The helots got it, got it for sure.

———◆———

Script Doctor: Voice-over now says I think we nailed down a new genre: American red & blue movies.

———◆———

Voice-over: Perhaps political movies have never previously risen to genre level, but now with a red and blue schism in the United States there may be no way of any movie avoiding the political.

———◆———

THE BLOGOSPHERE

Blog: www.whichbeast.com

Okay, take this moral mission Aristotle attributes to government and think of our post-9/11 policies. We go from Republic to Empire. But it's not just

propelled by a neocon positioning of America defensively and economically. There's a moral connect here, a militant Christian moral
connect. Remember that the neocon hegemony in the United
States post-9/11 isn't simply a market conservatism. All those
salaried voters who went for Dubya in 2004 didn't have their eye
on the Dow Jones. And they weren't even aware of the internal
battles among Republicans between traditional conservatives and
the neocons. Read Andrew Sullivan's blog on his Web site
(andrewsullivan.com) regarding how far the neocon agenda is
from the traditional Conservative one ("The Conservative Party:
Kerry's Democrats," August 29, 2004).

"Marketing is the beast that took America away from most of
us," Norman Mailer wrote in "Only in America," but it's not the
"beast" in the eyes of those same Americans. The "beast" is always
biblical in America, right out of *Revelations* 13:2: "And I saw a beast
rising out of the sea, with ten horns and seven heads, with ten
diadems upon its horns and a blasphemous name upon its heads."
The eyes of the salaried voter are on religion and moral issues. You
have to look for that connect in post-9/11 politics. And Mailer
does. And finds it: "From a militant Christian point of view, America is close to rotten. The entertainment media are loose. Bare
belly-buttons pop onto every TV screen, as open in their statement
as the eyes of wild animals. Kids are getting to the point where
they can't read but they sure can screw. So one perk for the White
House, should America become an international military machine
huge enough to conquer all adversaries, is that American sexual
freedom—all that gay, feminist, lesbian, transvestite hullabaloo—
will be seen as too much of a luxury and will be put back into the
closet again."

Blog: www.americanexceptionalism.com

If the good life is found by promoting the common good, and politics is all about both of these, then every individual has to get
involved in politics in order to promote the good life. But note how
Dinesh D'Souza defends "American exceptionalism": "As the American founders knew, America is a new kind of society that produces
a new kind of human being. That human being—confident, self-
reliant, tolerant, generous, future-oriented—is a vast improvement
over the wretched, servile, fatalistic, and intolerant human being
that traditional societies have always produced, and that Islamic
societies produce now. In America, the life we are given is not as
important as the life we make. Ultimately, America is worthy of our

love and sacrifice, because, more than any other society, it makes possible the good life, and the life that is good" (*What's So Great About America*, 2002).

I'd probably call that new kind of human being *machina sapien*, although we're not quite there yet. Certainly we have created the new *homo economicus*. I doubt if the founding fathers could imagine a "market player" like Oliver Stone's Gordon Gekko in *Wall Street*. And it's clear that maybe the top quintile of Americans are "confident," but we've got a lot of insecurity, disaffection, fear and trembling, angst and concern right below that. "Self-reliance" has swerved a bit from the Emersonian belief that we aren't in a "war of all against all" waged by self-interest but rather each of us has within a shared truth that we must rely upon, and such reliance brings justice not only to ourselves but to all of society. Market-driven self-interest replaces Emersonian transcendentalism with a "trickle down" psychology wherein the huge winnings of the few will trickle down to the losers and thus I suppose keep them fit enough to be deployed by ever-venturesome capitalists.

We are certainly "tolerant" within the circle of our cell-phone memory and instant-messaging support group. Shift us, however, an inch either way outside our "self-interest," our networking circle, and "tolerant" isn't a word I'd use. Oblivious captures it. We are "generous" certainly to ourselves, losing no opportunity to add comfort, convenience, and speed to our lives. However, Americans now equate "the common good" with some sort of socialist scheme or federal entitlement program and, therefore, the phrase has gone out of fashion. As generosity involves others and we now exclude any concern for the plight of others, generous can hardly be a term applied to Americans—except, of course, *by* Americans. We are "future-oriented." Uncontested attribute. Madison Avenue's everlasting compaign on behalf of the "newest new" wouldn't have us oriented in any other way, certainly not toward the past where some reminder of this country's idealistic but nobly inspired origins might temper our shopping.

The "good life" for Americans results from looking out for number one, in doing absolutely nothing that would *not* show *me* the money. Perhaps the top 20 percent of Americans have attained this money-is-the-good-life Good Life and, therefore, we could claim a 20 percent American exceptionalism. But this hardly connects ethics with politics in the Aristotelian fashion, unless, of course, we hold on to the notion that the wealthy getting wealthier and the poor getting poorer somehow has an ethical dimension to it. Global capitalism has also sprung free of politics in so far as

American democratic politics has no built-in deterrent to what Marx called capitalism's inevitable savagery, and he, of course, was not referring to our new globalized, computer-serviced capitalism that has kicked that savagery up to global levels. I would like to point out that China does have an economic dimension to its politics, one that may make it difficult for the Chinese to eventually become as "exceptional" as we are. Islam also bears within it an infiltration of ethics into politics, as well as everyday life, and, therefore, capitalism cannot, at this moment, bring the Middle East to our American level of "exceptionalism." Mr. Wolfowitz, among others, continues to work on this problem.

In our post-9/11 world we have witnessed a great deal of political legerdemain by which the "common good" is served by a Republican guarantee of our survival, the political is held bound to the same "politics of survival," and, ethical concerns are adroitly brought into CSPAN view at Republican National Prayer Breakfasts during which prayers of invocation ask the Supreme Being to safeguard us from "self-interest" and inspire us to gather together in communal sharing for it is in togetherness and community that we truly shine.

Blog: www.collateralmensch.com

Similar to the Pixar blockbuster film *The Incredibles*, boasting of the *Übermensch*, is *Collateral*, starring Jaime Fox and Tom Cruise. A political dimension, yes. "Max the cabbie" is just "temporarily" driving a cab; he escapes his "loser" life by periodically staring at a photo of a tropical island and going through limo ads for this future "all-luxury limo" service. A loser living on dreams but without enough initiative to realize them. When asked by Vincent, his well-dressed passenger, how long he's been driving, Max replies, "Twelve years." Not temporary at all. This is his life. He's settled for a cabbie life because he "doesn't just get out there and do it." He doesn't take advantage of opportunities; he has no capacity for instantaneous adaptability; no readiness to take what chance throws his way and turn it to his advantage. He's passive and reactive, not proactive and creative like Vincent. Vincent's a "player" perfectly poised to meet the challenges of a postmodern world, a world where fads and fancies rule one day and are gone the next. Vincent isn't "nationalized" or "territorialized"; he's "globalized." He doesn't show any attachment to any existing "order of things" because he knows order is a human concoction and humans have no talent for anchoring their concoction in anything trustworthy or permanent. Vincent's code is the play of the *I Ching*. He's a winner, a knight of entrepreneurial quest, turning every opportunity his way, maximizing his return on every endeavor.

Too bad he's a sociopath. There's the rub, the downside so to speak. Vincent was a criminal lawyer, and now he's a lawyer who's a criminal. He's gone over to the dark side, but then again so have all the CEOs and corporate execs presently being prosecuted by the Justice Department after the corporate scandals that began the new millennium.

In the end, Max the loser has a shootout with Vincent, and Max wins. Vincent, the bad guy, meets his deserving end. It's a moral ending; evil is vanquished. But wait . . . this is a Hollywood box-office blockbuster. The first requirement here is that bad guys get theirs, and good guys walk off with the special lady. That's given. That's like the mandatory health warning on a pack of Camels. It's there to be ignored, is what I mean. It's our Soma tablet, the stuff we recite without reflection.

Do a grand delete of all that and what do you have in this movie? Another *Mr. Incredible*, this time it's Tom Cruise as a sociopath, who has "superpowers," who can just fly by all the moral concerns of the 2004 red state electorate. But, hey, so do all the winners in the global capitalist game. Is a good guy like Max running Wal-Mart? Did he run Enron or World Com? The "virtues" of the sociopath, unfettered by what fetters the ordinary guy, aren't winning virtues. Why should big government regulate our lives? That goes without saying in the mind of the players. But why should the player not think, like Vincent, that he's a speck on a planet spinning in a universe for a short period of time with no one watching and no one caring? He's not going to pretend there are laws out there that trump his own self-made laws, somebody else's interest that he should put before his own, some plan of self-realization that somebody else has developed for him. You have to not care about anything but a maximization of self-interest to be a winner in our free market world. If there's also an alibi out there that points out how your self-interest pursuit helps your neighbors, helps the whole world in fact, why that's wonderful.

You can't be ensnared in a whole host of do's and don't's that prevent you from seizing the moment and wringing from it the most that it can give you. It's like an entrepreneur seeing a potential market and then going full tilt to establish it despite the protests of unions, environmentalist, consumer advocates, federal regulators, and Kantian moralists. Christians won't get in your way; you are, in fact, who they vote for. But the Kantian ethic that asks you to consider whether you'd allow your fellow to do what you allow yourself, and if not, restrain from your act—that's a roadblock between you and your self-realization.

Being absolutely free of the constraints—religious, moral, psychological, familial, social, legal—that rule the lives of men like Max the cabbie is like being a superhero. You have an incredible advantage over the Maxes of the world, who may be Maxes but fail to maximize. In the hearts and minds of every viewer of *Collateral*, Vincent is incredible not because he kills people wantonly but because he has a power that this world now calls upon us to unleash and we didn't realize that until now. Vincent is the guy Trump wants to hire; Max is us and we greet that fact with dismay. It's not strange then, in a year in which Bush went cowboy and filled the world with imperialistic "shock and awe," that two box-office hits, *The Incredibles* and *Collateral*, almost transparently espouse the cause of the *Übermensch*, the Superman. I mean the sociopathic *Übermensch* that the world has seen before. Unfortunately.

I don't' know why the writer of "This Genre Doesn't Exist" backs off from revealing the post-9/11 film as a film celebrating a particular kind of American hero, a strong man not overburdened by thought and doubt but ready to act, clearly and decisively, a man who can transform the world and turn a new page in the history of the world. Incredible.

THE BLOGOSPHERE

Fearscape/Thrillscape/Nightscape

> . . . what in me is dark . . .
> —John Milton, *Paradise Lost*

> [F]ear is by its very definition terrorism's principal ally; its aim is precisely to draw its enemies into . . . a "theatre of terror" that can literally scare them to death.
> —Benjamin Barber, *Fear's Empire:*
> *War, Terrorism, and Democracy*, 2003

> Every loss is a win for a regime supported by fear, an administration which feeds, like a vampire on blood, on terrorism, a terrorism indelibly grounded in the terrorist act of 9/11.
> —Norman Mailer, "Only in America,"
> *The New York Review of Books*, March 27, 2003

Characters: Prince of Filmtides and his psychiatrist Lowenstain Lowenstain, both parodies of characters from The Prince of Tides *(1991); Harry Favorite, private investigator, a parody of Mickey Rourke's Harry Angel in* Angel Heart *(1987).*

———◆———

Voice-over: "What in me is dark" may find its way to the screen and scare the bejeezus out of me. Maybe we fear falling back into alcoholism, or cheating on our wives or husbands once again, or not having enough of a retirement pension to get by, or that mole on our back becoming a melanoma and eventually killing us, or having someone run a red light and crashing into us, or someone finding out we pursue some weird sexual fantasy in secret, or a stranger who raped us and was never caught coming back for us, or the phone ringing and that one person we love with all our hearts has been killed, or Anthrax sent to you in the mail, or, a dirty bomb going off not too far away, or, the airplane you're on suddenly bursting into flames and spiraling toward the dark, cold waters of the Atlantic . . . whatever your mind now touches and you feel fear.

Can we call these personal fears? Surely, whatever the origin, they occupy the private spaces in our minds. We bring it inside and become haunted by private fear. This is fear privatized, and the genre of fear starts here.

———◆———

PRINCE OF FILMTIDES (free associating as he lies on the couch): Only two movies in all of cinema history—*Night of the Hunter* (1955) and *Mulholland Drive* (2001)—lock you into a nightscape of dream, like a dark room without a window, and though both promise to let you out and indeed seem to release you in the end, in the end you remain haunted. The light in those movies never comes from the sun; the sun is hidden. "No light, but rather darkness visible" (Milton, *Paradise Lost*, I, 6). At first you think you are witnessing a new picture of the world, but somehow in the back of your mind you know this is not the world. You don't know this place; you don't belong here. But you stay because a bond has been forged: The dark recesses of your own mind and what you see on the screen.

"Out of a misty dream our path emerges for awhile and then closes within a dream" (Ernest Dowson). The mist is on the moor; Sherlock Holmes is deducing and inducing what murderous entity is hidden in that mist. But he is the detective of daylight; when the hound is haunting us from within (Francis Thompson), when the world is invisible to the mind's eye, opaque to the light of reason, when the mist is primordial and archetypal, when it is Blake's tyger burning bright in the forests of the night, not to be solved or resolved—a fearful symmetry—then we are closest to where we began. And to where we end.

I hear the itinerant preacher: "Trailing clouds of glory do we come, from God who is our home" (Wordsworth). Not a mist but clouds of glory. Perhaps. But can the darkness be made visible in our lives while the clouds of glory that remain are only dreamed of? What is sleep? I hear a child ask. How do we get there? Where do we go? Am I sure to return? Is it a pleasant thing to be under Walt Whitman's bootsoles, a blade of grass, one among an infinite number of grass blades? Or is it more Shakespearean?: "To die—to sleep—/To sleep! perchance to dream:—ay, there's/the rub;/For in that sleep of death what dreams may come,/ When we have shuffled off this mortal coil,/Must give us pause . . ." (*Hamlet*, III, I).

I see the preacher all in black and riding a stolen white horse, singing a hymn, coming over that hill, in the moonlight. And I am hidden, but now I know I am not hidden well enough and must run. To the banks of the Ohio River where my boat is. Push off into the night, into the river, away from the darkness that pursues me.

That's a scene from *The Night of the Hunter* (1955); a mythic scene, a dreamscape, nightscape scene. I hear the voice over at the movie's beginning: "Inwardly they are ravening wolves." They hunt us and they haunt us.

LOWENSTAIN LOWENSTAIN: Okay, Prince. You know what's clear? The second person plural "you" that you use is really a first-person personal "I." You, second-person singular, are caught in some kind of nightscape that those two films play into. So you're filled with fear. We need to explore further what the connect is.

PRINCE OF FILMTIDES: I get lost inside the mind of that girl in *Mulholland Drive*. Diane. Betty. She tries to kill herself but she doesn't die right off. I wish she would have. But no. She draws us into her last minutes. The whole movie. She lies to herself. Tries to tell her dying self that she didn't do anything bad, that nothing bad ever happened.

LOWENSTAIN LOWENSTAIN: It's like your sister, Savanah, trying to kill herself. Trying to erase what happened to her. It's like you trying to kill yourself in another way. I mean, by rejecting your wife, your family and friends, your life. You're the young boy in *Night of the Hunter* running from something dark. But it's not that preacher in black. There's no ravening wolf outside, Prince. The ravening wolf is a fear, a demon you have locked up inside you. You need to release it.

———◆———

Script Doctor: Interject a summary of Barbra Streisand's film *Prince of Tides*: The brother of a woman who is hospitalized after a suicide attempt winds up revealing to the psychiatrist a long repressed memory of rape and murder.

———◆———

PRINCE OF FILMTIDES: The trouble with you, Lowenstain, is that you refuse to see that the world is shit and that people . . . like me . . . are entitled to their anger. I didn't make up my demons, Lowenstain. They're out there. They're not just inside my head. They're real. You want to look for clues? Read the goddamn newspaper. Turn on the TV. You don't have to be a detective of the psyche to see what's wrong here.

———◆———

Script Doctor: Now Harry Favorite, a knock-off character from *Angel Heart* (1987), a seedy detective played by Mickey Rourke is hired (by the devil?) to find a man who ran out on a debt to be paid (his soul?) and discovers that he is the man he is looking for.

————— ◆ —————

HARRY FAVORITE: He's a headcase, Doc. Your Prince of Filmtides. Anyway, *Nightmare Alley* (1947) with Tyrone Power as Stan, the carny, who becomes the great Stanton Carlyle, mind reader and spook medium. You get lost in the carny world, in there with the geek. What is it but a dark alley inside a nightmare? That's the world. That's the terrible interior of Stanton Carlyle's head. Darkness that's visible. Like the Prince here said. A nightmare is just reminding you that you're on the Devil's side. The Prince of Darkness. Not the Prince of Filmtides. That's nothing, doc.

LOWENSTAIN LOWENSTAIN: Are you offering the thesis, Harry, that we get trapped in a world of dark fears that the devil leads us to?

HARRY FAVORITE: Doc, we're thinking here we are in a world that runs on time, that we can time the ebbs and flows of the tides. But what if we're just on a tiny island where the sun shines and the tides ebb and flow but all around is a dark unknown?

LOWENSTAIN LOWENSTAIN: Freud showed us that the *terra incognita* of the medieval world was the deep recesses of the human mind itself. It wasn't the dark pit of hell waiting to suck us in. If you recall that in neither Hitchcock's film *Spellbound* (1945) nor *Psycho* (1960) does anything other than early trauma generate pathology. In *Spellbound* Gregory Peck's own mind has locked him into a world of dark fears. We feel his fear; we go in search of the key that will open locked doors. In *Psycho* Norman Bates' assimilation of his mother's tyranny after he murders her is masked by an exterior that sporadically gives us glimpses of the dark state of affairs beneath.

HARRY FAVORITE: Doc, the devil works through your head. What's inside comes from the outside. You fear your plane being hijacked and flown into a building? It's a fear based in reality.

LOWENSTAIN LOWENSTAIN: The fear is not in the reality. The devil didn't put it there. You did.

PRINCE OF FILMTIDES: Forget about the devil, Lowenstain. You don't have to come up with one bad guy. That's a political gimmick to wag the dog of the electorate.

LOWENSTAIN LOWENSTAIN: So we agree. The devil isn't a personal or a public figure. It's the use we make of what's dark that we have to deal with. President Bush can only make use of Saddam or bin Laden to haunt us because we are already haunted on the personal level.

———◆———

Script Doctor: If the *whole* culture is haunted on the personal level it obviously means that we are culturally haunted. We need to interject something about a mass American cultural psychic fear probably resulting from our false womb of isolated security and the fire wall we've built out of property and possessions to protect us from our own mortality. Fear is the soft spot in the American cultural psyche and it's a fear of death. Bin Laden touched that spot. He wouldn't have been as successful anywhere else in the world where death's head shadows every life.

———◆———

HARRY FAVORITE: That's more than half the U.S. population, Doc, that's haunted on a personal level cause Dubya put enough fear into them to get himself re-elected. The only fear the less than half had was that he would be re-elected. Fear of bin Laden trumped fear of Dubya, and why not? Dubya seemed such a friendly, regular guy from the ranch, and bin Laden looked a lot like those tall mythological creatures haunting the woods in M. Night Shamalyan's *The Village*. Am I wrong, dude?

LOWENSTAIN LOWENSTAIN: I've already told you, Harry. Fear is private, not public. It's personal, not social. It's not the devil's work and it's not a political campaign . . .

HARRY FAVORITE: Or 9/11? Or a preemptive war that can never be won with a country that had nothing to do with 9/11, a war that has already killed thousands of American soldiers and more than a hundred thousand Iraqis?

LOWENSTAIN LOWENSTAIN: Harry, when it comes to the individual psyche you have to be prepared to accept personal responsibility. And you're not. You're not because you know you're guilty; you know if you go in search of evil, you'll find it inside yourself. If you go in search of a monster, it will turn out to be you. Now, Prince, what if I told you that the world was neutral, and that it was just you who projected good and evil or dark and light into it?

PRINCE OF FILMTIDES: Just out of the blue?

LOWENSTAIN LOWENSTAIN: Not out of the blue. Out of a plot. In your mind. But what's in your mind isn't self-generated. It's a jumble of responses, linkages, associations, and interpretations of what you make of the world. You know what experience is, Prince? It's what we say we get when something out there gets brought into you in some way. When we're healthy in our minds it just means that none of that hangs around in any special way. But when we begin to feel like somebody put a dark shroud over the sun, that means something is hanging around in our minds in a special way. My job is to find out what it is.

PRINCE OF FILMTIDES: So I've got some tangled wiring? My reception channels are screwed up? The world's totally neutral and I just misinterpreted it. Is that what you're saying?

LOWENSTAIN LOWENSTAIN: I should have said nature is neutral. The planet is neutral. The cosmos is neutral. But you put people on the planet and that neutrality gets overlaid with a lot of plots of what the world is. Some of them good. Some of them bad. I think you and your whole family ran into something bad and instead of keeping it outside yourselves and dealing with it, you took it inside where it's festered over the years, and is now malignant. Whatever it was didn't kill you or your sister then, but it's killing you now. With your help.

HARRY FAVORITE: Fear is universal, Doc. What you're saying is that only a few whackos know what fear is. Fear is universal. Which means you need a universal cause. The devil. The dark side. Where the dead go who ain't happy. You close your eyes, Doc, for the last time and you go someplace. Maybe it's a happy place; maybe it's a dark place. But it ain't no place. Why? Because if dead people were going no place for all these centuries the story that we go some place would have dried up a long time ago. In point of fact, Doc, that story would never have been told. Do you see any other creature on the planet trembling in the dark? What separates us from them? I'll tell you. We're jumpy. And we've got a right to be.

PRINCE OF FILMTIDES: He's crazy but he's right, Lowenstain.

HARRY FAVORITE: Being crazy keeps me from going insane.

PRINCE OF FILMTIDES: There's this movie that scares the bejeezus out of me everytime. *The Uninvited* (1944). I'm filled with fear, and I know that fear has nothing to do with this personal malignancy that you say I got inside me. In this movie there's a spirit filled with malignancy in this one room. The spirit lives in this room. The room is always ice-cold. You know she's in there and she makes it cold and clammy. Like a grave. Fresh flowers immediately whither in that room. You know why that movie scares me, Lowenstain? It's because death scares me. Maybe I'm ice-cold about life because I got some dark repressed thing eating away at me. Maybe I don't care if I live or die. And you're treating me for that. But when I see this movie, I'm scared.

LOWENSTAIN LOWENSTAIN: Ghosts, zombie, spirits at a séance. . . . It's what we may become. But we all become dead bodies. Anything that reminds us of that fills us with dread because we know dead bodies go into the deep bowels of the earth and rot and turn to dust. Or are plunged into a cremation oven and incinerated, like the day's garbage. That's a fear shared by the whole human race. Some overcome it with belief. Or think they do. And you ask, Harry, why other creatures have no such fear? They have no consciousness of being alive or of being dead, nor do they have consciousness of being in the present or what the future might be like. The price we pay for our human consciousness is our consciousness of a time when that consciousness will be no more, when darkness and deafness destroy our awareness.

HARRY FAVORITE: You know, Doc, I just thought of something. Did you ever see the movie *Angel Heart* (1987)? Mickey Rourke is a private eye named Harry Angel. He gets hired to go look for a real sadistic pervert killer named Johnny Favorite. No relation to me. Guess what? Turns out the guy Mickey is looking for is himself. He's Johnny Favorite. He's the sicko. And the devil—that's Robert DeNiro—shows up to clue him in that he's one of his. But Mickey thinks he's the good guy looking for the bad guy. And he doesn't face up until the end.

LOWENSTAIN LOWENSTAIN: Your point is?

HARRY FAVORITE: Here's another one. *The Sixth Sense* (1999). Bruce Willis is this shrink who gets shot by a demented patient. When he gets better he takes on a case of a kid who seems paralyzed by fear. Then the kid tells him he sees ghosts. The thing is the ghosts want the kid's help. For this or that. Turns out Willis is dead. He's a ghost. He ain't helping the kid. The kid's helping him realize he is dead. Get the point now, Doc?

LOWENSTAIN LOWENSTAIN: I've been hired to help the Prince of Filmtides here, but I'm either the cause of his problems or he's helping me realize I'm the one who's in trouble? That's like thinking the cause of 9/11 wasn't fanatical religious terrorists but U.S. support of Israel or U.S. support of undemocratic regimes in the Arab world. Or that it isn't al-Qaeda that's in trouble but the United States.

HARRY FAVORITE: My point, Doc, is that you want to fight a war that you think you can win that's going on in Prince's head and that to me is like Dubya thinking he can fight a war against terrorism that he thinks he can win by attacking Iraq. It's inappropriate, is what I'm saying. In both cases. Prince's head isn't in a private space connected only with private memories. It's got the World Trade Towers brandished high like Caesar's golden eagle in it. It's got a "why were we lied into Iraq?" in it. And Iraq and bin Laden and al-Qaeda aren't in a private space of fanaticism and terror. The United States and all it's capitalist oil policies and antidemocratic sheik support are in that space, too. You're not the problem, Doc. You're just committed to detaching your patient here from a culture both you and he share. And that means your mask of neutrality is a problem, an obstacle. It keeps us from tracking down an out-of-control capitalism, a deranged neoconservative ideology, and a religious fundamentalist irrationality that supports both.

LOWENSTAIN LOWENSTAIN: Haunted and darkened psyches greet all world events in a haunted and darkened way. Good and bad events. The root causes are not outside but inside.

HARRY FAVORITE: You know what I think, Doc? We're afraid of ourselves. Our fear comes from knowing that we're the bad guy we're looking for. We set up all kinds of bogus wars against stuff you can't war against. And we know it. Why do we do it? A war on terror?

LOWENSTAIN LOWENSTAIN: Because we know darkness from light, Harry. And we won't give up seeking the light.

HARRY FAVORITE: By dropping bombs on an "axis of evil"? We're the major component in that axis, Doc. We need a war on terror because we know it can't be won. Dubya said so himself one time when his string to Karl Rove was cut. We can't win it the same way Harry Angel can't find Johnny Favorite. He can't find himself. We can't win a war against ourselves. We've armed the terrorists, given birth to the terror, and have re-elected a president who ensures that the war will go on. It has to go on. And ending would mean we would know what our part was and who we really are. America can't face that. The Dow Jones would slide.

LOWENSTAIN LOWENSTAIN: You're quite an analyst of warped psychologies, Harry, but then you start from a warped perception. I think our session, Prince, is at an end.

PRINCE OF FILMTIDES: You know, what you said about the belief thing intrigues me, Lowenstain. Makes you think faith will make you fearless. But here's what I'm thinking. If you already are prone to believe in the supernatural, aren't you just set up for belief in all kinds of irrational things, from vampires and werewolves without souls roaming around looking to suck your blood to houses haunted by spirits looking for their souls?

HARRY FAVORITE: All those sick murders in the movie *Seven* (1995). Who did them? A guy who wants to cleanse the world of people who are guilty of any one of the seven deadly sins. He's doing God's work. But he's a psycho. A demented serial killer. He's like a guy who votes for Dubya comes out and says he voted for him because of moral issues, which is code for he don't like gay marriage. So he's doing God's work in voting for a guy who is, first thing he gets elected, going to raze a city of three hundred thousand people. You know, the war on terror, which is God's work too except I say it's the devil's work.

PRINCE OF FILMTIDES: I seem to know from the beginning of that movie *Seven* that whoever is killing those people doesn't threaten me. For all the dark atmospherics of that movie and the claustrophic sense you get, I followed it like a police procedural. No fear. Tell me, Lowenstain, was that because the film didn't touch my personal psychodrama? Or was it because, following what Harry's been saying, our serial murderer fascination distances us and distracts us from what's going on in our own country that we should really be fearing? I mean, the fact that corporations are privatizing our democracy, befouling our environment for a profit, demonizing a federal government established by the founding fathers to protect us . . . I mean we get to think evil is just there with those serial murderers, those rare sociopaths, and psychopaths but . . . but it's in our government, in our corporations, in the people we've elected. We're living in some deranged, mesmerized, frightening picture of America we've created. But it's a picture that doesn't frighten us, and I don't know why. It frightens the rest of the world.

LOWENSTAIN LOWENSTAIN: I'll say it again, Prince. The world isn't the picture you have in your head; your head is making something dark and depressive of the world. Your time's up, gentlemen. If you want, I'll put on a DVD you might like. A colleague of mine, Dr. Cannibal Lecher, being questioned by an FBI agent, Agent Starwing, who suspected Dr. Lecher was a serial killer. You'll notice how Dr. Lecher gradually becomes the questioner, trying to turn the tables on Starwing.

—— ◆ ——

Script Doctor: At this point we turn the tables on Lowenstain; she wants to run a tape pushing her privatized view of fear. But we can trace fear to time and place—the insane, psychopath Angie Dickinson runs into in Brian De Palma's *Dressed to Kill* (1980), the natural-born killers on a mindless killing spree in Oliver Stone's *Natural Born Killers* (1994), the walking dead in George Romero's *Night of the Living Dead* (1968), *Dawn of the Dead* (1978), *Day of the Dead* (1985), the inbred, murdering, rapacious hillbilly cretins of John Boorman's *Deliverance* (1972), Wes Craven's *The Hills Have Eyes* (1977), *Wrong Turn*. The fear of death is a culturally relative fear and thus in the present the product of a marketing campaign.

——— ◆ ———

DVD is played:

CANNIBAL: Do you fear swimming in the ocean, Agent Starwing? Because I think you'd fear swimming in the ocean. Not knowing what might be below you. What dark presence might be lurking just beneath your wiggling toes.

AGENT STARWING: It's an archetypal fear, Dr. Lecher. We came out of the oceans. We had eons to develop fears of what swam in deep waters. It's carried over to present day. I've seen *Jaws* (1975) a hundred times, Dr. Lecher.

CANNIBAL: Very good, Agent Starwing. Do you know why *King Kong*, I mean the original 1933 version, not the mechanized farces of 1976 and 2005, so fills us with dread as those natives chant and beat their drums high on a wall they've built to keep something unknown coming toward us, breathing heavily, knocking over the trees in its path?

AGENT STARWING: I don't know. I suspect it's also an archetypal fear.

CANNIBAL: Right you are, Agent Starwing! It is indeed. Something monstrously huge coming out of the darkness toward us. And Kong. So like us. Walking upright. Is this the monster from which we descended? Or perhaps the fear is simply the small mammal's fear of the giant creatures whom for eons, as you say, ruled the planet. And the night, Agent Starwing. When monsters hunted and their prey hid and waited for the light of the day. We are that small, humble prey that once cowered in fear.

AGENT STARWING: But now we rule the earth, Dr. Lecher.

CANNIBAL: Trailing our fears I'm afraid, Agent Starwing. As you do. In spite of your very professional appearance.

AGENT STARWING: You promised to tell me why our sense of suspense can never seem dated . . .

CANNIBAL: Yes, indeed. We feel the same dread when faced with a certain arrangement of events and mood and sounds and looks. . . . The atmospherics of eeriness, Agent Starwing, are not subject to time and place. Because our plight as humans suspended in a dark void lit by stars far apart is fundamentally a mystery. The moon perched in that darkness is eerie; the diminishing light of day in the forests is eerie. We walk quickly passed the graveyard at night. And every year at All Hallow's Eve we costume ourselves in disguise and challenge the eeriness with a trick or treat! I see you've watched too many of those kind of movies, Agent Starwing.

AGENT STARWING: What makes you think I watch movies, Dr. Lecher?

DR. LECHER: Why, Agent Starwing. I can smell it on you. Bucket popcorn with cheap, imitation butter. Did you make out with all the boys in the back row? Did you put out in the dark movie theatres, Agent Starwing?

AGENT STARWING: Go #@##$ yourself, Dr. Lecher.

DR. LECHER: Why, Agent Starwing, you're getting a foul mouth. What would all your friends back in the 'holler think. Do you know why audiences screamed in fear and some even passed out when Lon Chaney's mask was pulled off in the *Phantom of the Opera* (1925)?

AGENT STARWING: It looked like a skull?

DR. LECHER: Not quite. It was a human face with death peering out. Beneath the most beautiful eyes, Agent Starwing, lurk dark, empty sockets. Behind the loveliest smile lurks the bony, toothy grin of death. Cheeks that blush now will be hollowed; the smoothest skin will fall away and reveal a bony gauntness beneath. *Memento mori*, Agent Starwing.

AGENT STARWING: That face doesn't frighten us anymore, Dr. Lecher. I just don't know whether we've overcome our fear of death.

DR. LECHER: That face has become familiar. Overexposed. We're used to it now. Being used to a representation of death doesn't imply that we have a new, postmodern arrangement with death. On the contrary, Agent Starwing, we are more vulnerable than ever. Can you tell me why?

AGENT STARWING: No, I can't, Dr. Lecher. And I don't want to play your games.

DR. LECHER: The guy with the most toys in the end wins Agent Starwing. The mantra of the moment. Do the toys keep the grim reaper away? I think not. Do the toys mean anything after you're dead? I think not. Then it must be that death doesn't matter to the living. It doesn't matter not because we've overcome the fear but because we're preoccupied. With our toys. There's not enough time in our lives, Agent Starwing. There's not enough space on our mental shelves for death, filled as they are with our Wal-Mart purchases. Isn't that wonderful, Agent Starwing? The first rule of global market capitalism is there is no death. The thought of death erodes the bottom line.

AGENT STARWING: But you're saying we fear more than ever.

DR. LECHER: A man doesn't spend his whole life building a wall because a wall is a good thing itself regardless of whether it has a purpose. The wall supports something. Or keeps something out. Every moment the wall is being built, its purpose is before us.

AGENT STARWING: Shopping is like building a wall.

DR. LECHER: Very good, Agent Starwing. If we don't shop, our economy collapses. We shop not motivated by need but rather propelled by subconscious desires and fears. Sexuality is detached from any frank, open discussion, thus driving desire into the dark recesses of the mind. We go surreptitiously hunting for it. Where to find it, Agent Starwing? Where? There. There it is. Now attached to products and services.

AGENT STARWING: So you're saying that we barricade ourselves against the fear of death by buying stuff. Death isn't attached to the product?

DR. LECHER: That would be the death of successful marketing, Agent Starwing. The opposite is sought: Totally detach product and services from death. Funeral services are growing shorter and shorter; wakes are almost obsolete. You are not to spend days wailing over a coffin of a loved one. Quick cremation; no body but a stylish urn of ashes. A memorial service like a testimonial. No body to perfume the air, Agent Starling. No keening permitted in the new millennium. When we see those Middle Eastern women wailing in grief on the TV we find it tacky. Tacky. Death, Agent Starwing, has become tacky.

AGENT STARWING: Times change.

DR. LECHER: The medieval ages fought death with a strategy of bringing it to full presence. They took it into their homes; they brought it to their lips; they took it on their journeys; they began their feasts and holidays with pilgrimages to graveyards; they held masses for the dead; they prayed for souls in purgatory. They sought heaven and shunned hell. Death was a companion. It shadowed birthing; it was more likely to find one before one found old age.

AGENT STARWING: I remember my mother saying that when her younger brother died when she was no more than eight or nine they put his body on ice and kept it in the living room for three days waking it.

DR. LECHER: The dead may awaken at a wake, Agent Starwing. But not to this world. We are engaged in a strategy of bringing death to full absence. And the more strenuously we pursue this strategy the more fearful do we become.

AGENT STARWING: I don't know, Dr. Lecher. It seems it takes an awful lot to scare us at the movies these days. We've seen it all. I mean you've got all those computer hijinks making ghosts and werewolves and such more realistic. But they've got to keep topping that or otherwise it looks pretty sad. Dated. I mean if we're so full of fear how come the movies have to work so hard to scare us?

DR. LECHER: They didn't work very hard with *The Blair Witch Project* (1999), Agent Starwing. Hand held cameras and no computer pyrotechnics. It isn't difficult to see that relying on computers and technical virtuosity is just throwing stuff at the task at hand—creating fear in an audience. The belief is that sophisticated production will generate fear; fear itself is a product to be so manufactured.

AGENT STARWING: But stuff is supposed to not generate fear.

DR. LECHER: There's no path to fear through things and products and computer ingenuity. There's also no path away from fear through the same. But what would you expect, Agent Starwing, from a society whose answer to everything relies on the sophisticated ideology of "pushing product"?

———◆———

Script Doctor: Comic relief moving us toward the post 9/11 mass psyche fear. Bring in a parody of Ash—call him Brash—from Sam Raimi's *Evil Dead* series.

———◆———

AGENT STARWING: Excuse me, Dr. Lecher. The man in the cell next to you just threw something at me.

BRASH: To get your attention, sister. I'm tired of listening to all that hogwash. Who fought the Armpit of Darkness? Me or you? Who's that? Me, that's who. Brash.

DR. LECHER: I have a doctorate in fear. I graduated summa cum laude in Halloween studies from Oxford. My great grandfather was Dr. Von Helsing. My maternal grandmother was the bride of Frankenstein. My paternal grandmother was Maleva the Gypsy in *The Wolf Man* (1941).

BRASH: Well, hullo, Mr. High and Mighty. Here's an update on your high-and-mighty life: You're not studying anything now but jack and shit. And jack left town.

AGENT STARWING: Mr. Brash, can you tell me why Freddie Krueger is so frightening?

BRASH: To who or whom? It's a generational thing. *Nightmare on Elm Street* comes out in 1984. White suburbanite kids nestled in a world soccer moms and Republican dads have made for them. This is not the fifties rebel without a cause. This is the eighties. Causes are dead. The only rebellion going on in the suburbs is in your dreams. That's where Freddie shows up. They need a boogeyman from the dark to get them. Why? They couldn't put it into words. I call it bourgeois guilt.

AGENT STARWING: Dr. Lecher, can you tell me why Michael Myers in *Halloween* (1978) is so frightening?

CANNIBAL: Put a man in a mask. Or wrapped like a mummy. Give him a slow gait. Put a long knife in his hand. Or set his hand out like a claw. Set him loose in a darkened world. Introduce folks. Just plain folks like you and me, Agent Starwing. Going about their everyday lives. When will our frightening friend appear? Suspense carefully orchestrated.

AGENT STARWING: But why, Dr. Lecher?

CANNIBAL: You should be able to decipher this by now, Agent Starwing. You're not a very good student, I'm afraid. In a society that makes "I Shop Therefore I Am" it's raison d'être, death must become the absent presence. Nothing must evoke it or summon it. But death, like conservative taxes on the payroll class, is an inevitable presence shadowing life. It is, therefore, a potent but absent force. Popular culture taps into it to push the products of popular culture. Marketing strategies have built a dam in our mass psyche behind which the waters of fear have risen. Tapping into those waters is very profitable, Agent Starwing.

AGENT STARWING: Death can arrive at any moment. And his face is shrouded in darkness. That bedrock fear is where Hollywood pitches its tent. I understand that. But it all seems timeless, and you seem to be saying our fear just has economic roots in corporate capitalism.

BRASH: Timeless my butt. 1932. *The Mummy.* 1999. *The Mummy.* Why has the 1999 film turned into an Indiana Jones farce? Why can't they just have a guy in bandages creep around like Karloff did in 1932? I'll tell you why. The 1999 audience is hyperkinetic; they're wired; they're digitalized. They want all the mummies the computer can generate in ten seconds. They want the Mummy video game with all the latest high-wire acts. Times change audiences.

AGENT STARWING: So you're saying we don't fear death any more?

BRASH: You saw *Final Destination* (2000). I saw *Final Destination* (2000). What do these kids fear? Losing. It's like they're on the *Survivor* TV show and competing to see who's going to survive, which means who's the winner, who gets the bucks. Death is going out of business, getting voted off the island. They don't want to go. They're trying to outwit him. It's death comes to Melrose Place. What I'm saying is that how you stage fear has all to do with where and when. Michael Myers and the mummy can only show up for laughs in *Scary Movie* (2000). Or they can show up as in *Scream* (1996) as "old school" and "old school" is fake and dead but what you're watching now is *now*. And now is *real* and where it's at. Why the need to be constantly reassured about what's real? Because reality is on camera; the mummy isn't walking toward you; he's walking toward the camera. And that little tweak in our perception makes us immune to old fears while sitting in a darkened theater and watching Karloff as the mummy. And leaves today's Jacks and Jills with a whole bunch of new fears. Like what? Who would know? I'm guessing it's not like death is an extreme makeover but more like death cancels your makeover appointment. It doesn't get any deeper than that.

AGENT STARWING: So you don't think a psychopath with an IQ of 200, a pulse of 40, and no conscience has evoked fear in his fellow citizens since the beginning of time.

BRASH: Then time must have started with the premiere of *Silence of the Lambs* (1991). If it fits into the profile of the moment, friend, then it'll register. Does the history of the present moment generate a fear of the serial killer? Does Jeff Dahmer baffle the mind and summon fear in us because we can't figure out what makes him tick? Sure. But to understand fear of Jeff you have to understand that in a divided society in which one half is a mystery to the other half, anything can emerge from that mystery. Both sides think the worse of the other. Were you paying attention to the 2004 U.S. presidential campaign?

AGENT STARWING: Is that why are we all of a sudden breeding these psychotic serial killers? I don't know. The nineteenth century had its Jack the Ripper, and every century before that was equally infested with psychotic murderers. I'm thinking that our fears are endemic and archetypal and that marketers aren't creating those fears but taking advantage of them.

BRASH: Jack the Ripper was a media sensation for sure, and he was a serial killer, but what made a serial killer back then is not what makes a serial killer now. I'm not saying they weren't around. I'm just saying they were different societal products off different cultural shelves. They were there in every century, but you'd have to be living in those centuries to be able to profile them. The reason why serial killers didn't stand out in previous centuries was because they got lost in a world of slaughter and guts. The homicide unit is a fairly recent invention. It only gets its start after the majority of people stop coming to a brutal end on a daily basis. Before that they get lost in the crowd.

AGENT STARWING: And they don't get lost in the crowd today. . . . I mean, we're fascinated with them today because we live in the opposite of a world of blood and guts all around us?

BRASH: Manicured lawns, diversified stock portfolios, remodeling projects at the summer cottage, cozy, secure and reliable cell-phone networking. Get the picture? World of televised football game blood and guts. Botoxed world to keep the lines of death invisible. And so far removed from being us, they look like Dr. Lecher here. He's what we fear and he's not real nor anything like us nor does he in any way connect with our real fears at this moment. He's the simulacra of what we should fear.

DR. LECHER: I don't have to fry up your brains, Mr. Brash. I fear they're already fried.

——◆——

THE BLOGOSPHERE

Blog: www.guiltridden.com

You want a movie that registers Americans' fear after 9/11? This from Luke Thompson writing in *Express*, January 7, 2004:

"Back in January of 2003, New Line Cinema released *Final Destination 2*, a horror movie in which the antagonist was the unseen hand of death itself. All the main characters knew their time was up, but they didn't know how or when, so they existed in a constant state of fear, never knowing from which angle death might suddenly claim them. Real life has felt a bit like that for a while now. If that vaguely worded terror alert that switches to Code Orange doesn't make you paranoid, there's always the possibility of suffocation via government-approved plastic sheeting and duct tape."

This is not the fear of a people absolutely confident that they are innocent victims, of those who in the deepest regions of their hearts and souls fear harm from those they have never harmed. I think not. Post-9/11 fear is a guilt-ridden fear; somehow we know that we had a chance to consume less and share more, that we had our chance to oust despotic regimes in the Middle East but it wasn't in our interests, that we had a chance to help the former Soviet Union at its most needy moment in 1989 but we allowed it to sink into chaos, that we had our chance in the 1990s to transfer huge stock-market wins into campaigns against AIDS, tuberculosis, malaria, hepatitis, dysentery, malnutrition, illiteracy, and poverty throughout the world. We had our moment, but in every case we opted for the newest new in the shopping aisles and fashion salons. We chose ourselves as the only target of our interests. And now someone is choosing us as a target of their interests.

Blog: www.bushwa.com

Hollywood is making a profit on our fear *and* on the very opposite—putting fear so far off the screen we think we're in Disneyland. Then you can also see fear working glibly in Republican politics. Bush-wa plays it like it's the only note on his piano. But how do you get an intelligent person to put aside a critical reasoning capacity that trumps Bush-wa's "automated reactions"? Here's how Terry Eagleton (*After Theory*, 2003) describes the Bush-wa response to 9/11: "Since September 11, a number of anti-theoretical terms have been in vogue in the United States. They include 'evil,' 'freedom-loving,' 'bad men,' 'patriot,' and 'anti-American.' These terms are anti-theoretical because they are invitations to shut down thought. Or, indeed, in some cases, imperious commands to do so. They are well-thumbed tokens that serve in place of thought, automated reactions that make do for the labour of analysis." If thought hadn't been closed down we might be spending some time in working out, as Eagleton puts it, "why they hate us so much." Instead, we're at the moment looking to fire a tenured Colorado university prof for making a connection between Eichmann, who was a willing functionary of the Nazi nasty, and those financiers working in the Trade Towers on September 11. His point, clearly, is that we have invested in a kind of globalized capitalism that is more insidious than the colonializing imperialism of previous centuries. We have no need to set up a Raj or a Vichy government; shareholders profits can be maximized by the operation of those transnational corporations a small percentage of the world's population is fortunate enough to be invested in.

But Eichmann was aware of his complicity in the Nazi horrors, which, of course, he rationalized in some personally amenable way, having to do, I'm sure, with the self-realization of the German people, their need to find liberty and freedom by working their way out of the tyranny of Jewish banking and other "evil" perpetrated by "evil men." He, like his *fuehrer*, was a freedom fighter. What nonsense such an alibi seems to us now. Did the brokers, financiers, bankers, investment analysts, and so on who died on September 11 see themselves as soldiers of capitalist imperialism? Had each of them concocted a defensive alibi story that protected them against

THE BLOGOSPHERE

such a charge? Had they adopted the voodoo economics of "trickle down," by which all the world's poor would one day benefit from venture capitalists seeking short-term return on investment, CEOs downsizing and outsourcing in a quarterly rush to maximize profits, and shareholders voting against workers' rights, environmental protections, and consumer protections to maxmize their own portfolio profits? Had they simply been just good market conservatives, following a reigning creed in the United States since Reagan?

Clearly enough Americans believe this creed will eventually "raise all boats," expand the middle class and expand the creation of democracies all over the world. But a distinction must be made between those who benefit directly, as shareholders and investors and those who serve them, and those, say, the next 80 percent of the world's population, who are not presently benefiting from the same, and, unlike Dickens's Mr. Micawber, see nothing fortunate on the horizon. You can see that the top 20 percent have no need to stretch to meet and, thereby, accept and support the "automatic reactions" of the White House. Those reactions benefit them. There is no profit, so to speak, in their investigating Eagleton's query: Why do they hate us? That's a road they don't want to go down. On the other hand, those not reaping present rewards in our severely wealth-divided country really do have to stretch to accept the White House's "automated reactions" urging them to be filled with fear. Only if fear were to abate would one ask the question "why do they hate us?" At present, the administration's automated reactions disconnects causes from 9/11 and, therefore, fear is left to roam, floating free of any rational interrogation and, therefore, forever floating. You might say this is a blockading of intellectual inquiry we've been dedicated to since the Enlightenment.

Enough Americans have stopped at the outset of inquiry to give Bush-wa another go at being President of the United States. Thomas Frank in *What's the Matter with Kansas?* is desperate to track down the logic his fellow Kansans employed in voting for the man who had already in his first four years proven he wasn't going to do anything good for the working man and maybe a whole lot that would be bad for them. The same kind of astounding ignorance led them to accept Bush-wa's "automated reactions" and that unthinking acceptance has put them into a "theater of fear" they can see no way out of because they have short-circuited the critical thinking process that would examine causes, responses, and remedies.

Once you get enough Americans into that "theater of fear" you can push any number of hate campaigns. You can see this scenario working in what Thomas Frank calls the "backlash conservatism," which has gone on in the United States since Reagan. The backlash here is against the supra-liberality and valueless politics of liberals. There's a fear in the heartland that liberals will unground their Christian morals, trample on the sacredness of heterosexual marriage, turn "family values" into "Feminazi" values, legalize pot, abort future Bush-wa's, and drink café lattes while the United Nations invades Montana. All those fears, and many more new ones being spun everyday, have created an Us against Them divide. Liberal Polluters of the Soul vs. Godly Conservatives. This is not the Marxist class warfare of proles vs. capitalists. This divisiveness is economics-free. "The erasure of the econonmic," Thomas Frank writes, "is a necessary precondition for most of the basic backlash ideas" (128).

So what we have is an American populace amazingly side-tracked from the role corporations relishing a global free market game board have on their lives. And instead these Americans buy into the fear and hatred of a backlash mythos. They bought it because it was marketed to them by a business rationality they can't critique because critique is the one thing that capitalism doesn't market. Before 9/11 Americans were already on a daily diet of fear and hate, the kind of diet that put critical thinking and history out of sight. It's not surprising then that the same tactics that torched liberalism would torch Iraq, a flame that can spread anywhere.

This is now an American style honed on conservative backlash tactics and now globalized. What else could explain Bush-wa's victory in 2004 but this linkage—not between Saddam and bin Laden—but liberals and al-Qaeda, liberals and Saddam, liberals and bin Laden, liberals and the Arab world, and liberals and treason, as Ann Coulter asserts. Electing a Massachusetts liberal—John Kerry—trying to sound like a past Massachusetts Liberal—JFK—whose New Frontier turned out to be the countercultural frontier of the 1960s, would be the last thing an American populace long fed on fear and hatred of liberals, would ever do. That 2004 election showed that there were some three million more Americans who accepted Bush-wa's "automated reactions" than Americans who didn't. Bush-wa was elected by those whose fear and hate had trumped reason and ignored what lessons history teaches.

Blog: www.rageon.com

I would like to comment on the Bush-wa blogger who seems to think that fear and hate after 9/11 are unjustified. I quote an editorial from *The New Criterion*, April 2003:

THE BLOGOSPHERE

"[W]hat most Americans felt after September 11 was rage, not guilt, and it wasn't an 'odd' rage, either. It was the perfectly justifiable rage any normal person feels when his country is attacked and 3,000 innocent people are slaughtered by a gang of ravening lunatics."

If liberals take the view that Americans are, first of all, too stupid to see who's hitting them, and, secondly, that mainstream Americans just transferred their dislike of liberals to al-Qaeda, then they're more out of touch with the real world and real people than anybody thought. I, for one, had been giving liberals too much credit. Now I do think they're anti-American. Who needs a political party like that at a time like now?

Blog: www.911adrenaline.com

I ask the Bush-wa blogger whether it was ultimately in the interests of the victims of the Holocaust to ponder Hitler's reasons. What the Bush-wa blogger condemns as "automated reactions" may simply be the instincts of survival, which were on display recently when animals obeyed their "automated reactions" and avoided the Indian Ocean tsunami. Fear has its purposes; biologically it spurs the release of adrenaline, which enables an accelerated physical response to danger. The president's supporters didn't go through the kind of "critical reasoning" that left the liberal candidate Mr. Kerry just about incomprehensible on every issue. There's certainly no problem with changing one's views, or being torn equally between positions for a time. But now is not the moment in U.S. history for such indecision. President Bush won a second term because he's displayed and advocated the same kind of survival instincts and responses as a majority of Americans. His instincts are alive and healthy, whereas it became quite clear that Mr. Kerry's weren't.

Blog: www.scaryworld.com

Where has Europe's Hamlet-like incapacity to act left them at this moment? France and Germany have done numerous soliloquies off the stage of action, in-depth analysis of the United State's "automated reactions," and have broadcast enough reasons why the whole world hates the United States to satisfy even the Bush-wa blogger. Unfortunately, at this moment, for all their enlightened responses, the Europeans now suddenly realize what game they're in. It's called the Survival Game. It matters little how socially democratic The Netherlands may be, how wonderfully pluralistic and tolerant, how well they have engineered a society in which no loser need go without a bed, or a yearly income for that matter. But the death of Theo Van Gogh, a fringe, independent filmmaker who couldn't get distributed in the United States—unless he was ruthlessly murdered by an Islamic fundamentalist and everyone got curious about his films—has shown the Dutch that progressive social policies are no defense against religious zealots. Victor Hanson, writing in *The New Criterion*, January 26, 2005, puts it best:

"Europeans may brag of soft power, but in the scary world to come let us hope that they can bribe, beg, lecture, or appease Iranians, North Koreans, Chinese, and others to appreciate the realities of their postmodern world that has supposedly transcended violence and war."

THE BLOGOSPHERE

American Cool

Since having sex in the 1960s was a kind of sacred obligation, like wearing mascara or worshipping your ancestors, morality rapidly gave way to style. Or, indeed, to politics. The ethical was for suburbanites, while the political was cool.
—Terry Eagleton, *After Theory*, 2003

You're money, man. Don't you know it?
—*Swingers*, 1996

"Michael Moore vs. Mel Gibson. Hilary Clinton vs. Newt Gingrich. Smarter kids vs. Smarter bombs"—these dichotomies between cool, liberal "metro America" and vulgar, conservative "retro America."
—Michael Lind, "Red State Sneer," *Prospect*, January 2005

Can we be square again? We were last square half a century ago. Then we were, more or less, successively, hep, hip, cool, wild, beat, alienated, mod, groovy, radical, turned-on, dropped out, ironic, Clintonian, and, finally, postmodern, which is to say exhausted—and who can blame us? In all these states we were, first and above all, not square.
—Michael Kelly, "Getting Hip to Squareness," *Things Worth Fighting For*, 2004

[T]he cool universe of digitality has absorbed and won out over the reality principle.
—Peter Pelzer, "Dead Man—An Encounter with the Unknown Past," *Journal of Organizational Management*, 2002

Voice-over: There is no film genre called "American Cool" but "coolness" is the number-one item that we now merchandise globally.

Nobody does it better. No country pictures "cool" with what Joseph Nye calls "soft power"—the power to attract, to persuade, and to influence—anywhere near the level that the United States does. As we slowly (and painfully for "outsourced" workers) move out of domestic manufacturing, we continue to manufacture pictures of "coolness" consumed globally. When conservative economists herald the coming of a post-Fordist consumer capitalist service economy (a global computer network—cyberspace—is the *sine qua non* force here) they foresee American workers as brokers in every field, neither growing nor manufacturing but providing essential services for sellers and buyers. They foresee American workers working as "symbolic analysts," providing the necessary information for sellers and buyers. Perhaps this future has already been sabotaged by the energy broker Enron's scandalous example, but that may be a questionable assumption. There is no question, however, that we do succeed in manufacturing consumers domestically and internationally. We produce a product— "coolness"—that we have found the international code for. Code?

In a *Frontline* titled "Persuasion" Americans were introduced to a French market strategist who was paid by Fortune 500 companies to find the "code" for luxury. This "code" would describe a set of values and meanings existing in the American mass psyche of the moment, on both conscious and unconscious levels. Rapaille seeks to find this "code" within the reptilian part of the brain, the brain of irrational desire, repression, trauma, and delusion. Once advertisers create advertising campaigns that fit this psychological code they can push their luxury products. But Americans haven't overwhelming "soft power" in regard to luxury. In fact it may turn out that Rapaille's secret "luxury code," the psychological impetus drawing Americans to luxury items, even if they can't afford them, may have connections to our inferiority in the face of the deep cultural class-riven distinctiveness of European luxury. You have to look to the "coolness" code to find overwhelming American soft power. There is an eye-opening connection between American movies and coolness that does not exist for luxury. We picture "coolness" on that reptilian level Rapaille seeks.

Another *Frontline* special entitled "The Merchants of Cool" focused on marketing "cool hunters," marketers who went in search for what "coolness" was in the world of teens at that moment. Once they had a finger on the pulse of "coolness" they too could "push product," until the view of "coolness" changed. MTV, for instance, became an indicator of what coolness might be, or, more precisely, MTV entered the teen's world so thoroughly that it was the place teens went to find cool. Hollywood, however, has been the capital of cool for decades and now that coolness has become our primary export it's about time we recognize this powerful new genre of American Cool.

———◆———

Script Doctor: Hollywood linked coolness with rebellion. Who's cooler than Rick in *Casablanca* (1942)? Or John Garfield in *Body and Soul* (1947)? Who's cooler than James Dean in *Rebel Without A Cause* (1955)? Who's cooler than Peter Fonda's Captain America in *Easy Rider* (1969)? Who's cooler than Donald Sutherland and Elliot Gould in *MASH* (1970), John Travolta as Vincent in *Pulp Fiction* (1994)? Who's cooler than The Dude in *The Big Lebowski* (1998)? Who's cooler than Jack Nicholson in *Five Easy Pieces* (1970), or Linda Fiorentino in *The Last Seduction* (1994) when she goes into that redneck bar? Rebels all. Totally American. And why not? Who's a bigger rebel anywhere than Tom Paine? We didn't have a revolution; we had a rebellion. Rebellion is in our blood, in our roots. What are Americans rebelling against? "Whatya got?" Brando responds for the whole country in *The Wild One* (1953). Young blood, young guns. Every guy willing to fight the law when the law always wins, from Billy the Kid, Clyde Barrow, John Dillinger to Jesse James, Jack Kerouac to Bob Dylan, Elvis to Snoop Doggy Dog and Tupac. Who's cooler than Paul Newman as *Cool Hand Luke?* Ask them that.

———◆———

Characters: Vincent Le Big Mac: a filmscape character based on John Travolta's Vincent Vega in Pulp Fiction; *Jules Kung Fu: a filmscape character based on Samuel L. Jackson's Jules in* Pulp Fiction; *Jack Honeyimhome: a filmscape character based on Jack Nicholson; Linda Seduction: a filmscape character based on Linda Fiorentino in* The Last Seduction.

———◆———

LINDA SEDUCTION: @#$*#@ off.

JACK HONEYIMHOME: What we definitely got here is a failure to communicate. You remember when Strother Martin tells Paul Newman that in *Cool Hand Luke* (1967)? So, let's back up. I'll take the chicken salad on toast, no lettuce, no tomato, no mayo. Then give me the number-two scrambled eggs. Hold the chicken, give me the toast and the scrambled eggs.

LINDA SEDUCTION: You're a jerk. You think young rebels began with *Easy Rider*. So what was the real Jack—I'm talking about Jack Kerouac—and not you, jackoff, doing on the road? The Fifties, Jack, the Fifties. Ever hear of James Dean? Rebel at home, at school, on the road, and east of eden. And before that you never saw a John Garfield movie? Forties. And he's on the road, wandering into that greasy little diner with Nick the Greek and his hot wife, Lana Turner. And Bogie? "Tampico, what a town." A cool expatriot in *Treasure of the Sierra Madre*.

JACK HONEYIMHOME: The thing that you fail to understand, Linda, is that the real rebels don't go around mumbling in their navels or running out a toilet paper roll of bullshit.

VINCENT LE BIG MAC: What she's saying, Jack, is that James Dean made you feel his pain without saying a word.

JACK HONEYIMHOME: Put a hold on the teenage angst, will you? What you got there in those Dean movies is the so-called generation gap hitting the screen. It's the dark side of Ozzie and Harriet. It's like Ricky Nelson and his dad Ozzie can't communicate. Okay. Send in the clowns. Is this something grown-ups can care about? So what did we do with that kind of rebellion? We turned it into the Osbornes, Ozzie and his family, the comedy of family dysfunctionality. We kicked the whole "I never sang for my father" angst up to postmod parodic levels. Give me an angst sandwich, hold the 1950s and James Dean.

VINCENT LE BIG MAC: I don't care what you say, man. The Dean does it for me. He nails the rebel-without-a-cause thing.

JULES KUNG FU: I think you'll have to admit, Vincent, that compared with the vagrant, nomadic, down on their luck, discarded by the American capitalist system outcasts like Garfield . . . and let me remind you, Vincent, I'm talking about films like *Body and Soul* (1947), *Force of Evil* (1948), *They Made Me a Criminal* (1939), and *The Postman Always Rings Twice* (1946) . . . what the 1950s rolled in was the rebellion of decadent capitalism. The youthful spoiled products of an inhumane economic system were dazed, confused, frustrated, angry, and disappointed. So what did they do, Vincent? They pouted and mumbled under their breath or they went out by the quarry and did "chicken" races with their souped-up cars. The Dean did both so he was doubly sure to get your attention.

VINCENT LE BIG MAC: You are totally missing the coolness of The Dean's rebellion, man. It's existential; it's ontological. It's a rebellion from the gut. It has to do with the whole universe, man. Sure Bogey's got that Depression-era edge in *Sierra Madre*. Fred C. Dobbs. Panhandling expat in Tampico who's trying out the American Dream of Greed. His humanity gets totally eaten up—that's if he had any in the first place. He's a victim, not a rebel. Same with Garfield. He's always trying to work his way inside, where the success is, but he always winds up on the outside. He's a victim, not a rebel. They run into a social order that's like a wall. They're two steps away from being Tom Joad in *The Grapes of Wrath* (1940). And how cool is he? Zero cool is how cool.

JULES KUNG FU: My rebellion moves up from teenagers fighting with their dads to adults clashing with the evil by-products of economic inequality. That's all I'm saying, Vincent.

VINCENT LE BIG MAC: And my rebellion doesn't have anything to do with the forces of outside evil but all to do with a deep, inner rebellion against the nature of things. That's all I'm saying, Jules. It's a rebellion of the cool gesture, the cool look, the cool lighting of a cigarette. You can see it and hear it in Brando in *The Wild One* (1954) when the counter girl asks him what he's rebelling against and he says "Whatya got?"

JACK HONEYIMHOME: I got to admit that was cool.

LINDA SEDUCTION: You would. Testosterone on motorcycles? Coolness now is nothing more than a stupid image thing. Real-world problems are real problems, not image problems. Unfortunatey, we live in an age of hype, which you boys eat up. For you it's all about how something appears on the screen, not what it may be in reality. Coolness is one of the pictures we're forced to live in, and it has nothing to do with the world. What I'd like to see is the fat Brando on a Harley. That would be less than cool, right Jack?

JACK HONEYIMHOME: *Less than Zero* (1987). Great film showing that cool rebellion you're always talking about, Vincent.

VINCENT LE BIG MAC: That's not coolness, Jack. That's just a bunch of have-it-all kids who have their little fits when having it all doesn't cut it. The 1980s is filled with flicks like that. Why? Because if you take a decade that makes Gordon Gekko from *Wall Street* (1987) your cultural role model you're going to wind up with youth only appearing in your profit analysis report. Those 1980s kids are not trying to find where they fit in the universe; they're trying to get back in as something more than marketing targets.

JULES KUNG FU: No, Vincent. They've given up trying. Trying means you're responding to a certain situation that exists in the world at that moment. It means you have intentions, if not ambitions. Rebels may be naturally born or man-made, but if they don't know what society means by an outlaw and they don't know when they're being outlaws, then they're not rebels. They're just insensible.

VINCENT LE BIG MAC: You're talking about the 1986 film *The River's Edge* where these kids are like totally affectless when they find the body of a friend naked at the river's edge and she was killed by another member of their clique.

JACK HONEYIMHOME: Beautiful clash of rebels from different generations. Dennis Hopper is the old 1960s rebel who tells these kids that unless they know what the rules of the game are they can't be rebels. And they don't know. They're in that less-than-zero zombie state.

VINCENT LE BIG MAC: Oblivious. Manufactured oblivion. Twentysomethings and younger in Iraq wondering when an IED is going to blow them to kingdom come. Twentysomethings on TV's *Survivor* shows pretending their lives are in danger. The mock survivors are totally oblivious of the real death their generation is facing. And the people watching them? Thinking they're so cool and they'd love to be on the show pretending to be a survivor so they can be cool? Something died with these kids, something totally human and real, and that ain't cool.

JULES KUNG FU: *Frontline* did a special called "Merchants of Cool." What was it about? Selling coolness to teenagers. Once a product gets linked with being cool, then it's boomtown. I am pleased, Vincent, that you now see that the economic order that the rebels of the 1930s and 1940s fought has in the 1980s discarded, disenfranchised, and destroyed youth in this country. To be young is nothing more than to be an easy mark for advertisers of cool.

LINDA SEDUCTION: Can we call it round one with you two? I threw up on *The Breakfast Club* (1985), and if I ever feel like getting into the mood to cut my wrists I'll rent a Molly Ringwald film like *Pretty in Pink* (1986) or *Sixteen Candles* (1984).

JACK HONEYIMHOME: Pardon me, Ms. Seduction, but those are just teeny bopper I-got-a-pimple-before-the-prom movies.

VINCENT LE BIG MAC: *Ferris Bueller's Day Off* (1986) . . .

JACK HONEYIMHOME: Pardon me once again, but let's get to the 1960s when rebellion wasn't you against your pop, or against the winds of fate, but a rebellion by one generation against the corporate/state of another generation. Ladies and gentlemen, it's a countercultural moment in American history, a moment when true radicals and rebels were born. This is not the inarticulate mumbling of James Dean or the existential angst of Jack Kerouac. This is a new revolution; a new romantic revolution incited by the free speech movement, Vietnam, civil rights, feminism, the New Left, Pope John XXIII, the Greening of America, the Chicago Seven, the Port Huron Statement, Free Huey . . .

LINDA SEDUCTION: If you mean drugs, sex, and rock 'n roll, why don't you say it? You want to see a couple, three, guys sitting around a campfire off an Interstate smoking weed as rebels doing a rebel thing, go for it. Personally I walked out on *Easy Rider*. Got a low tolerance for alienated guys on Harleys searching for the "real America" but really heading for a whorehouse in New Orleans. Coolness is a male thing, and males are infants fed infantilizing images.

VINCENT LE BIG MAC: The real Captain America is Peter Fonda? That movie took itself too seriously, man. That's not coolness. The 1960s thought it was cool but I don't see anything cool up there on the screen. Some very uncool movies were big rebel movies back in the day. All those Billy Joe Jack movies . . .

JULES KUNG FU: Billy Jack. *Born Losers* was in 1967, but then *Billy Jack* came out in 1971. And then *The Trial of* . . . and then *BJ Goes to Washington* . . .

LINDA SEDUCTION: For my money, you get deeper portraits of sociopaths in 1960s films like *Cool Hand Luke* (1967) and *Cape Fear* (1962). You keep talking about what's cool and what isn't, Vincent, but you don't know what you're talking about.

VINCENT LE BIG MAC: And you do?

LINDA SEDUCTION: Yeah, because I know why Vincent Vega was so cool in *Pulp Fiction*. He's a sociopath. And so is Linda Fiorentino in *The Last Seduction*. They seem cool to you because they do what they want, when they want, and they don't cry, moan, or bitch. They're cool about it. Why? Because things don't register with them the way they do with normal people. They're a disconnect between head and heart is the way some people put it. It's like they heard the preacher and the teacher but it went in one ear and out the other. No conscience, none of your normal fears and worries. They're cool, Vincent, because their hearts never beat fast. They don't beat for anyone or anything. People, society, memories. Blank. They don't get caught up in the hype. Nobody spins them. They're detached.

JACK HONEYIMHOME: Yeah, Frank Sinatra came up the hard way and couldn't conceal his edge, but Dean Martin, he was detached. Cool.

JULES KUNG FU: Yeah. I get it. So that means there's really one real rebel in the 1980s. Mickey Rourke in *Angel Heart* (1987). Breaks all the rules, God's and man's, and goes looking for the guy who's done it 'cause he's a detective and he's hired to find this guy. He's hired to find himself. Very, very cool.

VINCENT LE BIG MAC: Then the truest sociopath of them all. Kirk Douglas in *Lonely Are the Brave* (1962). Very first scene: man on horseback. Kirk Douglas. Cowboy hat. Rides up to barb wire fence. Can't go any further. No trespassing. It's 1870 and he's riding fence out in Wyoming. No. A plane flies overhead. It's the present. Kirk takes out a pair of wire cutters, cuts the wire and rides through, rides across an Interstate, rides up to the back door, dismounts, goes inside. He's riding through.

JULES KUNG FU: How does he wind up?

VINCENT LE BIG MAC: Jules, I swear to you, he has a whole police force after him after he escapes from jail. He got himself locked up so he can talk a friend of his who's in jail to escape with him. Kirk has to escape alone. Rides over the high mountains, chased by cars, horses, helicopters. Makes it to safety. Almost. Horse spooks crossing an Interstate and they get hit. They kill the horse and Kirk just lies there in the road looking up at us. Lonely are the brave in a world that crushes the free and independent spirit.

LINDA SEDUCTION: Next you'll be telling me Marlon Brando with his snakeskin jacket in *The Fugitive Kind* (1959) is the same kind of romantic spirit. But you know how David Lynch mocks the hell out of that with Nick Cage's performance in *Wild at Heart* (1990). He wears the same snakeskin jacket symbolizing his rebellious spirit. You don't realize how stupid and silly all that is until you witness how stupid and silly what goes on in Sailor Ripley's—that Cage's character in the film—head is. There's nothing Hollywood romantic about the kind of independence and difference you see in a true sociopath.

VINCENT LE BIG MAC: Elvis is Sailor's hero. You could say Elvis was the first to really rock the foundations of the whole American culture.

LINDA SEDUCTION: Yeah, the fat Elvis wound up rocking the foundations of a Vegas stage.

VINCENT LE BIG MAC: You are one tough lady, Ms. Seduction.

LINDA SEDUCTION: I'm not so tough, Vincent. You're just used to Rayette women.

VINCENT LE BIG MAC: I am? What's a Rayette woman?

JACK HONEYIMHOME: That was the stand-by-your-man-momma in *Five Easy Pieces* (1970). Film where they were getting into the nitty gritty of sociopathic behavior. Jack Nicholson can't work up any interest in his talent—he was a classical piano prodigy—his family, his life or his girlfriend Rayette. Except for the sex that is. Which is not confined to Rayette.

LINDA SEDUCTION: Then they went and put a "never sang for my father"—remember that movie?—tag to his behavior and screwed it all up. But that's what America was prepared to hear about sociopaths in 1970. They got their way because they just never had that "man-to-man" talk with their dad, Judge Hardy. Pathetic. A person detached herself and she's a sociopath. Give me a break.

VINCENT LE BIG MAC: Look, if it was a Depression-era movie Jack would be that way because of society, the hard economic times, the crush of capitalist oppression. If Jack were in the postwar years of the 1940s he'd just be facing the sudden dark tragedy of an accidental life in an accidental universe. If Jack were in the 1950s he'd be the rebel son; 1960s he'd be society's rebel. The 1970s is a totally divided decade. Midway Watergate and Nixon disconnects the whole cultural memory from the 1960s so the decade finishes with Travolta and disco fever, full polyester, and a born-again Prez.

JULES KUNG FU: Until Ronnie Reagan pulls his Frankenstein—the market player—out of the laboratory.

VINCENT LE BIG MAC: The way I see it, *Five Easy Pieces* targets those guys in the pickup truck who waste Captain America and Billy on the highway at the end of *Easy Rider*. *Five Easy Pieces* is trying to show that there's disaffection, anomie, and estrangement in the redneck trailer park segment of society. But remember: Jack lives like a redneck but he comes from an upper-middle-class culturally elite background. It's that class that provokes the rebellion of the hippies and the rednecks.

JULES KUNG FU: I don't agree with that, Vincent. Class warfare isn't the root 'cause of Jack's estrangement. It's personal; he could never be what his father wanted him to be.

VINCENT LE BIG MAC: Okay. So the film retreats to the I-never-sang-for-my-father motivation but not before it shows us what a bunch of boobs the so-called elite are. This is a movie that wants to deal with class warfare, Jules, but it doesn't want to look like Clifford Odets's *Golden Boy* (1939) or *Dead End* (1937). It's like movies went through their socialist phase, went all dark with Joe McCarthy and his blacklist, and now in 1970 that's all extinct. Old, over, and adios.

JACK HONEYIMHOME: I'm sorry, fellas, but I gotta defend the 1970s. I mean, look at Woody Allen's flick *The Front* (1976). He takes all the nonsense of that Joe McCarthy era and implodes it. You gotta respect that. Political rebellion is not dead in the late 1970s.

LINDA SEDUCTION: Maybe you should take your dark glasses off some time, Jack, and see what's actually up there on the screen. The disco duck late 1970s segue nicely into the roll out the red carpet for the rich era of the 1980s. So @#$##!! that. The thing that bugs me is that you get a film, *Kalifornia*, in 1993 with a sociopath—Brad Pitt as redneck Early Grace—and the film is all about this writer—David Duchovny as the naïve Brian Kessler—trying to find out what makes sociopaths tick, and he winds up with nonsense explanations. Here's the plot: This writer and his girlfriend hook up with Early and his girlfriend Adele on a drive to California with stops along the way at places where a serial killer killed. Early and Adele are brought along to defray gas expenses. But Early is a genuine sociopath.

JACK HONEYIMHOME: That's because in 1992 you put a sociopath in as prez. But don't get me wrong. I liked the guy.

VINCENT LE BIG MAC: So what are the nonsense explanations for what makes this Early Grace a sociopath?

LINDA SEDUCTION: First, Duchovny is probing for the father thing. Early hated his father. Early should take a good look at the face of the cop he's about to shoot and see that he's not his father. What does Early say? Crap, I know he's not my father. He's just a cop that's hurting bad and I gotta put him out of his misery. So what does the smart writer finally conclude about sociopaths? "These people are evil. Plain and simple."

JACK HONEYIMHOME: I could see how the moral tag would annoy you, Ms. Seduction.

LINDA SEDUCTION: It doesn't annoy me, Jack. It just makes me think how stupid some people are. Do you know that for centuries a rich man could sleep with another man's wife on their wedding night because it was a perk of the rich? Did you know during the Spanish Inquisition you could torture a supposed heretic until he confessed and then you'd kill him because he was on the devil's side and the devil always lies. Did you know none of that got tagged "evil"? It's an empty word, a whore word that fits the needs of the times. When you hear it used, watch out: Somebody is trying to hide something.

JACK HONEYIMHOME: Which, in the case of our friend Early Grace, is what?

LINDA SEDUCTION: "I'll never know why Early Grace became a killer" is what the dumbass writer tell us. "When I looked into his eyes I saw nothing. No guilt, no remorse, no confronting your conscience. Early never did."

VINCENT LE BIG MAC: That reminds me of Hannibal Lecter in *Silence of the Lambs* (1991). No conscience, a resting pulse of 40, and an IQ of

200. That's the most dangerous creature on the planet. Seldom available for observation. Why? 'Cause they're too smart to be detected by the lame bureaucratic procedures of the police.

JULES KUNG FU: So is Hannibal the typical sociopath of the 1990s, Vincent?

VINCENT LE BIG MAC: He's a sharp surgical tool used to take apart the privileged order of things. He's the ultimate deconstructor in a decade on the march against false constructions of reality and truth. His kind fill the 1990s: Max Cady in Scorsese's *Cape Fear* (1991); he's the Joker played by Jack Nicholson in the 1989 *Batman* directed by Tim Burton. And the two are larger than life; they're all over the place. In the 1962 *Cape Fear*, Robert Mitchum's Max Cady is an evil to be clearly separated from Gregory Peck's goodness. The 1991 evil interpenetrates every character and every incident, including Nick Nolte, the 1991 version of good guy Gregory Peck. What's happened? Modernity makes every effort to distinguish good from evil, true from false, sane from insane, ugly from beautiful and so on. Postmodernity sees us living in stories of these which change over time and from place to place, run into each other, change moral valences and keep running a bridge across the safe spread between the cape of goodness and the cape of evil.

JULES KUNG FU: It sounds like you're making the sociopath the cool dude of the 1990s, Vincent.

LINDA SEDUCTION: Why not? We're in a world fast turning us into products that we're forever shopping for. Who escapes? The person who can't be targeted. What will that person do? Whatever suits them and not the bottom line of some Fortune 500 corporation. There's nobody left in the mall to seize the day. Except the sociopath. What we're exporting to the world is the coolness of sociopathy.

JACK HONEYIMHOME: I love it. I just love it. Spoken like a true sociopath. What did Linda Fiorentino say in *The Last Seduction*? Murder is commitment?

LINDA SEDUCTION: What's the matter, Jack? Scared to move across the capes of fear?

JACK HONEYIMHOME: Call me old-fashioned, but James Cagney's Cody Jarrett in *White Heat* (1949) is my kind of nut job, the tough, little guy fighting a world that deserves to be fought, that won't give him a break, a me-against-the-world world. And he's nuts; his mother's nuts and she passes that on to Cody, the obedient, loving son. You know where he's coming from, where he's going to wind up and along the way his anger dazzles you and you cheer at the end when he gets on top of that tower and yells "Top of the world, Ma!" and then blows up you think "crazy bastard." You don't think, maybe I'm just as crazy as he is. You know where you are in the moral order and you know where he is. I like that.

LINDA SEDUCTION: It does make it convenient for the sheriff, Jack. Not to mention the power brokers who made him sheriff.

JACK HONEYIMHOME: Jeez, who's talking about the sheriff? What sheriff?

JULES KUNG FU: I think you can clearly see that Patrick Bateman in *American Psycho* (2000) is just a psychopath. It's hard to find anything redeeming in his actions. He's not a romantic rebel or even a quixotic sociopath who can find a clever way to get what he wants in a diner. He's just a madman.

VINCENT LE BIG MAC: I agree with you, Jules. He's like Mr. Orange in *Reservoir Dogs* (1992). Or the hit man James Gandolfini plays in *True Romance* (1993). Nothing of those guys crosses over into normal life. You can't make heroes out of those guys. They're not cool.

LINDA SEDUCTION: You take your big-market-player hero, add a dash of the sociopath's blindness to what we call the moral order and you get Patrick Bateman. He's not a member of Fight Club. He's not going to join Project Mayhem. He's not going to blow up the credit card companies. He's just going to clobber people who get in the way of his corporate success.

JACK HONEYIMHOME: So you liked *Fight Club* (1999)? Tyler Durden was your kind of sociopath? You know, he's a waiter who pisses in your soup. He's a projectionist that flashes a penis on the movie screen. Then he finally blows up credit card companies. He's a fun guy.

LINDA SEDUCTION: "What you own winds up owning you." You know, Jack, for a guy who played with great relish a psycho who wants to chop up his family, you . . .

JACK HONEYIMHOME: If you remember the film, Linda, you'll remember that the guy goes berserk because the place is haunted. He wasn't a member of Fight Club. He didn't enlist; he got drafted by fatal forces outside his control.

LINDA SEDUCTION: I love the way you guys will hunt up some fable to justify your actions. It's fate or destiny that made me a sociopathic killer. Tell me, guys, did your doctor give you permission to leave the ward?

JACK HONEYIMHOME: No, I'm saying what Truman Capote said when they asked him whether those guys who killed those people in cold blood should be executed. Capote wrote a whole book explaining how they were almost fated to do what they did. You know what he said in the courtroom? Capote? He said hang 'em high. You know why? "'Cause their lives weren't just a chain leading them to those murders. There were other links in their lives. They just chose not to hook up."

JULES KUNG FU: You're talking about *The Shining* (1980)? Or about *In Cold Blood* (1967)?

VINCENT LE BIG MAC: You know, Linda, that your love affair with sociopaths gets ripped in *Natural Born Killers* (1994)? I mean, every time two young lovers get in a car and race across the Midwest killing wherever and whenever they want . . . I mean from *Gun Crazy* (1949) to *Bonnie and Clyde* (1967) to *Badlands* (1973) to *Kalifornia* and *Natural Born Killers* . . . people think something quintessentially American is going on. It's like the glamour of outlaws from the old West has been revived. And these people are just thrill seekers, looking for their ten seconds in the spotlight. They're not professional. They're not cool. They're media creations. The outlaw as celebrity. People see through that hype. Cool can't be hyped. It's either pure or it isn't cool.

JACK HONEYIMHOME: All I gotta say is that you guys are in my opinion very cool. And sociopathic. I saw *Pulp Fiction* (1994).

VINCENT LE BIG MAC: That wasn't us.

———◆———

Script Doctor: We're missing the code. You think cool, you think youth. Youth when? *Now* because youth *then* is age, not youth. What's the surround now? Post-9/11? Rebel? The opposite. Poll showed that most young people get along with their parents, don't mind living at home, have traditional moral values, think of shopping as a purpose in life, think much better of the Fortune 500 then they do of the federal government, see Donald Trump and Bill Gates as heroes and not Che Guevara or Jim Morrison, think liberals are radicals, and would rather build a personal stock portfolio than wipe out poverty. Okay, if teens and twentysomethings respond to coolness hypnotically, what are they responding to in this present conservative American clime? And, wouldn't young-blood movies reveal this connect between conservatism and coolness? How can there be a connect between square and hip, between a moral values, flag-waving red-state conservatism and coolness? If a growing majority of the country is conservative, does this mean the end of U.S. "soft power" in regard to coolness? Will coolness move to China too?

———◆———

Characters: Vince Money, parody of Vince Vaughn in Swingers *(1996); Johnny Knothead, parody of Johnny Knoxville in* Jackass— The Movie *(2003); Ice Cubit, badass of New Black Cinema; Slacker, a fan of the film* Slackers; *Captain Trip, a parody of Captain America in the film* Easy Rider; *and, Tucker Crossfire, a TV Smashmouth warrior.*

———◆———

SLACKER: Right now I'm thinking we're really the lost generation, because what do we represent? But if I was my age and it was the 1950s, I'd be like James Dean. A rebel without a cause.

ICE CUBIT: Slackers ain't got no cause.

SLACKER: Yeah, but that's the thing. Not having a cause is a cause. I'd be a natural rebel. Without needing a cause. That's cool. But now the question of cause doesn't come up. We're acausal. If I were in the 1960s I'd be part of the Woodstock generation. You know, just out there, not even on the road. Just like off the road. Smoking dope around a campfire and getting into how way out everything is. Like the stars.

CAPTAIN TRIP: You do your own thing in your own time, man.

SLACKER: See what I mean? Just like that. So cool. You do your own thing in your own time. See? We can't say that anymore.

CAPTAIN TRIP: Why not, man? Just say it.

SLACKER: "Why not, man. Just say it." See how cool that is. But it can't be said anymore. It can only be quoted. I can't be Captain America or Billy. I can only sample them from *Easy Rider* (1969). I can only be hyperconsciously cool.

ICE CUBIT: You ain't cool, man. You just a bum.

SLACKER: Okay. Okay. Even when I go back before cool. I really dig Andy Hardy in the 1940s talking to his old man who's a judge and can solve all his problems. And having, you know, love problems and being love sick like Andy Hardy and having a buddy named Buzz and wearing hokey hats and stuff like that.

VINCE MONEY: This Andy Hardy money?

ICE CUBIT: See what I'm saying? Got everybody today thinking that it's all about the benjamins. But what I'm saying is Bill Gates cool? Them Yahoos that started up Yahoo is cool? No way. That ain't cool. And look at this sucker here. Knothead. He ain't cool. Tom Green ain't cool. Being a mook ain't cool.

JOHNNY KNOTHEAD: I'm Johnny Knothead and I take it to the max. Push the party hardy and take the mean to the extreme. Continuous spring break and wildness in the mosh pit.

ICE CUBIT: Don't listen to this knothead. Send his jackass to Iraq he want some mayhem. What you looking at, Bowtie?

TUCKER CROSSFIRE: I'm trying to understand your definitions here. All blacks are cool? Or only blacks are cool? It's in the skin color? Or the clothes? I wear a bowtie so that automatically makes me not cool.

ICE CUBIT: Wearing a $300 Abercrombie shirt ain't being cool. Cool don't come out of GQ or MTV. Cool is a vibe that you lay down from the inside. And when you kick in some attitude that makes it clear you along for the ride in this world but you ain't buying it, then you hip. You put an edge to cool and you got hip. Black folks invented hip. They got the edge automatically from the white man.

TUCKER CROSSFIRE: Then, according to your definitions, Indians would be the first hipsters. But that aside, what I want to know is the difference between cool and hip. We market coolness but we can't market hip? Am I right?

CAPTAIN TRIP: Maybe I can help you out here. Take Captain America in *Easy Rider*. He's a cool dude no doubt. But he's naïve. He's mellow. He's let the flow flow, do your own thing in your own time. Your bag may not be my bag. Come on people smile on your brother everybody get together right now. Inner peace and total self-possession. Harmony.

TUCKER CROSSFIRE: No edge? What about at the end of *Easy Rider* when the rednecks shoot them dead?

CAPTAIN TRIP: A bummer, man. It's the Christ thing all over again.

TUCKER CROSSFIRE: Example of hip?

ICE CUBIT: Richard Pryor. Then after him Eddie Murphy doing the ghetto Mr. Rogers. Jack Nicholson doing his order thing in *Five Easy Pieces*. Lawrence Fishburne with them cool glasses fighting the Matrix. Ice Cube in *Boyz 'n the Hood*.

TUCKER CROSSFIRE: So the hipster is the cool guy with a bit of rebel? If that's the case, then the hipster is dead in America, and if you want to find the cool guy just look for the latest fashion. Coolness is apparel. Or the ride you drive. Coolness is in products, not in people, therefore, coolness is a product. And rebels, whether they're mellow like Captain America or angry like Ice Cube, are just as dead as liberals.

ICE CUBIT: It's history like that gonna lead to a revolution.

TUCKER CROSSFIRE: The historical trajectory is clear regardless. Drugged-out romantic idealists in the 1960s, dazed and confused by the end of the 1970s, waking up to market realities in the Reagan 1980s, creating the New Economy in the 1990s, and so far in the new millennium making sure the next century is ours.

SLACKER: Andy Hardy wasn't dazed and confused. He was just a teenager in movies made just before and during the Second World War. They had family dinners. His dad was a judge and the undisputed head of the household. Andy would get into trouble and then go talk to his dad and get straightened out. He was like a little gentleman who ran amok sometimes and got reeled in.

TUCKER CROSSFIRE: That was a time family values meant something. But we're returning to that now after the nightmare of radical social engineering that advocated condoms and not abstinence, gay marriage and not real marriage, murder and not adoption, taxation and not private accounts, socialized medicine and not private practice, spotted owls and not American workers, unions and not the right to work . . .

SLACKER: I get dazed and confused like those kids in the movie *Dazed and Confused* (1993) in the late 1970s. They didn't know they were dazed and confused then in 1976, but the guy who made the film in 1993 looked back and said they were dazed and confused. But he could only say that because he had already made a movie in 1991 called *Slackers* where the slackers were beyond dazed and confused. They're like: Cut me some slack on those issues, man, because we already saw the movie and are totally clear and focused about how they were dazed and confused. The director, Richard Linklater, was looking back to 1976 for a beginning to slackerdom.

VINCE MONEY: Here's the deal, Slacker. You're a slacker. You've got a time and place. A window of opportunity. Message: The window closed. You're 1980s. I'm 1990s. You're like the . . . the breakfast club.

SLACKER: The Breakfast Clubbers were like Hollywoodized slackers. I mean, Hollywood gave each of them dysfunctional issues and then resolved them. Slackers don't have issues. We're issueless.

VINCE MONEY: A riff on the Beats. You know what some dude said in *No Exit from the Breakfast Club*? Hell is having Anthony Michael Hall, Judd Nelson, and Ally Sheedy representing young blood.

TUCKER CROSSFIRE: I'm not a liberal multiculturalist so I don't mind pointing out that a white boy, James Dean, was the first hipster in *Rebel Without a Cause*.

VINCE MONEY: That's because The Dean is money. He's old money, but he's money. How many foxes can he get? How many does he want? He's vintage. He's iconic. You think a white T-shirt, chinos, boots, and a red jacket with a turned up collar, Harley, cigarette hanging out of your mouth is not hot commercial property, you're nuts. He's totally Madison Avenue MTV. You, Mr. Slacker, are not money. You're a loser. You're just a guy who doesn't want to be rich, doesn't know how to be rich and will never be money. The dot.coms blew you away, baby, and you disappeared from the American landscape.

CAPTAIN TRIP: You know, I'm beginning to see into this thing. It's like a vast conspiracy thing. Cool is rebel, rebel is cool. In the 1950s. Juvenile delinquents. What happened to them? The whole world went delinquent, man. In the 1960s. The family went delinquent. The country went delinquent. *Wild in the Streets.* Teenager becomes prez. Delinquent becomes the norm. Marriage is a preface to divorce. It's a wild world. And it hits its peak with Watergate. We go into a recession; the rebellion went nowhere. Hip and cool are up for grabs. Dazed and confused. Reagan brings the squares out of their hiding places and we get the dawning of the age of conservative America. Young rebels are now "righteous dudes."

VINCE MONEY: Righteous, dude. Like in *Bill & Ted's Excellent Adventure* (1989), *Dude, Where's My Car?* (2000), *Wayne's World* (1992), followed by *Wayne's World 2* (1993), and *Dumb and Dumber* (1994). It all gets dumb and dumber, like being dumb is cool. But here's the miracle move, baby. *Swingers.* You connect coolness with money. I mean I'm telling you saying somebody is "money" is like saying they're "cool." Money owns coolness. It owns the word.

ICE CUBIT: Airheads. *Dumb & Dumber.* Slackers to Airheads to Jackasses. Loserville. But the rebellion ain't dead, brother. Step up to a flick like *Boiler Room* (2000). Grand delete for the PG ending, but here's a hard slam at giving up the fight just for the benjamins. Ditto *American Psycho* (2000). Patrick Bateman is hanging with the Dubya crowd. The haves and have-mores. Bateman is one of them. He ain't cool. He crazy. The cool dudes are Edward Norton in *Fight Club* and Kevin Spacey in *American Beauty.* Cool and hip ain't dead. They abide.

CAPTAIN TRIP: You know when the Dude in *The Big Lebowski* tells the cab driver to turn off the Eagles because the Eagles represent what went wrong with the 1970s? That's like the way I feel about those nerd raunch movies. Totally bogus nerd dudes like in *American Pie* (1999) and *American Pie 2* (2002). You take young people trying to do their own thing and make some peace in this world and you slowly turn them into jackasses watching endless hours of reality TV where other jack-asses sit around and talk "she said" and then "he said" nonsense. Their brainspace is full up with T&A.

ICE CUBIT: Disco did it. The market was solid behind that. Clothes mat-tered. Tony Manero puts a down payment on a shirt. A shirt. The shop-ping fever is something the hippies didn't have. They was a homegrown-only bunch. They shared the shirt, is what I'm saying. They didn't go all up-scale Abercrombie on the shirt, is what I'm saying.

VINCE MONEY: You just don't know the power of Saturday night fever. I feel it, babies. They were staying alive. Style. I shopped a shirt for a month, but it was worth it. You tell me why Raves are so big now? Looking good is about money; money is about looking good. There's coolness in there somewhere.

ICE CUBIT: Disco Duck ain't cool, man.

SLACKER: I think you have to put the slackers of the 1980s on the rebel side. Well, maybe the slack side of the rebel side. But they didn't sell out to the seductions of watching MTV to see what coolness was. And slack-ers don't shop. They can't seem to get worried about stuff. They're con-cerned with not being concerned about stuff. I kind of wish I was mel-low. You know, like chill. But I kind of let it go and wait for it to happen. I think that's more heavy than mellow. But you know, like I said, the heavy is always like me saying that Captain America in *Easy Rider* said something like, "You do your own thing in your own time, man." But that's not me being heavy; that's Captain America. Heavy is like already happened. For the most part. So it's slack. Not heavy. It's after the fact. Already happened. We're like living after it's all happened and then when it happened, it happened on the screen anyway.

ICE CUBIT: That's some white shite is what it is. You keep your eyes peeled when you live in the hood. You ain't gonna live long, but you is alive when you is alive. You like after the orgasm, brother, not after the fact. Slack is what you is, and that's what I'm saying. It was you slack-heads that cued things up for this jackass generation.

VINCE MONEY: You get the clash of hippy mellow and slacker disaffect in *The River's Edge* (1986). Dennis Hopper is this remnant druggie biker type from the 1960s who can't identify with the total apathy these kids have. One of them is killed and just left there by the river's edge, naked, dead, and they just stare at her and go on like nothing happened. It's like anything real doesn't compute. They look at her like they're watching old TV reruns.

———— ◆ ————

Script Doctor: That's a rerun. Outtake it.

———— ◆ ————

SLACKER: And you've got an explanation?

VINCE MONEY: Here it is. Look at the top teenage movies of the 1940s, the Andy Hardy films. He's an uncool jerk but he doesn't know it so it's all good for him. Why, every girl in Carvel thinks he's the cat's meow. Now James Dean. He's money. The 1950s. What's he rebelling against? Now we say, "Andy Hardy's world" but The Dean is just reactive: Judge Hardy, Andy's Dad, has turned into Jim Backus in *Rebel Without a Cause*, and this is a Dad who's a ragmop The Dean's mom's tossing around. Social and family protocols are disintegrating, but The Dean's no activist. He's not hyperconsciously aware of being a rebel, and he's no natural born sociopath. But he's about to explode. By the time you get to the 1960s you get a "movement." It's a self-aware protest and rebellion. It's a countercultural movement. It's got leaders and gurus; it's a little bit Eastern; it's a little bit left; it's a little bit Dr. Leary, Frank Zappa, Gandhi, Thoreau, Chicago Seven, and the Hippy Dippy Weatherman. The Dean didn't know how to drop out, turn on, tune in. The Dean is just running away; there's no social vision. No vision thing. By 1968 with *Wild in the Streets* when the voting age is lowered to 14 you get a guy the same age as James Dean is in *Rebel Without a Cause* being elected the prez of the United States. And that guy, Christopher Jones, is a Dean lookalike. Anybody over thirty is not to be trusted. This is a countercultural movement with a politics.

CAPTAIN TRIP: That's what I've been saying, man. Hipster coolness went radical social and political. It was like the Youth Reformation, and then with Reagan you got the beginning of the Conservative Counterreformation.

TUCKER CROSSFIRE: You fellows want to come back to Earth? Market forces step in when there's a sudden break in fantasy. After Operation Babylift in 1975 when the United States shamefully got out of 'Nam because youth protestors had undermined our war effort, Ronald Reagan was elected and the whole country felt as if it had come out of a nightmare. The mood of the young became what the mood of youth should always be: enthusiastic, positive, and full of hope. Youth could now listen to the Bee-Gees, watch Tony Manero dancing in *Saturday Night Fever*, and buy polyester suits and platform shoes. Ronald Reagan took us back to wanting to be rich, to wanting to succeed and not rebel. Coolness became a construct of a profit to shareholders' mentality. Slackers and retread hippies got sucked into a vacuum while the rest of us saw the light.

CAPTAIN TRIP: There's no light in the dollar, man. It leaves like those kids you were talking about in *The River's Edge*.

VINCE MONEY: There's losers and victims, brother. It's a high-stakes game. Some people are money. And some are not. It's as simple as that.

ICE CUBIT: So this jackass here is what, in your view?

JOHNNY KNOTHEAD: I'm Johnny Knothead and I'm going to set off some fireworks at 3 A.M. in my dad's bedroom.

ICE CUBIT: I'm Ice Cubit and I'm gonna cap your ass.

TUCKER CROSSFIRE: There's nothing wrong with people who work hard looking to play hard. I'm sure Johnny understands he has to assume personal responsibility for his actions. Bad behavior is expecting the federal government to give you a handout. Bad behavior is being free to choose, and consistently making the wrong choices, and expecting society to reward those bad choices. Johnny Knothead's behavior doesn't attack conservative values. He might hurt himself, but I'm sure he doesn't need liberal legislation to protect him from making his own choices and accepting the consequences.

ICE CUBIT: I seen that Jackass movie. It's racist. What I'm saying is they can't do that crap in South Central or Crenshaw because this whole country is phonyass PC. So they go to Japan and be racists over there with them people. They got a fat guy and a little dwarf guy they play that crap with. This whole youngblood generation of white boys is bad news, is what I'm saying. They vote to bring back slavery them boys do.

CAPTAIN TRIP: I'm still wondering how we wound up with *Jackass—The Movie* (2003). How do you go from Reagan to Dada? I know it's a marketing move but I can't figure it out.

SLACKER: The way I see it when a whole culture gets caught in a real divide in values, say, between mutual aid and interdependence, and greed and competition, then youth get caught in the whirlwind. But when a whole society opts for greed and self-interest and can't recall what else there is, then the youth just reflect that. It's like Huxley's *Brave New World*. People go around saying stuff that's been put in their heads and they never question what they're saying. Jackass pranks come out of the biology of being young. There's no cause but raging hormones and high energy levels. The pranks are raunchy and mean, the total vibe is protocretin and mindless because a culture reveling in selfishness doesn't produce anything else. You could say that since pranksters have no politics and are no threat to the status quo, they're a whole lot more acceptable to that status quo than say Abby Hoffman's Yippies were. They were pranksters with a revolutionary purpose. These jackass pranksters are clearly not a threat.

ICE CUBIT: I saw that movie *Kids* (1995). What's up with that? Twelve-year-old punk kid going to deflower all the virgins he can find. Some cold shit coming down in that movie.

VINCE MONEY: White man's *Menace II Society* (1993).

ICE CUBIT: That's where you're wrong, sucker. You live in Watts you got to know how to survive. This is the jungle, man. Those punks in *Kids* living in the lap of luxury. So what, their parents ain't got time for them? So what, their parents feel guilt 'cause they can't spend any quality time with them? What's that? At least they got parents and their parents got money. I say, get over it. Ain't nothing on the street forcing that punk to deflower them virgins. All that badness come from the inside. All *our* badness we got coming from the outside and we just responding. Black folks ain't making no preemptive strikes. We just defending.

TUCKER CROSSFIRE: Like random drive-bys?

ICE CUBIT: You all got a random drive-by going against a whole country, is what I'm saying. And you reelected the fool behind the wheel. Anyway, we come here random and we be random in return, is what I'm saying.

TUCKER CROSSFIRE: The future of coolness is in conservatives' hands, gentlemen. And why shouldn't it be tied to profits to shareholders? President Bush's "ownership" society will make shareholders of every American. And what is a real gift to youth—the chance to begin accruing compound interest from investments at an early age—will very soon in the new millennium replace the negative associations of coolness and hipness that all of you seem to applaud.

CAPTAIN TRIP: I don't know, man. Do you know what it was like to be sitting there with a joint watching *Alice's Restaurant* (1969)? I mean, man, this was just a song by Arlo, but it was all connected. Song, movie, freeform style, politics, power to the people. We're talking total solidarity of the whole generation.

JOHNNY KNOTHEAD: Come on. All you potheads sold out for a stock option.

VINCE MONEY: First you get the shake, rattle 'n roll out of your system. You face up to the fact that the guy with the most toys in the end wins and not the guy who dies young and leaves a good-looking corpse. After you realize all this, you let greed show you the money. Then you get the power. Then you get the honeys. The guy with the most money and honeys at the end wins. *Jerry Maguire* (1996) is *not* about giving up your lucrative job as a sports agent and writing a bleeding heart mission statement. It's all about "SHOW ME THE MONEY." That's what we took away from that movie.

SLACKER: I liked the way he said she completed him. I thought that movie was all about love, not money.

VINCE MONEY: Show this guy to the shredder, somebody. Back to reality. The truth of *Boiler Room* (2000) was revealed at the beginning: You want a million before you're thirty and you don't have a wicked jump shot and don't want to sling hash cocaine, you better become a stock broker and learn how to spin nimrods out of their savings.

CAPTAIN TRIP: There are signs of a resurrection, friend. Have you seen *Good Will Hunting* (1997)? Will Hunting is a genius, but he has other values besides making money.

VINCE MONEY: That's the loser version. Will is a winner. He's got the competitive edge. That film just shows his loser buddies and all their buddies in the audience that winners deserve their winnings because they've got more of what it takes. It's a natural state of affairs. There's nothing natural in money being shared equally. We just aren't equal. The film lets that sink in. He drives off at the end without the girl and in a beat-up car but you know where he's heading and I know where he's heading. Honeys and Hummers. Survival of the fittest. Winning is cool.

ICE CUBIT: That's why they got all them survivor shows on TV. White guys win. Black guys not surviving, even if one of them do show up on the program. They get voted out right off.

VINCE MONEY: I watch the show where Paris Hilton and Nikki Ritchie live the simple life. Just to show how stupid and unreal that simple life is. It's like coolness meets squaresville. You watch it to see what not to be and what you should be. It's makeovers, nip and tucks, and shopping sprees.

CAPTAIN TRIP: But what do you make of a film like *Clerks* (1994), Vince?

VINCE MONEY: Classic Slacker flick. Losers talking loser talk.

JOHNNY KNOTHEAD: Here's my vote for the best all time coolest movie: *Animal House* (1978). Bluto Belushi began the whole Mook movement. Gross 'em out for tomorrow you're a CPA. Tom Green in *Road Trip* (2000) carries on the jackass journey.

SLACKER: You know when George Lucas went back to the 1950s in *American Graffiti* (1973) he extracted the rebel edge. I think he did it because he was doing the movie in the 'Nam era and was waxing nostalgic, which means he created a 1950s that was full of "happy days." Cars. Cruising. Sound track. Chicks. Burgers. Forever young.

ICE CUBIT: That's all white-bread rebel posturing. All candy stuff. What I'm saying is that you got those Soccer/Security Moms living in the wealthy 'burbs and their kids go on automatic rebel. They make that white boy Eminem their hero. They wanna be rappers and hang out in the hood and then go home to the wealthy 'burbs. They Wal-Mart rebels. They ain't hip and they ain't cool. You can't buy either one but they think they can. *Straight out of Brooklyn* (1991). *Menace II Society* (1993), *Boyz n' the Hood* (1991). It's all real is what I'm saying.

TUCKER CROSSFIRE: *Where the Boys Are* (1960) tied with *Beach Blanket Bingo* (1965). Full of fun. Not rebels, not hip, and certainly not trying to be cool. Cool is what liberals think they are when they refuse to join the team and assume personal responsibility. Even Elvis went from rebel to conservative.

CAPTAIN TRIP: Colonel Parker turned E into a product.

SLACKER: You can't totally turn hip into product. Hip strikes back. Like Jay and Silent Bob in *Jay and Silent Bob Strike Back* (2001).

ICE CUBIT: What you talking about? I seen *Mallrats* (1995). They ain't striking back. They striking out.

VINCE MONEY: *Swingers* (1996). Money for the honeys.

ICE CUBIT: I'm gonna name my cool dude, and he ain't no white boy talking about bling bling all the time. I'm saying Tupac was one cool dude and standing right beside him is Snoop. They was cool and they was hip. They knew what was going on.

VINCE MONEY: Bruce Campbell. *Evil Dead* Trilogy. Cool and hip.

SLACKER: The Dude in *The Big Lebowski*. The Dude abides.

JOHNNY KNOTHEAD: I'm Johnny Knothead, and I'm going to rent a car, total it and bring it back and say they're liable and then run away. All on camera. Now that's cool.

TUCKER CROSSFIRE: Patrick Bateman. *American Psycho* (2000). You've failed to factor in breeding. You have no idea that good breeding and a strong stock portfolio are what's hip in America today. Poverty, a sullen attitude, and boorish behavior is never a ticket to success.

CAPTAIN TRIP: I don't know, man. Breeding is like what they had before the revolution. Any revolution. Take your pick. Bloat ain't cool, man. No, I think cool is an Eastern thing. Like Caine in *Kung Fu* on TV back in the day.

VINCE MONEY: No way, baby. Look at Jules in *Pulp Fiction*. Total coolness. Is he hip? Does he have the edge that bites? Quoting Ezekiel and then pop! pop! Blows the little piggies away. But when he turns over to the born-again side and wants to walk the Earth like Caine in Kung Fu he loses it. He goes from being cool to being a sucker.

TUCKER CROSSFIRE: He develops a moral conscience and he's a sucker. Then I ask you, Mr. Money, was Christ a sucker, too?

ICE CUBIT: Latinos think it's cool wearing a big gold cross round their necks. And they all love Jesus. Jesus this and Jesus that. What you got in Iraq right now but all them Jesus patriots fighting them Mohammed patriots. I say you just make a law over here that says you can't name your kid Jesus and a law over there that says they can't name your kid Mohammed and they ain't gonna be anymore war. No time, no place. Holy war ain't cool, man. It's older than old school.

Voice-over: Why did those young Japanese kids go all the way to Memphis to visit Graceland in the movie *Mystery Train* (1989)? Because they were visiting the home of the King, the king of coolness, the rebel king, the hipster king. Elvis was packaged cool and American marketers have been packaging it since for worldwide distribution. Why is coolness American? Because our language dominates and our cool-making factories and distributors are the most well financed and advanced in the world. Can conservatives disconnect coolness from rebellion, hip from dissidence? They already have. You get a tattoo and you also get coolness. "Pimp your ride" and you're cool. You shop upscale and patronize your servers and you're automatically hip. Showing contempt for losers is showing how hip you are. Going through a red light because public space belongs to you and not the government is hip. Running your SUV into the staff at a Hamptons bistro is hip. It shows that you've assumed personal responsibility for your privileged status. Have the marketers repackaged cool and hip away from the homeless outsider, the uncouth rebel, the mellow, laid-back idealist and dreamer? Sure. Coolness has been privatized; it's corporate. It's a fashion statement, not an ontology. The most obsolete thing in America today is the "cool radical." What we have now is "radical cool," and that's a seasonal creation of the fashion world.

———◆———

Script Doctor: You start with a search for the coolness code and wind up with a bunch of views tearing each other down. You get no place, which is where postmodernists take us, but we've got no time left for going no place. Here's the code for coolness—*betrayal*. Coolness after 9/11 means being cool about the future, about being secure, about the social compact, about the American dream. A deeply submerged sense of betrayal by country, history, reason, reality, words, and pictures puts Americans places where they can't be betrayed again: virtual realities and realities emptied of real thought. These are realities in which you become one of the survivors in exotic locales far from the real America, or realities that are so flagrantly unconnected with the real world that they are sadistically referred to as "Reality TV." Coolness is now no more than being cold about the world you live in.

——— ◆ ———

THE BLOGOSPHERE

Blog: www.hipster.com

Norman Mailer's 1957 essay "The White Negro" opposed the Organizational Man of the 1950s with The Hipster, who was a rebel existentialist looking at conformity and permanence like they were death and choosing instead a "life-giving answer," which was "to divorce oneself from society, to exist without roots, to set out on that uncharted journey with the rebellious imperatives of self." The "Negroes" were already on the margins; they had already been excluded from the "Organization," kept out of "The Club"; they were already on a societally "uncharted journey." Escape for the white man, in Mailer's view, was to take the same path that the Negro was on.

Maybe it was a bogus cultural division between conformist, consumer capitalism and The Hipster, but the fact remains that nobody after Reagan could be called a hipster by Mailer's definition, least of young people, who had, ironically, been the ones to respond, in the 1960s, to Mailer's call. Take a look at the film *Boiler Room* (2000). It's not a hip thing to *not* be a player. The Player is "hip," but since the word carries a rebel baggage it's been replaced with "cool." "Hip" and "The Hipster" are last year's "old, over, and adios." But the film that really nails the Hipster's coffin is *Good Will Hunting* (1997). Will Hunting is a rebel trying to wander away from the "show me the money" creed but there's not a fragment of Mailer's Hipster story in Will's surround. It's all been swept away by the newest new out of Madison Avenue. The Hipster journey is not only uncharted, it's now unmentioned, nonexistent. What Will needs is a little bit of psychiatric counseling to get him back on the right path.

Blog: www.coolbusiness.com

I agree with what Thomas Frank writes in *The Conquest of Cool* regarding a false thesis "that hip constitutes some kind of fundamental adversary to a joyless, conformist consumer capitalism." Frank doesn't buy the notion that consumer capitalism just co-opted or commodified hip ("If you can't beat 'em, absorb 'em"), finally calling it "cool."

Here's Frank: "The curious enthusiasm of American business for the symbols, music, and slang of the counterculture marked a fascination that was much more complex than the theory of co-optation would suggest. In fields like fashion and advertising that were most conspicuously involved with the new phase of image-centered capitalism, business leaders were not concerned merely with simulating countercultural signifiers in order to sell the young demographic (or stave off revolution for that matter) but because they approved of the new values and antiestablishment sensibility being developed by the youthful revolutionaries. They were drawn to the counterculture because it made sense to them, because they saw a reflection of the new values of consuming and managing to which they had been ministering for several years. Hip capitalism wasn't something on the fringes of enterprise. What happened in the 1960s was that hip became central to the way American capitalism understood itself and explained itself to the public" (Frank, 1997).

Blog: www.liberatedshopper.com

Coolness is a product of capitalism, which means in this playscript "American Cool" that it's really not cool but tainted. Coolness is maybe something to do with being on an unmarked journey that is existentially liberating as Mailer thought. But it's capitalism that's liberating. "[M]odern capitalism was positively liberating; by its very nature it rejected all traditions and embraced desire" (William Leach, *Land of Desire: Merchants, Power and the Rise of a New American Culture*, Pantheon, 1993).

"Revolution"—a sudden break with the old and the creation of a "new line"—is essential to capitalism. "Creativity" is the wellspring of new product creation. "Unleashed desires" augment the creation of new desires, which become new needs, which are then satisfied by new product production. Capitalism is on an uncharted journey into the heart of human desire and its fulfillment. Why would capitalism preach a postponement of desire? Why would it seek to ground society with any kind of unchanging security or certainty? To do so would terminate the ceaseless pursuit of "The New," of something better, of something faster, easier, of something that promises "more"—all of which every shopper is engaged in pursuing.

Blog: www.oldsocialist.com

I quite agree with the liberatedshopper blogger who knows that capitalism eats hipsters, rebels, and assorted "cool dudes" for breakfast. I, however, am not as happily transformed by this as liberatedshopper, although I, myself, an unrepentant socialist, have long since been eaten up by capitalism. Why did socialists get eaten up? I suppose because their notion that self-realization is not only goalless but reciprocal (as Terry Eagleton puts it people "achieve their deepest fulfillment only in terms of each other") countered capitalism's unrelenting unleashing of human desire, desire for everything and anything. The socialist was bringing into view an unbraidable braiding of the economic, the political, and the moral. The moral goal was a self-realization dependent upon not just one's own free development but the free development of all. Politics then becomes the venue to accomplish this. Boundless desires fed by the boundless capitalist quest for ever-increasing profits seem highly unnatural within this socialist vision. Socialists advocating a realization of our nature as an end in itself and not linked to functionality or instrumentality in which life is a means to this or that particular end, such as a Bentley sports car or maybe several, were in capitalism's way. How effective has capitalism's assault on socialism been since the collapse of the Soviet Union, which was taken to be socialism's corrupt product? Since 9/11, when any critique of capitalism (and where would it be launched except from the left?) was at once support of al-Qaeda? Socialism is as far off the American radar screen at this moment as Norman Mailer's "Hipster." In regard to rebellion, however, one must understand that capitalism is not conservative; it abhors the status quo, tradition, long-term commitments to yesterday's stylings, and the confirmed conservative's belief that what is essential in society has an unchanging authority. Capitalism, however, feels that one's wardrobe needs a constant purging; one's vehicle needs to be traded in for something newer; one's wife . . . and so on.

Once again Eagleton on all of this: "Capitalism wants men and women to be infinitely pliable and adaptable. As a system, it has a Faustian horror of fixed boundaries, of anything which offers an obstacle to the infinite accumulation of capital. . . . No way of life in history has been more in love with transgression and transformation, more enamoured of the hybrid and pluralistic, than capitalism. In its ruthlessly instrumental logic, it has no time for the idea of nature—for that whose whole existence consists simply in fulfilling and unfolding itself, purely for its own sake and without thought of a goal" (Terry Eagleton, *After Theory*, 2003).

THE BLOGOSPHERE

blog: www.mrincredible.com

If there's a discussion in "American Cool" of a post-9/11 "coolness," I must have missed it. Follow the "cool" stars to see if there's been a post-9/11 rewrite of "coolness." Brad Pitt becomes Achilles in *Troy* (2004); Colin Farrell becomes Alexander the Great in *Alexander* (2004). Both warriors played by the hottest—and therefore the "coolest"—luminaries Hollywood is producing. "I'm a war president," George W. Bush says. Connection here?

What about the box office hit of 2004, *The Incredibles*? If Mr. Incredible is not a personification of the U.S. of A., I'm a Pixar jackalope. He's a superpower. Doing good. One guy. But he gets taken out of business by a whole bunch of stupid, greedy malpractice suits. Mr. Incredible is the victim of a legal system that needs reform. If we had had some good-old tort reform preventing anybody without up-front money from hiring a lawyer, Mr. Incredible wouldn't have been forced out of business. But forced out he is. He's sued into fifteen years of hiding his superiority behind a desk of bureaucratic mediocrity. He becomes another cog in Max Weber's iron cage of bureaucracy. He's surrounded by losers ready to go "postal." Mr. Incredible! Can you imagine that? Mr. Incredible and his whole family of incredibly talented, top-of-the-genetic-line, best and the brightest, have to live like "ordinary folk." This means they have to be like everybody else, be leveled to a universal sameness in which no one is better than anyone else, in which everyone is equal.

The truism of the movie? "When everybody is special, nobody is." But Mr. Incredible resurrects his super-self, as does his whole family, and defeats an evil doer. The scene where a destructive flying machines hovers over the Manhattan skyline did it for me. 9/11 all over again. Thank God, Mr. Incredible broke free of a pernicious egalitarianism and asserted his *Übermensch* self. Who's the coolest guy in 2004? Mr. Incredible, which is what we now call George W. Bush. He's *Time* magazine's Man of the Year. Mr. Incredible. I mean, George W. Bush.

Blog: www.whohatesyoubaby.com

I really don't see how we're peddling "American coolness" as some kind of "soft power" all over the world when it would be hard to find a country that really likes us since Iraq. What it comes down to is that our economic hegemony was in play at the Digital Dawn. Our English language is now cyberspace's language of choice; e-commerce is in English. What's "cool" in China? Will "Chinese

Cool" go along with Chinese economic and military hegemony? Or, will we all have to learn Chinese for that to happen? If it all goes on in English, "Hollywood" and its "coolness" will continue.

Blog: www.nocoolness.com

THE BLOGOSPHERE

Are we exporting coolness? Even George W. Bush doesn't think so. He said this to university students in Beijing: "As Americans learn more about China, I am concerned that the Chinese people do not always see a clear picture of my country. This happens for many reasons, and some of them of our own making. Our movies and television shows often do not portray the values of the real America I know" (February 22, 2002).

Of course, George W. Bush's "real America" is a picture of America he has in his head. "Born on third base and he thinks he hit a triple" is where his head is at, which means his "real America" is a good place because it's a place where he's at the top of the pile. As Mel Brooks as King Louis XIV in *History of the World Part One* remarks: "It's good to be the king"—in Bush's case a U.S. president who's the son of a former U.S. president.

But Bush wants to attack Hollywood because he sees it as attacking him. Hollywood and Madison Avenue are the two largest spin-making enterprises in the country, if you exclude Karl Rove. Bush's image as a decisive, tough, plain-speaking, plain-dealing, regular guy is about as real as Brittney Spears's virgin image was. They're both marketable creations. You could say that the Madison Avenue image factory is on a leash, and why not? Bush is, as Nader said, a corporate president. He's all about "pushing product" and in turn he's aided in pushing himself as a presidential "product." But Hollywood is something else. It's a revisiting of the days when Joe McCarthy found a nest of communists and communist sympathizers swarming Hollywood. At least that was the picture of the picture capital of the world that McCarthy wanted to paint.

George W. Bush sees Hollywood through the same lens. A picture is worth a thousand words here. The new *Manchurian Candidate* is all about the influence corporate lobbyists have in Washington. The film commits an unpardonable sin from a conservative point of view: It replaces the Soviet empire as the culprit with a Halliburton-like corporation. It's not government we should fear but corporations. They're brainwashing us, putting us all on a diet of Soma tablets.

If this was an op-ed piece in the *New York Times*, it would be half as troubling to Republicans as a Hollywood film working on the passive, receptive channels of the average American. Like Chance the gardener in *Being There* (1979), we all now "just like to watch."

So the deal with "purveying coolness" is more complicated than "American Coolness" represents it. Marketers rely on their simulations of coolness to help push product; our conservative regime wants a "no-holds barred" treatment of product pushing. At the same time, Hollywood is using its simulating genius to reveal the "uncoolness" of this conservative regime, or, once again, the Bush administration believes this. There's no timidity in 2004's *Manchurian Candidate* nor in Oliver Stone's *Alexander*, in which an imperialist drags a democracy toward a lunatic dream of world conquest. But there is, for the most part, a reluctance on the part of Hollywood to satirize post-9/11 America. Pixar animations, the café latte world of self-centered "friends," or Jackass-like productions of mooks and midriffs on mindless jaunts into a remarkably unterrorized world are brought to the screen over and over again. Hollywood is certainly not putting out a film like Lars von Trier's *Dogville*, which David Denby calls "an attack on America." It's a very sad day, civilization-wise, when satire and critique are no different than the 9/11 attacks on the Trade Towers.

There's no "coolness" in *Dogville* for sure, but then again there's no "coolness" in America right now either.

Blog: www.coolgroupies.com

"Coolness" *is* a countercultural creation *but* where's the counterculture?

Like everything else it's a product of "business rationality." This is a quote from Thomas Franks' *What's the Matter With Kansas*?

"[C]ounterculture is so commercial and so business-friendly today that a school of urban theorists thrives by instructing municipal authorities on the fine points of luring artists, hipsters, gays, and rock bands to their cities on the ground that where these groups go, corporate offices will follow."

THE BLOGOSPHERE

Epi-Blog

Post-Hurricane Katrina

www.heretichere.com

It seems that the Invisible Hand of God the Father has trumped the Invisible Hand of the Efficient Market here in New Orleans. There's a third possible primary force: nature itself. I can see the Deep Greens, devout Pantheists all, attributing Hurricane Katrina to the Visible Avenging Hand of Mother Nature. And for the devout agnostics and atheists there is, of course, the Visible but Always Unexpected Hand of Pure Contingency—Uncle Chance.

What Bill Maher calls "the Christers," who came out in such numbers in the 2004 election to stop gay marriage by re-electing Son of Bush, blamed not God for the Hurricane but "natural forces," the dark side of Nature that the good God doesn't choose to challenge or can't challenge. *Ab uno ad omnes*: You're a heretical Manichean if you think God has nothing to do with bad things happening. If you believe he chooses not to step in, then you're choosing the view that somehow the people of New Orleans and/or all those watching on TV are being tested, ultimately for their own good. Something spiritually good will come out of Katrina. All along, New Orleans has been Heaven's waiting room. Or perhaps in a Falwellian view, it was Hell and now it's gone.

All of this is a two-millennial-old quandary and too tiresome for a blog, but the Market's Hand vs. God's Hand is of the moment, some call it a Reagan Moment. The Christian Coalition/Christian Fundamentalists/born-agains have aligned with the Republican Party, whose think-tank cockamamie grounding idea is that all will be well if we simply allow market forces to rule. (*Nota bene*: No mention of God.) Liberals and leftists who want to "socially engineer" by intervening and "correcting" the market will only corrupt the market's miraculous efficiency. These liberals and leftists know not what they do for the market is "self-correcting" as long as it is not interfered with and proper oblations are made. Counsel: Think like a pagan.

Government is the big interferer, not local and state government that can be bought off with the promise of "new jobs," but the Feds, who have all these regulatory agencies set up to interfere. I shall only mention in passing all those Fed entitlement agencies set up to disrupt the ultimate dispensations and allotments of market rule. You know, take some money from the winners and give it to the losers so one immortal in our egalitarian democracy doesn't wind up with the whole pot, as in a Monopoly game. Some fear our cloning Louis XVI and heading down that inevitable path to the Reign of Terror. But poor Louie wasn't the problem; it was the entrenched Aristos, who after all kept the really good stuff from being trashed by Trash.

Apparently, Christers believe that Christ is a market conservative, that God the Father is fond of Reaganomics, that a sacred imprimatur has been placed on supply-side economics, that it isn't voodoo after all but foundationally Christian. As a heretic, of course, I could be wrong.

I dissent though, heretical as I am. I think what Hurricane Katrina washed up for TV view were the waste products of market rule—and they were people, poor people, mostly people of color, who didn't choose to have their lives taken or destroyed by a hurricane, and who didn't choose to be poor in wealth, health, education, and prospects. I know another conservative think-tank big idea is that the poor are "free to choose" and have chosen to be poor and, therefore, should assume "personal responsibility" for their plight. One then voted for Son of Bush because he *ab ovo* chose to be born into wealth and power and not in the Lower Ninth Ward in New Orleans, that he chose to go to Yale rather than street hustle, that he chose to be bailed out of his failures by relatives rather than be a homeless drunk, that he chose to send his daughters to university rather than Iraq, that he chose not to need Social Security, public education, public highways, Medicare, Medicaid, Public Health, the minimum wage, union support, HUD, food stamps, rent control, Roe v. Wade, the progressive income tax—not to need, in short, the Federal Government.

And, of course, Son of Bush chose instinct over reason, ignorance over knowledge, spin over truth, hypocrisy over compassion, the rich over the poor, cronies over competence, smirk over words, private profit over the commonwealth, empire over republic, oligarchy over democracy, and freedom to choose and personal responsibility over obvious conditions/constraints/opportunities outside our realm of choice and the difficulties of determining personal responsibility that proceed from such.

The wealthy are born-again not only in gratitude for their priv-ileged circumstances but as protection, as a protective mask that puts their (earned or unearned) privilege to the background and their moral compass and compassion to the fore. It wouldn't work, of course, if the market losers were atheists or at least agnostic. But you will find a good deal of faith in the spiritual world among the New Orleans poor; such Christian faith has been a bedrock of African Americans since slavery. Their faith gives solace to and con-soles them, gives them a future (though not on this earth), gives them the strength to go on, the strength to reconstruct their lives after such a disaster. New Orleans was too much of Heaven's wait-ing room after all.

There were more believing souls than lusting looters on our TV screens. And this is their tie to the Bushies and the privileged class who publicize their breakfast prayer meetings, their talks with God, their faith in Jesus, their born-again bond with the poor, their com-passion for the "unfortunate." The oligarchy plays the faith card as deftly as it has played the racism, homophobia, patriotism, greed, hate, and sexism cards. Unfortunately, this mutual bond of faith between rich and poor has not prevented the poor from losing 80 percent of what they had in 1985, transferred notably to the rich. And that transfer began with Citizen Reagan and has gone on industriously with Son of Bush. Hurricane Katrina, like 9/11 before it, becomes an opportunity to continue that pursuit.

One wonders what the world would be like if there was more belief in God's invisible hand than in the market's. Or, better yet, no belief in either.

www.juryisout.com

After August 30, 2005, when Hurricane Katrina hit New Orleans, the United States rocked with a cultural tidal wave of its own. This cul-tural tidal wave may subside and wash out to sea, or it may bring down the Bush-wa regime, anti-Federal Government conservative politics, and neoconservative empire-building; end the ill-conceived war in Iraq; liberate us from a yuppie security mom Halloween Fear-fest and toughen us up; bring corporate greedy bastards to justice or bring justice to them; legislate some fuel emission standards that should knock gas guzzling SUVs and Hummers off the road; rebuild America's town-to-town passenger rail system with TGV and Eurostar high-speed trains; and hit Chinese imports with protective tariffs that will make Wal-Mart and other big-box stores stop push-ing U.S. manufacturers and U.S. workers into extinction.

www.stormingahead.com

What Hurricane Katrina exposed was the shameful by-products of a liberal "safety-net" governmental crusade that went on far too long and, unfortunately, still lingers. The survival fiber, the will to do battle no matter what the odds, was long ago taken from the poor of New Orleans and has left them waiting to be rescued. If Bush Jr. had followed through on Reagan's incisive beginnings in regard to shrinking the federal government, there would have been no FEMA agency to come to the rescue. It and all such governmental teats would have been pulled out of the mouths of the poor long ago. When those levees broke, the poor would have been able to swim and not sink. Bin Laden and his terrorists have long ago seen this collapse in strength and will, this slow deterioration of that inner mettle that this country was founded on. Fortunately, only the bottom quintiles of our population have been so infected for they are not the ones to decide whether this country will climb on a rooftop and wait to be rescued, wait to be fed, wait to be watered, wait to be housed. Fortunately for the preservation of this country, we do have neoconservatives who will not only *not* wait for another storm to hit but will take the storm to al-Qaeda.

www.mothernaturecomesknocking.com

I'll lay out the scene before the storm: A top 1 percent of Americans so obscenely rich and self-absorbed they make the French *ancien régime* look like a bunch of good-hearted paupers; the next 20 percent professional class serving in every way possible that equestrian class, including inventing alibis for them; the next 40 percent despicably adaptable to whatever racist, sexist, homophobic, hate-filled spin laid on them by the alibi-making class; the bottom 40 percent under the radar screen, only showing up on *Springer* or *Cops*, without shirts and with foul mouths. But nature put that Jerry Springer crowd on every TV station for a solid week so we could see what our hypocritical egalitarian, human rights, democratic, and free society really is. You know a corporate legislature, a corporate executive, a corporate media, a corporate Supreme Court isn't going to pull back the curtain and give us a good look at how our democracy has been stolen from us, how far we've come from caring a stitch about each other.

We're not going to rush out of Iraq because we need our National Guard at home; we're going to rush out because it's now too transparent that the democracy and freedom we're supposed to be bringing to them is something we first have to bring to ourselves. Then again, we won't rush out of there, because when our cultural ADD hits—and it's kicking in already—we'll be back to what we were.

www.Romeyes.com

Maybe for a brief moment when I was a child, I thought as a child, but reality kicked in quite early for me. I saw what human nature was, and is, and put aside my Bakunin and Proudhon and Stirner and Kropotkin and that whole anarchist crowd. You could have economic equality—how you got it I haven't a clue—for about as long as it takes for the bigger guy to want a bigger piece. Of whatever. I also put aside my Marx and the idea that for an indeterminate time some bullies calling themselves a party would tell everyone what to do and make sure that no one had more than anyone else—except, of course, themselves. Then after sucking 99.9 percent of the population's blood, the party would break up and we'd all be living in a utopia of political, social, and economic equality. Once I put this nonsense aside, I looked at what was, not what someone was wishing for. And what was is this: The United States has economic and, therefore, military hegemony, but China is closing fast, and God only knows what "freedom," "democracy," "human rights," "reason," "equality," "justice," and so on means to them. If you think few of us Americans knew Arabic or the history of Iraq or who ruled in any of the Middle Eastern countries, wait until the poll figures come out on what we know about China, including the language. So before China has enough economic and military strength to tell us what military actions we can take, say, in the Middle East, or not take, we—and I mean the bright boy neocons—seized the opportunity 9/11 presented in order to position us militarily in the Middle East. Could this reason be given to the American people? No. Why not? Walt Disney hasn't prepared them for real-world actualities. Would we be better able to stop al-Qaeda if we set up camp in the middle of his sphere of influence? Yes. Would this action antagonize to the point of action those in the Middle East not already antagonized by us? That's like asking whether the good Apaches would join Geronimo if we took the fight to Geronimo. Would we basically be just riling up al-Qaeda, already riled up? I think so.

We are now positioned to peer over Iran's shoulder as it prepares its nuclear weapons. Or tries to. We are now positioned along side our strongest military ally in the Middle East—Israel. We've established a formidable military outpost that will not only protect our oil interests from the Chinese, who will, with a population of a billion and a half, be looking for all the oil its military power can bring it, but we are protecting American commercial interests. The Middle East is backward and weak and yet rich in oil; it stands like a ripe fruit waiting to be plucked. We can fail to pluck—in order to keep us from thinking we're like the Roman Empire—and wait for the Chinese to eventually pluck us. Or, we can take advantage of a small window of opportunity and engage in a win-win-win situation: remove the tyrant Saddam, make an American protectorate out of Iraq, secure Iraqi oil, and create for ourselves an improved defensive posture for the future.

I would like to think that once China steps into our number-one position it will not threaten our way of life. But I left that sort of utopian thinking behind long ago. The Romans defended the Roman way of life for close to a thousand years against all comers, and though we are aware of its decline we must also be aware of its defensive success over such a long period of time. And yes, they did preemptively strike. The Roman genius was to strike when they could, not before they were ready. Or when it was too late.

www.securityfrogs.com

Does the fear and trembling, sickness unto . . . no shopping generated by 9/11 now after Katrina segue into increased fear and trembling? Does the regentrifying class now pull up stakes and move away from coastal areas as well as away from cities, nuclear power plants, fault lines, bridges, tunnels, poultry farms (bird flu pandemic is coming!), Superdomes, mosques, and Crawford, Texas? Statistics show that the elites and their families mourn 9/11 anniversaries while in foreign spas. They get out of the country. Soccer moms, whom I always associate with the upper-middle-class, are the ones you have to watch, rather like watching the migration and mutation of frogs to see which way the pollution blows. Security moms don't leave—maybe it's because they're patriotic; maybe it's because they can't envision nesting nice and secure on foreign soil, something oxymoronic about "nesting" and "foreign." I doubt if New Orleans registers as anything a security mom would mourn, blackened red fish trumped surely by the Roman bacchanal of Mardi Gras, New Orleans jazz trumped by a Sin City rep. Now, if that Sin City were transformed into a secure, well-policed, well-maintained, well-kempt Disneyland, a place where a security mom could take her kids, then . . . there you go!

www.pandorasbox.com

Hurricane Katrina may have broken through the New Orleans levees but hasn't opened up the Pandora's box the left thinks it has. Should we have fear now that our government can't protect us? We can put that fear on top of the fear we already have of al-Qaeda and what, among many very nasty scenarios, it may do to us. I, for one, do not fear that our military can't protect us. I don't link a natural disaster striking our Sodom and Gomorah all rolled into one city—New Orleans—with what we are doing in Iraq. The South since the War Between the States has not welcomed federal intervention. No one but the very oblivious was really surprised to discover that there are a lot of poor blacks without cars in New Orleans. But who's to fault there? Lyndon Johnson's "war on poverty" left poverty victorious in New Orleans and elsewhere. That "psychology of assistance" figured it best to give the poor a fish and then when they had eaten that to give another and yet another until you had not a mature individual but a permanent dependent.

The right's "psychology of assistance" is termed "tough love" or "compassionate conservatism," which means we'll teach you to fish in our privatized teaching institutions. Assistance here is totally "privatized"—no government handouts, no tax-supported public education, no federally mandated affirmative action. Now, while the left had its chance, the right hasn't seen its total "tough love" plan fulfilled. It's *tough* because you don't get anyone giving you a hand up, but it's *love* because it holds back that helping hand so you can keep your initiative, your incentive, your will to compete, your self-respect, your chance to bask in your own accomplishments, and your moment to assume total personal responsibility and reap the total rewards.

The left thinks Katrina has given them a chance to once again "do welfare" to cure poverty. And the right thinks it may get yet another chance to put its real strategy in regard to poverty into play: gentrification. When you gentrify or regentrify a poor neighborhood you replace poverty and the poor with wealth and the wealthy. What happened to the poor? Are they going to incorporate, hire lobbyists and spinmeisters, and pay for photo ops? Are they going to run a presidential candidate from wherever they are and run a campaign and win the presidency? Are they going to create the hot, new TV season filled with the folks you saw on TV in New Orleans? No and no and no. I suspect they'll be once again swallowed up by poverty and just occupy the periphery of our awareness. The guy in the gutter, the guy asking for spare change, the neighborhoods you don't ever go into, the characters washing your windshield, the kids under the Johnny pump in the summer, the "servers" at TGIF and so on.

Prominence is not a part of poverty. To be poor is to be peripheral and in a celebrity culture, to be peripheral is to be invisible. Maybe another disaster will put the poor on the screen again, but it will be an "already seen" screen and in our Culture of the newest new, old is over. Whatever. In the meantime we will continue to gentrify and reallocate. The metaphor, by the way, for clearing out the poor in New Orleans is Bush clearing brush. He's making room for the oligarchy.

www.eviltown.com

Sin City? Now there's a movie right out of bin Laden's imagination. How else do you think he sees us? But it comes from inside our heads, too. Somebody's taken our just-below-the-surface desires and pumped them up to the max: tough, kick-ass guys, hot, tough babes, odorous, slimy pervert villains, corrupted government, corrupted cops, twisted love, unreachable raw power. Is it the whole country? Naw. It's just New Orleans, and nature has purged that problem. It's like the Old Testatment God flooding the city, drowning its wickedness. Katrina was carthartic for this country, so I don't think we'll get out of Iraq because we've lost our white plume of virtue and integrity. We'll stay because we've excised the evil in us and now we're pure again. Poor blacks you saw on the TV screen will never be allowed back in New Orleans, because the evil that gets televised is also the poor's evil. Poverty breeds corruption; power breeds a corruption that keeps the poor poor but, we seldom get a camera up close to that evil. Ignorance, bad health, unemployment, and crime attend poverty, but with the moralists it's the evil and sin they see. Reconstruction of New Orleans will be a purging, a national redemption. We'll detour a notorious city of more heat than light into The Light. Black is the color to purge. Is this yet another visitation of racism? Sure, because in this country white is pure and good, clean and wholesome. White neighborhoods harbor security and safety; black neighborhoods crime and fear. When some of us went to New Orleans it was for the sin; a weekend away from our white lives. But now none of that fits our World Redemptive posture. Katrina, like 9/11, has provided an opportunity for us to stay the course 9/11 put us on. Everything is grist for those moral mills. But you never could find any Brownbacks in our Sin City.

www.heatingup.com

Hurricane Katrina has revealed the sickening underbelly of American hegemony and left us all with a feeling that we're blowhards,
hypocrites, too meanspirited to long occupy our privileged spot on
this planet. That being said, Horatio, one wonders who can brag of
a spotless underbelly? Play that game and you're left with this:
Every country has a bit of good you'd like to encourage, and no
country is without more than a bit of bad you wouldn't want to
encourage. We are no different, and a case could be made historically that we've got a bit more of a bit of good than the next chap.
I don't buy this neoconservative window of opportunity spin; all
too remote, too many variables, too much wiggle room for contingency. And since when have conservatives become super-long-term
players?

No, Iraq was a mistake. Could al-Qaeda have been nipped in
the bud? Water under the bridge . . . but a timely clipping of bin
Laden's wings might have been endgame, rather like shooting the
Indian Chief and all the warriors go home.

We should have gone corporate with bin Laden. What do I
mean? Target the objective, hire the best team, no holds barred, and
run him out of business. Strictly a for-profit venture. The Israelis
had the best team but no incentive to find the chap. The Pakistanis
and Afghans and Saudis love the chap.

And yet our corporate goals would not have ended there. Are
there no capable, Arabic-speaking souls throughout the European
Union? In France, England, Spain, Belgium, The Netherlands, Italy,
and so on? A dirty several dozen trained in the true James Bond tradition. Bin Laden would have turned up.

Now that's all water under the bridge. What to do with Iraq as
American sentimentalizes over New Orleans and ponders the
endgame there? Bush won't leave Iraq, but he will leave the presidency. In 2006, Congressional elections may end the conservative
Republican renegade regime and our attention can turn to the Clin-
tons at war with Howard Dean and John Edwards for the soul of
the Democratic Party. Meanwhile, a few more hard knocks from
nature with some subway bomb threats, a probable bird flu pandemic, and five bucks a gallon at the pump should heat things up
almost more than greenhouse gasses do.

www.gentrify.com

I agree with the *Sin City* blogger. New Orleans is the Iraq we can't
fix, but we can fix New Orleans. We can cleanse it; we can make

New Orleans tractable while we obviously can't make Iraq tractable, despite what the Bush people say. Iraq suffers from poverty, unemployment, lack of health care, lack of old-age financial security, crime, and ethnic and religious rivalries. Yeah, it is worse than our Sin City; in fact, it's clear to everyone but the Bush people that Iraq doesn't want to be pulled into democracy and freedom—buzzwords for globalized capitalism unhampered by religion or anything else—and will slide back into their own history at any moment. But maybe it is clear to the Bushies and they'll seize their own moment after Katrina to switch the whole deal to New Orleans. The only problem is that the Bushies have so botched Katrina that the parallel with Iraq is not one they want to make. We botched "shock and awe" insofar as everybody who was supposed to be shocked and awed just went underground and continued the fight later under their own terms. Like the Apaches did.

Will we recoup with the reconstruction of Iraq? Doesn't look good. But here's New Orleans, and we can, after a bad start, show our colors here. And black is not a color. If the TV cameras continue to focus on the New Orleans poor it's going to be difficult to fully disperse them out of the areas we want to gentrify. Of course, if a majority of those poor already transported elsewhere don't have the means to come back (similar to the way they didn't have the means to leave), the TV cameras won't have a subject.

www.obliviousgeneration.com

Watch the skies. No. Watch TV. Watch TV after Katrina and see the cultural response not just to Katrina but to the disaster that our mission in Iraq has become. And what did the 2005 Fall TV season show? People who saw dead people, but not the dead in Iraq or New Orleans. People who saw aliens, but not illegal aliens. And the Reality TV shows. *Survivor* is now in Guatamala. A bunch of Americans competing to survive and hoping to win the big bucks if they prove to be the fittest are now in Guatamala. At the same time we have a whole lot of soldiers in Iraq trying to survive. They're not competing with each other for a grand prize. They just want to get out alive. Why don't the TV show *Survivor* survivors sign up for a tour in Iraq and test their surviving skills?

The twentysomething instant-messaging reality TV shows do not abate; there is no end to the closeups of the oblivious networking with the oblivious. No one is present to tap a citizen of the Empire of the Oblivious and say "If you want raw reality without artistic or intelligent intervention, why don't you and your mates go to Iraq?" And all their viewers should follow them, inexhaustible it seems in their quest for reality without purpose, without plan, without an exit strategy.

www.yuppiesecurity.com

We've got fear. Fear has got us. Right here in River City. Since 9/11. No doubt. No argument. Robert Kaplan in *The Coming Anarchy* thinks long-term peace has softened us up so instead of getting past the fear bin Laden confronted us with on 9/11, we've been traumatized by it.

But not the New Orleans folks I saw on TV; they didn't have 9/11 fear. They had worries; they had tragedy and anguish and bro-ken hearts and deep sadness. But the poor don't have 9/11-level fear because there's no room for that remote fear. It doesn't help pay the bills or put food on the table or make the neighborhood safe or get you to the doctor or the dentist. When you're down so long you don't waste time on WMD fear.

Life may sometimes be less appealing than death, but just the thinking about death, knowing that it's the hard end of a hard life, knowing in your heart that death fits in with life, that life has shown you something of darkness, of the unfathomable, of the incomprehensible, of the unexpected, and the unwanted gives death a place at your table. It overshadows your life like a bill col-lector, like a steady pain in your insides your cash on hand says you have to ignore. You have a daily acquaintance with mortality. That up-close-and-personal familiarity, that bringing in death to your bosom, doesn't set you up for distant fear. Anger, frustration, and belligerence create an edge, not a fear.

9/11—that signaling of national vulnerability, that signaling of how death could reach us up close and personal—put fear into those who spend every minute of our day building a firewall between ourselves and our own mortality. It's the same class of folks who took flight from the crime and poverty in New Orleans and headed for the suburbs. They had fellow Flight Club members in Detroit, Philadelphia, Los Angeles, Boston, New Haven, Pitts-burgh, St. Louis, Dallas—in countless cities across the country. Wealth secures safety and security; gated communities with private security police, condos with doormen, compounds with perimeter surveillance, and so on are, on the psychological and ontological level, protective buffers against death. Ten thousand square feet of home and an acre of lawn and a "fully loaded" Hummer mean invulnerable nesting, a safe niche. Private schools and play dates for children, summer cottages to "get away to," 24/7 cell phone contact with everyone you know, a social networking religiously pursued via e-mail, problem solving through catalog shopping, country club crony power lunches, Oprah's "spirit" moments, "servant" problems—all of this and more estranges death, holds him off, out of sight. And in his place, there's fear. Maybe it's no more than a fear of the loss of property, one's life being yet another piece of property. Perhaps property is the root cause of this class's depression.

You remember the faces of the New Orleans Hurricane Katrina victims? You saw no fear; you saw no depression. You saw anger and bewilderment at being once again at their wit's end. But deep in their eyes you saw a resilience, a stubbornness, a look that told you they had been here before in different ways, and being down, so far down, was too old to surprise them. The security moms had already taken flight; it wasn't just that they had the SUVs to drive away and places to go. They psychologically needed to take flight, whether it's white flight from the insecurities of the inner city, or a 9/11 terrorist flight that they believe Bush is in charge of. Flight, spatial or mental, is their *modus operandi*.

For the poor who remained, it wasn't just not having a means of leaving. It was a sense of having no place to run to, that running didn't make things better, that not being able to run and just taking it was what you were used to. It was the poor's *modus operandi*. They weren't being stubborn; they were just hardened. Katrina was a level-four hurricane and they had level-five lives, level-five resistance.

When life is daily throwing you curve balls, you learn to take advantage of a soft pitch. Looting is what you do when those who are doing the pitching take flight and leave their stuff behind. It just didn't go on in New Orleans; the Pakistani quake in October generated its own flock of looters.

Who was terrorized and remain traumatized by fear after 9/11 is that part of the American demographic that votes, lobbies, legislates, and rules. They have too much stuff and their lives are too easy and soft for them to be on close terms with death.

www.postkatrina.com

If I could, with a perfect little Epilogue note to Mr. Natoli's book, sum up the post-9/11 and post-Katrina connection it would be like this: We now have proof that we're not exceptional in virtue, charity, human rights, sympathy, compassion, intelligence, justice, egalitarianism, or imagination. We are in fact living in a bloated image of ourselves, full of the kind of fears the pampered have of losing their toys, so blinded by self-interest we can't care about anyone outside our little "nests." What's left of our rugged, independent frontier spirit resides in Mr. Bush's cockiness and smirk, his arrogance and strut; we can only now hope for the fifteen-minute retention of Guy Pearce in *Memento*; Bush won't permit photos of the bodies coming back from Iraq because we've become a people who might stop shopping and going to Disneyland if we saw a dead body; and judging by the way we care about the 45 million people without health care, we've got all the compassion lying behind Bush's smirk and we've got Barbara Bush-level empathy. But we are cool, in fact we're icy cold, when it comes to Old Europe, the United Nations, nature, and anybody who's too stupid not to have an SUV . . . you know, as a sign of your freedom to go where you want. But maybe we'll rise above what we've become, get over our post-9/11 panic attack, and bring this country back to its egalitarian promise. We'd have to temper rabid capitalism, stop dissing Mother Nature, give up membership in the Oblivious Empire, rekindle the Enlightenment only enough to guard ourselves in the future from the willfully ignorant . . . and, oh yes, did I mention that we're like the Tin Man? We need a heart.

www.highnoon.com

We see a picture of a "smart bomb" diving into a target. Later, we discover it was computer animation. Smart bombs are not that smart—or, only as smart as the people who deploy them. We listen to Colin Powell go through his PowerPoint program: "Iraq Just Seconds from Deploying WMDs" and later discover there were no WMDs, just as the U.N. Inspection Team had been saying. We check Arthur Anderson's audit of Enron and see that they're doing well. We later discover the reality is very different. Someone has cooked the books.

These are pictures and not the world. We listen to Dubya's assessment of how things are going in Iraq: "We're bringing democracy and freedom to them." And then we remember that some 62 percent of the American population doesn't know what "democracy" is because that's the percentage that failed to vote in the 2004 Presidential election. And we recall, too, that Dubya doesn't know what "freedom" means, because he's been engaged in curtailing ours since the Patriot Act was passed by a Corporate Congress. Of course, the Iraqis have a clear picture of what "freedom" means. I quote the Koran. . . . Wait. I can't. I don't know what the Koran says, if anything, about "freedom" and "democracy," and I suspect none of the neocons who pushed this war know. "Democracy," however, is something both tribal ways and Koran beliefs have no handle on. The Middle East has not been moving toward democracy, nor does it yearn for it nor is it anything they can separate from "capitalism." We're not just "making the world safe for democracy" as in domino theory Vietnam days. Now we're making the world democratic through force if necessary. But not the whole world. Not Africa. Just an oil rich nation with a "bad guy" leader. Perfect setup for a swaggering Texan who doesn't prattle but just gets the job done, like Duke Wayne.

This is the most effective picture: Bush wearing a white hat on a white horse facing Darth Vader at High Noon. Not the world. Just a photo op. The reality is very sad: A small man saved from a drunkard's life by a special lady, propelled by family expectations and fate into a place he cannot fill and is, therefore, nothing more than a straw man waiting to be mastered, a puppet waiting for his strings to be pulled.

Ours is a transnationalized capitalist world whose interests extend no further than the bottom line. But this is a world we cannot picture because we cannot face that picture, we cannot accept it. We, therefore, collude with Bush and his neoconservative mentors in drawing a picture filled with magnificent, inspiring signifiers like "democracy," "freedom," "human rights," "equality," "progress," "education," "compassion," "Christian values," "family values," "moral compasses," and so on. A picture filled indeed with empty words, empty of all meaning and consequence in the United States today as they were in Rome in its decline.

We are bringing the metanarrative of capitalism to Iraq in the hope that it will trump their religious beliefs, as capitalism has trumped Christianity here at home. If anyone doubts that, poll the Christian Fundamentalists on what John Edwards calls our Two Americas, on 45 million without health care, on Dubya's assault on social security, Medicare, Medicaid, public education, welfare, on the bottom 40 percent who have lost 80 percent of their wealth since 1985, seeing it transferred to the top 20 percent, on Dubya's assault on our planetary environment, on an unnecessary war pushed by lies, on the use of racism and homophobia to win elections, on the demonization and disenfranchisement of the Underclass . . . I could go on and on.

What in America would Christ, the namesake of these born-agains, approve of? President Peckniff perhaps? Add a scene to the New Testament: Christ goes from whipping the brokers and bankers out of the New York Stock Exchange to Washington, D.C., where he whips out all the religious fanatics, Brownback and Frist and Dubya himself among them.

The picture is democracy and freedom; the reality is forcing capitalism on a part of the world that has been resistant to it, the lure of the almighty dollar displaced by what we can only conceive of as "tribal fanaticism and ignorance." And perhaps that's where all religious belief genuinely held leads a country in our modern globablized capitalized world. They are fanatics and we are hypocrites.

www.twopictures.com

Post-Katrina? Are we looking for a paradigmatic change in America, in the American cultural imaginary, in the American mass psyche because of this hurricane? It's already been forgotten, and all the "new" opportunities it offered for us to end poverty, racism, the wealth divide, global warming, the war in Iraq, neoconservatism, shopping, botox, Paris Hilton's influence on young girls, and sex without a condom have been handled very nicely thank you by that same production company that brought you the 2000 election, the 2004 election, and the war in Iraq. You didn't really think Karl Rove couldn't detour the whole storm his way? He relied certainly on our cultural ADD, our broad-based cultural variety, and our vulnerability to even the most implausible spins. A deeply entrenched political ignorance has created that vulnerability. We also have some cultural hot buttons such as homophobia, racism, greed, and self-absorption, which when pushed, move us where a spinmeister wants us to go.

No, Katrina doesn't set up any lasting pictures of the world for us to choose from. But 9/11 did and still does. One picture: Do we think we are a country, a civilization, a culture worth fighting and dying for—in spite of all our congenital defects like slavery and genocide of the native population, nuclear attack on civilians, no vote for women until the twentieth century, a rigged presidential election, a president who lied about sex, and a president who lied us into a war? For you to continue. A great many blemishes. But are we worthy enough to fight for? The other picture is bin Laden's: We are too evil to continue. Perhaps the Roman empire was. Perhaps the world would have been better off if Rome had ended quicker, quicker than some one thousand years. Rome goes and the barbarians rush in, anxious for the Middle Ages to begin, anxious to burn classical texts and shackle every man's and every woman's mind and heart and soul to Catholic dogma and feudalist hierarchy. Does bin Laden think global capitalism would end with the destruction of the United States? Would Europe go next? And then Japan? And what about the fast-emerging China? Wouldn't Chinese goods flood Islamic streets, tempting the holy from prayers?

We have to survive not because we're perfect but because what bin Laden represents is less perfect, more imperfect, than what we are. This is the root choice we have to make and the one that bin Laden has created for us. But having chosen the survival picture, we have yet to put aside bin Laden's picture and search for the Islamic world he presumes to represent. Islamic terrorists reveal very little of Islam. We've sent administrative and military heads who speak no Arabic to conquer and control Iraq. Our president had to be informed after our preemptive strike that that there were three major Muslim religious sects in Iraq. We have no idea how the Koran deals with the notion of "freedom," or whether indeed it does. Only our university Middle Eastern scholars seem to know that "democracy" has no historical precedent in the Islamic world. The Bush people certainly didn't know. They thought democracy creation there would be a snap of a finger. Why is that?

We live in a picture of survival, of winning, of success in Iraq, but we have no picture of the world we seek to alter. Are we at war with the Koran? Is the kind of secularized capitalism, the kind of conservative market rule, the kind of privatization we wish to bring to the Islamic world, essentially and totally incompatible with the Koran? Do we hope that we can turn believers into shoppers as we have done here at home? Are we hoping to get religion out of politics or at very least turn religion in capitalism's direction through bromides like "family values" and "tough love," as has been done in the United States?

It seems clear that we're dealing with two worlds: Al-Qaeda's and traditional Islam's. We need to picture both. We've been fervent in developing the al-Qaeda picture since 9/11, putting together the sort of profile that a criminal behavioral unit would use. But we've allowed that picture to shadow the world of Islam and have assumed that the picture of one—of al-Qaeda—will serve as the picture of the other—the nonterrorist world of Islam. That has led us into thinking there is no nonterrorist world of Islam, that we are naïve if we think we are not fighting a war against all of Islam.

Had the Bush team at once responded to 9/11 on another front beside pursuit of terrorists but a pursuit of a world we knew little about except that they had oil we needed, we might by this time have a way of interacting other than as an invading army. We need desperately to picture in great detail the world of Islam; we need to imagine their culture beyond and outside our terrorist imaginings. And that world needs to do the same with us, but the first move is ours for all the reasons that we present to ourselves when we imagine ourselves a culture worthy of survival.

I wish I could say the author of *This Is a Picture and Not the World* has found the beginnings of such attempts . . . even at the movies.

EPI-BLOG

Index of Film Titles